Drawings by American Architects

ALFRED M. KEMPER

ASSOCIATES: SAM MORI & JACQUELINE THOMPSON

A Wiley-Interscience Publication, John Wiley & Sons • New York • London • Sydney • Toronto

Library of Congress Cataloging in Publication Data:

Kemper, Alfred M.   1933-   comp.
  Drawings by American architects.

  "A Wiley-Interscience publication."
   1. Architectural rendering—United States.
2. Architecture—United States.   I. Title.

NA705.K45   720'.28   72-13428
ISBN 0-471-46845-2

Printed in the United States of America

10 9 8 7 6 5 4 3 2 1

Foreword

The drawings shown in this book are, for the most part, renderings of crystallized ideas of buildings prepared to satisfy the insatiable desire of every owner to "see what the building looks like." They record a point in time in the development of the project, have a unique life of their own, and remind all of the original intent of the design. This initial aim is then measured against the completed building, which is influenced by pressures of budget, client demands, municipal authorities' edicts, consulting engineers' advice, and draftsmen's ego trips.

Renderings are, of course, preceded by ideas translated into *sketches* (a few are shown in this book). These sketches (rather private in nature) usually indicate most accurately the true intentions of the designer. However, the hundreds of sketches prepared for any building are often thrown away, destroying the record of the thought process behind the development of an idea. The study sketch is revised, renewed, retraced, reassembled, made into montages, discussed with colleagues, and used as instruction to collaborators. The rendering is seldom changed. The sketch is made only to record a thought and to be modified by other thoughts.

The act of drawing influences the design process in many ways, some of which are outlined below.

1. Materials and techniques used in drawings often favor actual construction methods and, therefore, influence the design. A steel or wood frame is easier to draw in line than in washes or sprays, whereas a building that has continuous surfaces of concrete or plastics is more easily portrayed through the use of washes or sprays. It is difficult, but far from impossible, to depict glass reflections in line drawings. In general, materials with highly developed textures are more easily rendered with superimposed lines than with washes or sprays. The renderings shown in this book are concerned with nature's textures, often indicating them in a decorative manner, rather than indicating the spatial role of landscape architecture.

2. The peculiarly twentieth century spatial concepts (space-time) are clearly depicted in the smaller projects shown in this volume, with the inside and outside relationships shown simultaneously. Curiously, drawings of larger projects often emphasize exterior masses only, indicating little of the relationship between the inside and outside. Remarkably little drafting technique has been developed to depict sequences of space and large scale organization in three dimensions. Eventually, movie techniques will undoubtedly be adapted to the peculiar demands of depicting the unbuilt.

3. Drawings, unlike models, can easily indicate the *breaking down of scale*. Distant buildings are shown as mass or silhouette, while detail and texture near at hand is celebrated. This has sometimes led architects to substitute minutely depicted trivia, such as patterned clothing, decorative vehicles of all kinds, paraphernalia connected with the street, and so forth, for architectural scale. These idiosyncracies, currently so popular, will date the drawings. Such devices may "humanize" the drawing but they have little effect on the building itself. Indeed, this emphasis can be traced to the desire to "break down the scale" of the building itself, but in the absence of painting and sculpture the traditional means of attaining such ends means that twentieth-century buildings continue to suffer from scalelessness. In reality this does not humanize buildings, and such efforts do a real disservice to architecture.

4. Simple rectilinear and circular forms are easier to draw and, therefore, one who draws is encouraged, or tempted, to use them. Nonrectilinear forms are easy to use in models and this method of study leads to their use. In this sense the use of drawings may become a trap, unduly dominating the selection of final form.

5. Since renderings, which have a fixed viewpoint, tend to show the most striking or "photogenic" view of the building, undue emphasis may be placed on that single point of view, to the detriment of the rest of the building. It has been said that Frank Lloyd Wright studied his buildings from a single perspective, constantly changing and revising it. Buildings are created by using the imagination. Drawings may assist some to clarify their views, but they are not necessarily helpful to all. The limitations inherent in drawing should never be confused with the reality of the building. This may explain why many very good architects draw very little. For them the creation of a building is an act of imagination that is assisted very little by drawings. It is often possible for the rendering to have little relationship to the building itself.

6. When we actually visit a building its psychological impact has little or no relationship to the feeling we get from a rendering of that same building. The renderings do not indicate varying qualities of sunlight and shadow or atmospheric and climatic conditions. The mood changes, from rendering to rendering, very little indeed. They are rather, finally, an abstraction of an idea, an idealization, a fixed view that has little to do with the reality envisioned. The renderings show a highly idealized version of the truth, but that truth is not the only one, and it may not even be the important one. One is reminded of the psychological impact of Van Gogh's drawings and paintings of his hospital and its environs. These drawings give a clear idea of his inner feelings with regard to his environment and its effect on him. Similarly, the architect cannot be entirely objective when he draws his

visualization of a building, unbuilt or built. To draw reality as the human mind sees or imagines it is a far different thing from depicting the unknown for a client in as clear a manner as possible. The psychological impact of the architect's design will not be truly known until it is built and, even then, its meaning will vary for individuals and will also vary with the passage of time. The great limitation of these renderings is that they can never convey the psychological meaning, the building's true essence.

The age-old process has not changed much. The *idea,* transmitted to the *sketch,* often augmented by *models,* is developed into a *rendering,* which in turn is *translated* into *working drawings.* These evolve into a *building,* which is a basic part of urban design. Modern technology has modified the process and this modification will continue; but technology is only a means to an end. Finally, the quality of the idea is the only thing that matters.

Paul Rudolph

Preface

In architectural design ideas are materialized. Frequently, the realism of a drawing bridges the final communication gap between the architect and his client. Therefore, to the architect, the drawing—be it an elaborate rendering or a quick sketch—is still the most important sales tool. Architect Philip Johnson, F.A.I.A., has said that clients like drawings better than buildings.

The rare combination of both design and visual communication bridges the gap not only between client and architect, but also between architect and architect, who, after all, learn from each other. Since the drawings represent the professional skill of the architect, it is important for me to give full credit to the renderer. Few have been executed with any tricks and the only helpful tool illustrated in this book is the computer, which relieves the renderer of the more tedious tasks and allows more time for finding the most suitable location point or viewpoint of the project. However, the computer remains a tool in spite of its clattering, humming, and blinking, and the renderer's skill is still needed to make the drawing more representative. And somehow no computer will ever create any feeling near the excitement experienced when tearing off a clean sheet of yellow tracing paper, hearing it smoothly crackle onto the board, and then enjoying the softness of lead or the scratching of the ink pen gliding over it.

It is my strong opinion that the presentation of the design is an essential aspect of our profession. I have often found that the quality of the presentation is in direct relation to the quality of the work, and no matter how large or sophisticated the office, ultimately one person has to present the design and make a rendering.

The purpose of this book is to show the drawings of many American architects across the country, drawings executed in and for the office to present to their client. It provided excellent opportunity for the quality of the small office's work to be shown with drawings submitted from major firms. The selection does not include all the offices in the United States; those not represented here were unable to meet the publication deadline. Furthermore, the number of drawings per office indicates neither the size nor activity of the office. Because of the limited space I also selected drawings by as many renderers as possible, within each section of each office. No judgment of the design itself was made, since I have no information about the criteria used or the desired requirements of the client for whom the design was created. The drawings, however, remain timeless.

The resulting collection shows a variety of drawings produced in or out of the office, with a wide range of techniques, from various viewpoints, and for different types of projects. I purposely avoided all color drawings, from water to oil, since I believe that color detracts from the design and most certainly from the drawing. I left out any reference to the history of the drawings or the past great masters; there are a number of books available on each of them. To give equal credit and for ease of reference offices are listed alphabetically, with an additional index for the renderers. For any changes in the names of offices (merging, disassociation, or relocation of office) please contact the American Institute of Architects in Washington, D. C. I hope I have made no mistakes in placing the right drawings with the appropriate office and/or the name of the renderer.

My sincere thanks to Paul Rudolph, F.A.I.A., for taking time out of his busy schedule to write the introduction. My thanks also to Mr. Michael J. Elliott, Executive Vice President, Southern California Chapter of the American Institute of Architects, for his help in announcing this undertaking to the national membership. I appreciate the efforts of all the people in charge of public relations or contacts to the principal partners in the various firms represented herein. If this collection of drawings helps clients to understand the different ways of presenting architecture and also helps future clients of architects to see the importance of good drawings, my intensions have been fulfilled.

Alfred M. Kemper

January 1973
Century City
Los Angeles, California

Contents

Drawings by American Architects

The Rex Allen Partnership • Architects

259 Geary Street • Union Square • San Francisco • 94102 • (415) 982-9770

John G. Merrell

Stanislaus Memorial Hospital

The Rex Allen Partnership

1

Christopher Urah

Alta Bates Hospital

The Rex Allen Partnership

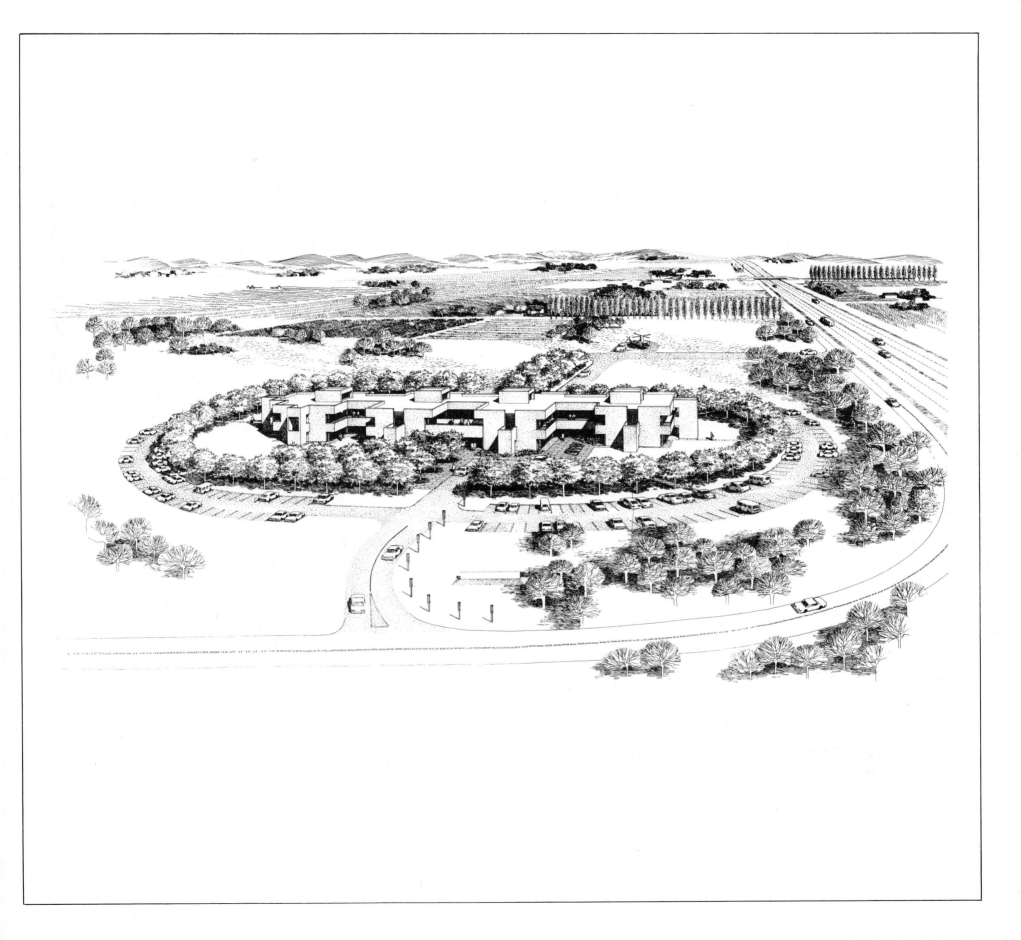

John G. Merrell

Madera Community Hospital

The Rex Allen Partnership

Humboldt State College, Physical Education Facility

The Rex Allen Partnership

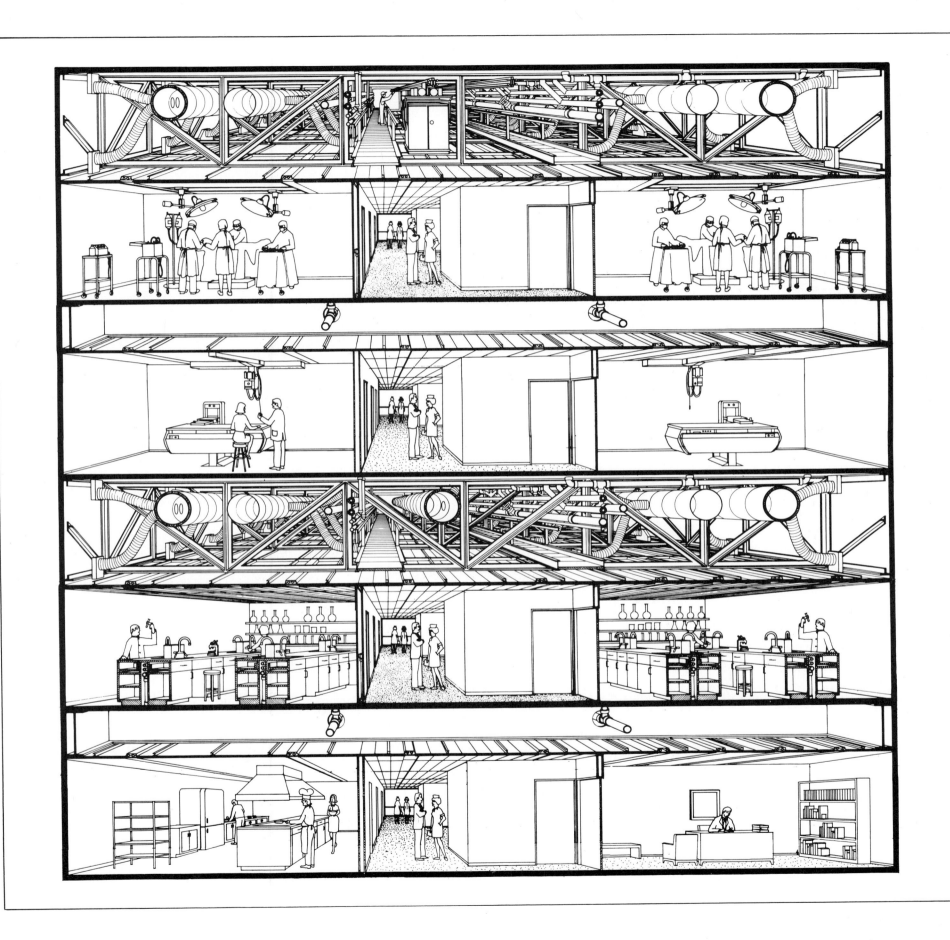

Tom Murphy

Sacred Heart General Hospital

The Rex Allen Partnership

ANGELIKIS & BAILLY 328 South Beverly Drive, Beverly Hills, California 90212 · 553-0030, 879-3838

VEHICULAR VIEW FROM ROOSEVELT DRIVE

PEDESTRIAN VIEW FROM WATERFRONT

VEHICULAR VIEW FROM FIRST AVENUE

PEDESTRIAN VIEW OF WEST NEIGHBORHOOD CLUSTER

PEDESTRIAN VIEW FROM PLAZA

Louis Angelikis

East River Urban Renewal Project

Angelikis & Baily Architects

Louis Angelikis

Glendale Place Apartments

Angelikis & Baily Architects

Louis Angelikis

Glendale Place Apartments *(Detail)*

Angelikis & Baily Architects

Louis Angelikis

Mission Creed Shopping Center *(Detail)*

Angelikis & Baily Architects

ANSHEN & ALLEN

ALLEN · PARKER · RICHARDSON · STROTZ · ARCHITECTS

461 BUSH STREET   SAN FRANCISCO   CALIFORNIA 94108   391-7100

Ernie Burden

Study: Natural Science Building, Univ. of Calif., Santa Cruz

Anshen & Allen

Ernie Burden

Residence: Sausalito, Calif.

Anshen & Allen

16

Ernie Burden

Natural Science Building, Univ. of Calif., Santa Cruz

Anshen & Allen

Ernie Burden

Natural Science Building, Univ. of Calif., Santa Cruz

Anshen & Allen

Ernie Burden

Natural Science Building, Univ. of Calif., Santa Cruz

Anshen & Allen

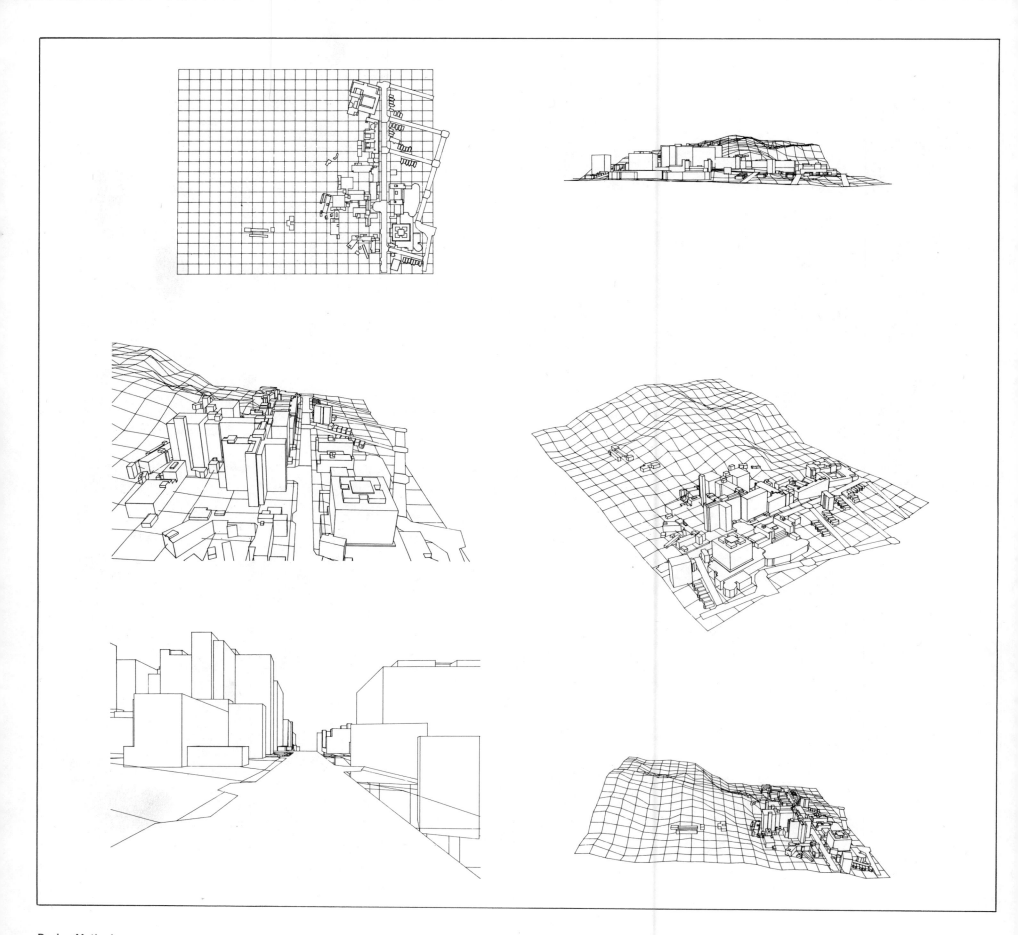

Design Methods
Sol De Picciotto

Berkeley Medical School

Anshen & Allen

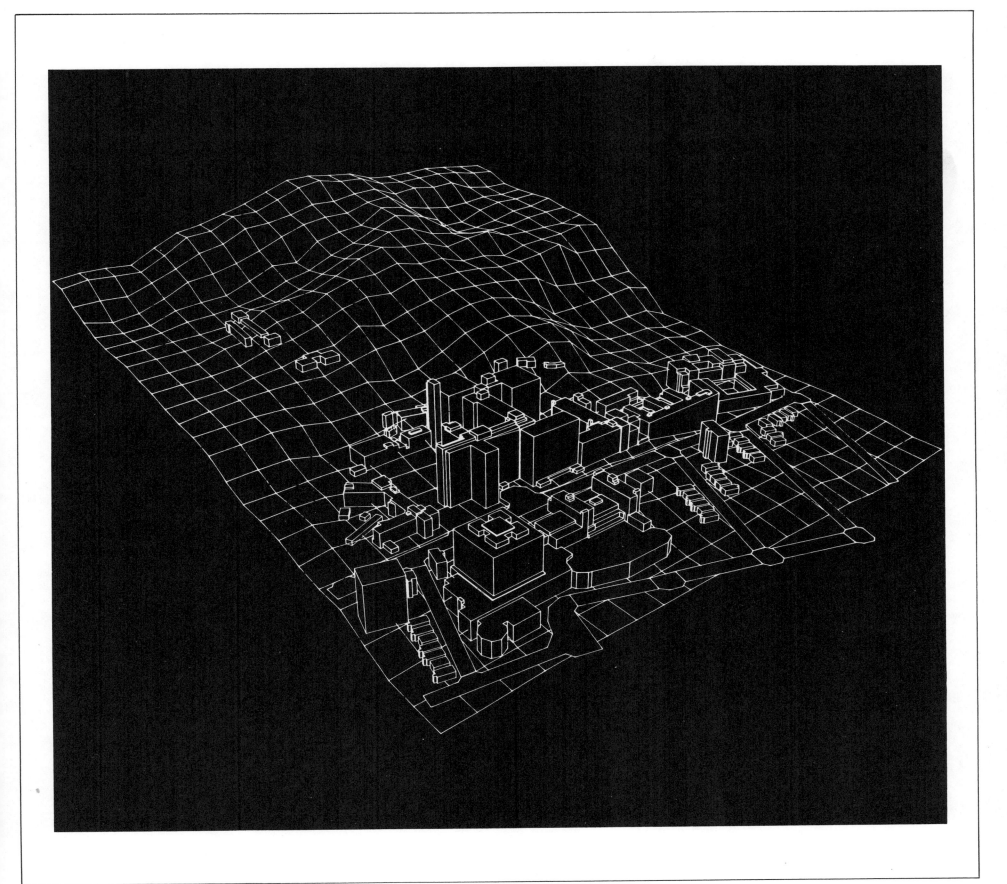

THE ARCHITECTS COLLABORATIVE INC.

JEAN B. FLETCHER
1945 ——— 1965
NORMAN FLETCHER
WALTER GROPIUS
1945 ——— 1969
JOHN C. HARKNESS
SARAH P. HARKNESS
LOUIS A. MCMILLEN

RICHARD BROOKER
ALEX CVIJANOVIĆ
HERBERT GALLAGHER
WILLIAM J. GEDDIS
ROLAND KLUVER
PETER W. MORTON
H. MORSE PAYNE, JR.

ERNEST L. BIRDSALL
TREASURER

46 BRATTLE STREET, CAMBRIDGE, MASSACHUSETTS 02138
TELEPHONE: (617) UNIVERSITY 8-4200 CABLE: TACCAM CAMBRIDGE

Thomas Larson

Boston City Hall, Competition

The Architects Collaborative

Thomas Larson

Boston University Medical Center

The Architects Collaborative

Thomas Larson

Resort Project, Turkey

The Architects Collaborative

Thomas Larson

Harvard Athletic Center

The Architects Collaborative

Thomas Larson   Harvard Athletic Center   The Architects Collaborative

Michael F. Gebhart

DCA Somerville Housing

The Architects Collaborative

Michael F. Gebhart

DCA Somerville Housing

The Architects Collaborative

Michael F. Gebhart

DCA Somerville Housing

The Architects Collaborative

Michael F. Gebhart

University of Minnesota Health Sciences Expansion

The Architects Collaborative

Michael F. Gebhart

University of Minnesota Health Sciences Expansion

The Architects Collaborative

H. Morse Payne, Jr.

Harvard Square Pedestrian Walkway

The Architects Collaborative

THE INN

H. Morse Payne, Jr.   Harvard Square Pedestrian Walkway   The Architects Collaborative

Howard F. Elkus

AIA Headquarters Building

The Architects Collaborative

Howard F. Elkus

AIA Headquarters Building

The Architects Collaborative

14 Arrow Street / Cambridge, Mass. 02138 / (617) 868-1800

Architects / Planners **Ashley Myer Smith** Incorporated

Fletcher Ashley AIA
John R. Myer FAIA
Douglas Cole Smith AIA
Richard I. Krauss AIA
Stephen Carr

Linos M. Dounias RA
Wayne I. Welke RA

Robert Fleischauer RA
Tyrus J. Porter

Linos M. Dounias

Luxury Housing Development

Ashley, Myer, & Smith with Homer & Rogers

Linos M. Dounias

Worchester State College Residences

Ashley, Myer, & Smith

Linos M. Dounias

Addition to Lawrence School

Ashley, Myer, & Smith with Smith, Sellew, Doherty

41

James Baker & Peter Blake, Architects

Studio 810, Carnegie Hall, New York City 10019, Telephone (212) JU 6-6440

Jay Walter

Library—Fine Arts Building
State University, College of Ceramics, Alfred, New York

James Baker & Peter Blake Architects

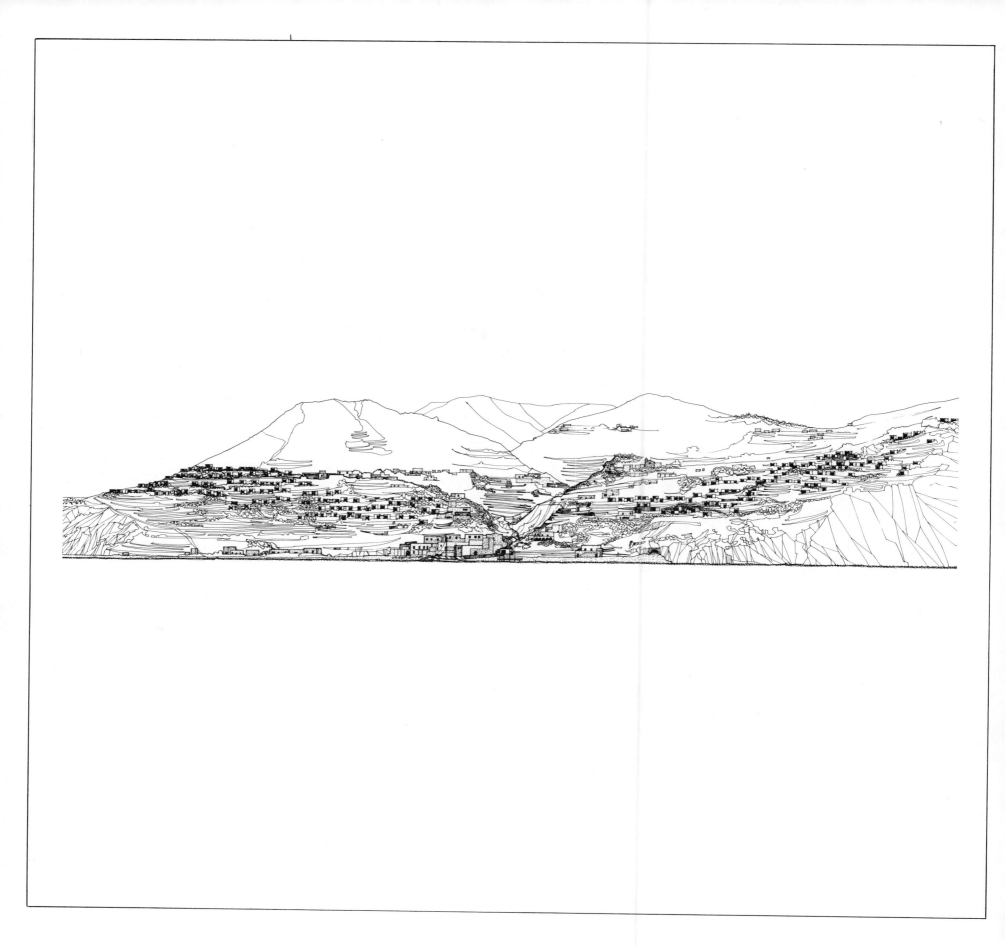

Charles Zucker

Proposed Island Development

James Baker & Peter Blake Architects

Brian Burr

Binghamton Rehabilitation Center
Binghamton State Hospital, Binghamton, New York

James Baker & Peter Blake Architects

Scot Jelley

Shafer House

James Baker & Peter Blake Architects

Ron Williams

Proposed Book Fair, Metropolitan Museum of Art, New York City

James Baker & Peter Blake Architects

47

ARMAND BARTOS AND ASSOCIATES, ARCHITECTS

200 MADISON AVENUE   NEW YORK, N. Y. 10016

212-889-6370

ARMAND BARTOS, A. I. A.
MATTHEW L. PRZYSTUP, A. I. A.
ROY FRIEDBERG, A. I. A.
MARTIN PRICE, A. I. A.

AUGUSTO MORPURGO, A. I. A.
ROBERT RHODES, A. I. A.

Helmut Jacoby

Mid-Westchester YM-WHA

Armand Bartos & Associates Architects

Helmut Jacoby

Physical Science Building, University Oswego

Armand Bartos & Associates Architects

Helmut Jacoby   Rehabilitation Center at Central Islip State Hospital   Armand Bartos & Associates Architects

FRED BASSETTI & COMPANY/ARCHITECTS

2027 FIFTH AVENUE / SEATTLE, WASHINGTON 98121 / MAIN 2-7725 / AREA CODE 206

PARTNERS:
FRED BASSETTI, FAIA
DONALD M. FROTHINGHAM, AIA
PHILIP C. NORTON, AIA

ASSOCIATES:
ROBERT H. ROSS, AIA, CSI
PAUL R. DERMANIS
KENT W. JOHNSON
JOHN ALVING, P.E.

KARLIS REKEVICS
HOWARD S. PETERSEN
JAMES F. HAMILTON

Kent Johnson

Regent's Hall

Fred Bassetti & Company/Architects

Jim Hamilton

Hotel at Seattle Center

Fred Bassetti & Company/Architects

Jim Hamilton

Seattle Center Hospital

Fred Bassetti & Company/Architects

Pete Petersen

United Church of Christ, Mercer Island

Fred Bassetti & Company/Architects

56

Karlis Rekevics

Loderi Place

Fred Bassetti & Company/Architects

Pete Petersen

Marina Village

Fred Bassetti & Company/Architects

Pete Petersen

Marina Village *(Detail)*

Fred Bassetti & Company/Architects

WB WELTON BECKET AND ASSOCIATES · ARCHITECTS

10000 SANTA MONICA BOULEVARD · LOS ANGELES, CALIFORNIA 90025 · TELEPHONE (213) 553-0555 · CABLE WURDBECK

LOS ANGELES · SAN FRANCISCO · HOUSTON · CHICAGO · NEW YORK

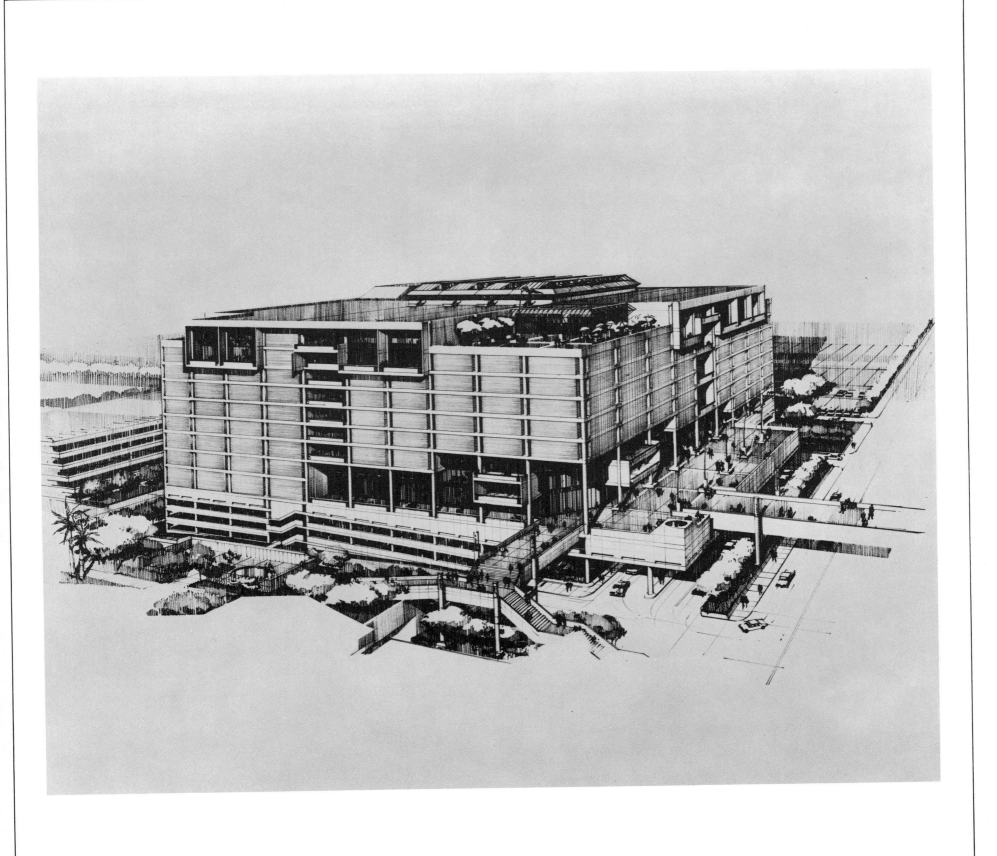

Robert Kaminsky

The Resource Center, Century City, California

Welton Becket & Associates

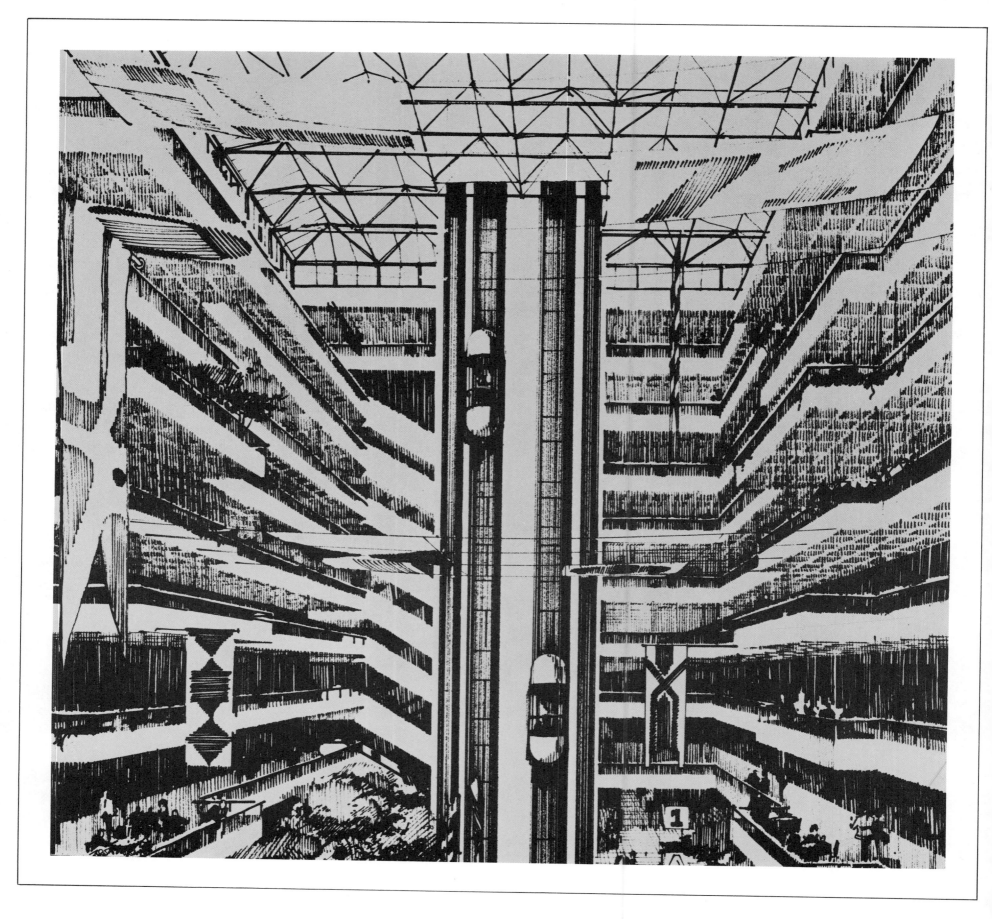

Robert Kaminsky

The Resource Center *(Detail)*

Welton Becket & Associates

Robert Kaminsky

The Resource Center

Welton Becket & Associates

The signs within the illustration read:

US AEROSPACE EXHIBITS →

FIRST AID
TELEPHONES
FOOD ↓

FOREIGN PAVILIONS ←

GRANDSTANDS FOOD ↓

PARKING →

Robert Kaminsky

Transpo/72, Washington, D.C.

Welton Becket & Associates

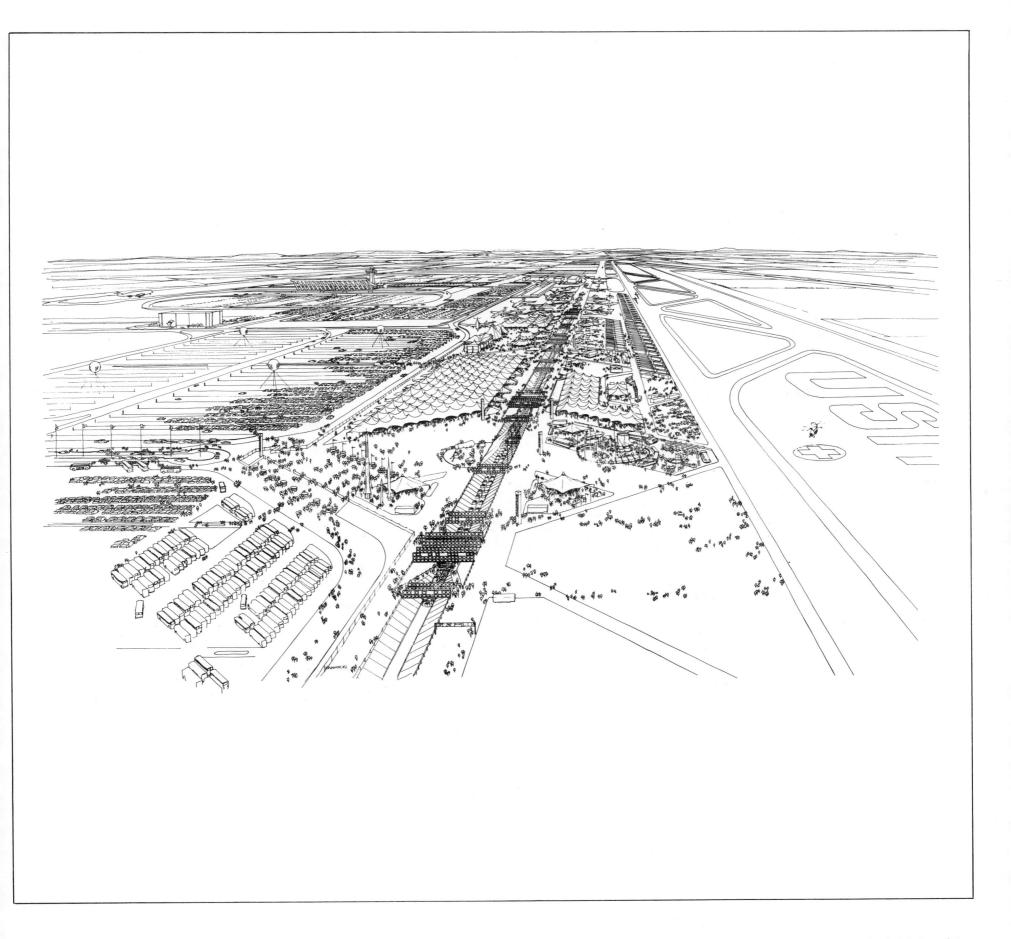

Robert Kaminsky

Transpo/72, Washington, D.C.

Welton Becket & Associates

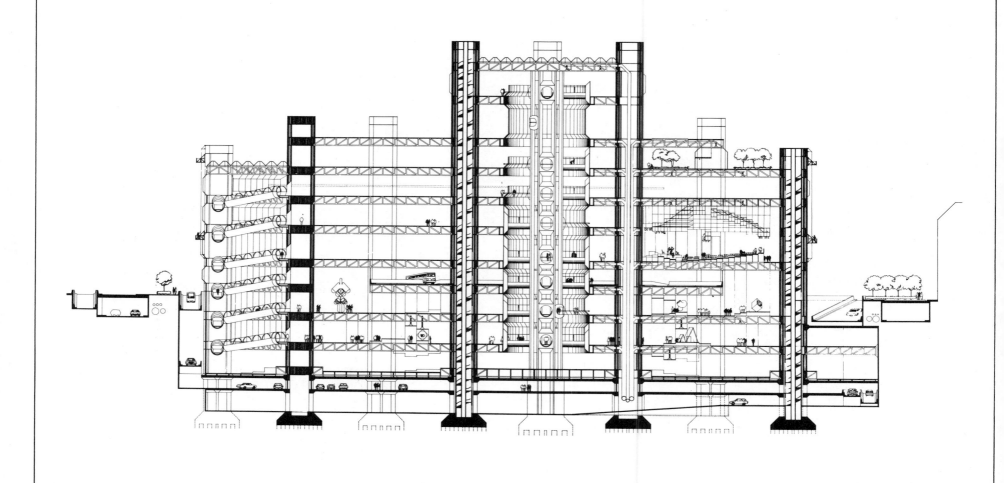

Pierre Cabrol Thomas Mathew
Samuel Tupaz Robert Kaminsky
Richard Ivine Michael Metcalfe

Paris Cultural Center, Competition

Welton Becket & Associates

Robert Kaminsky

Walt Disney Hotel, Florida

Welton Becket & Associates

william blurock & partners

architects   planners

1550 bayside drive / po. box 577 / 714 673-0300
corona del mar / california 92625

John W. McMurray

Federal Office Building

William Blurock & Partners

John W. McMurray

Willard & Lathrop Junior High Schools

William Blurock & Partners

Wally Arnold

Restaurant

William Blurock & Partners

JOHN S. BOLLES ASSOCIATES

Architects · Engineers · Planners
14 GOLD STREET   JACKSON SQUARE
SAN FRANCISCO CALIFORNIA 94133
415-392-4919

John S. Bolles FAIA · Richard E. Audsley AIA · Kurt Helmstaedter ISP · Robert L. Huck ISP · Len H. Teasley CE
Peter Rooke-Ley AIA · H. William Nilsen · Harriet Johns

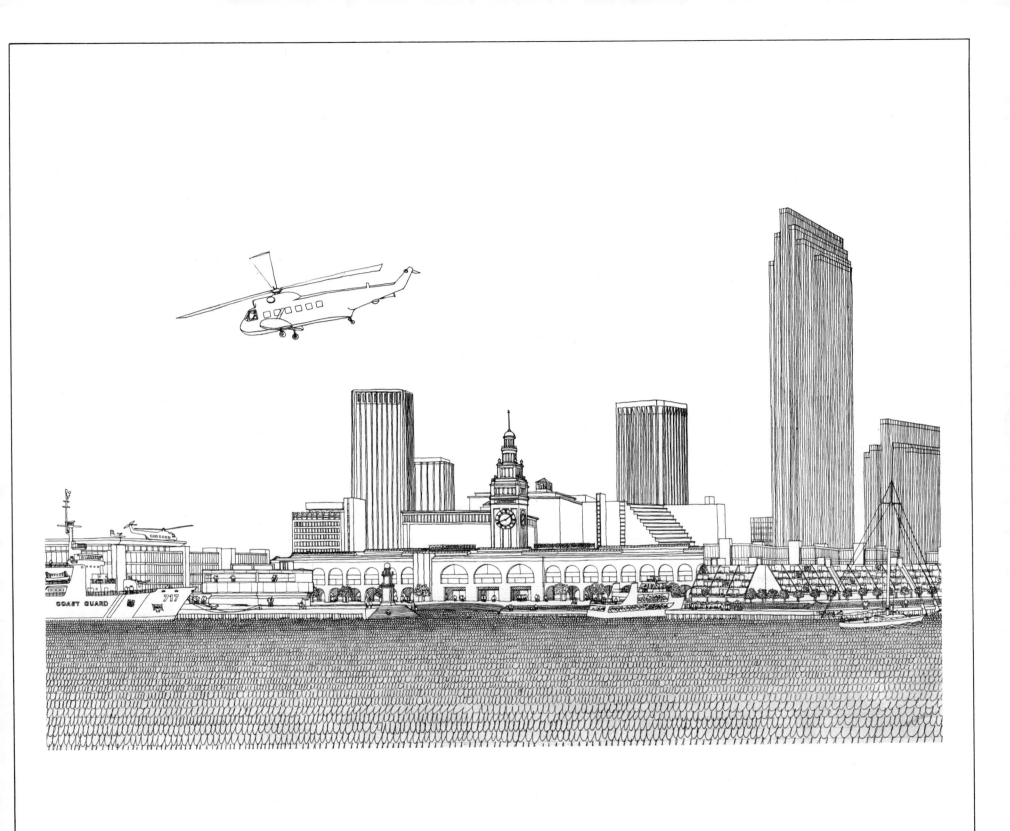

Charles D. Rushing, Jr.

Northern Waterfront Plan, San Francisco

John S. Bolles

Charles D. Rushing, Jr.

Northern Waterfront Plan, San Francisco

John S. Bolles

Charles D. Rushing, Jr.

Northern Waterfront Plan, San Francisco

John S. Bolles

Douglas Chun Chun, Ishimaru & Associates   Lakeside Haven, Konocti Harbor, Clear Lake, California   John S. Bolles

Al Sanchez

Civic Center Competition, Thousand Oaks, California

John S. Bolles

77

Roger Owen Boyer
Carl A. Scholz
     Architects
     & Planners   215 Leidesdorff Street   San Francisco, California 94111   (415) 398-3870

Roger Owen Boyer   Seal Rock Park   Roger Owen Boyer, Carl A. Scholz Architects & Planners

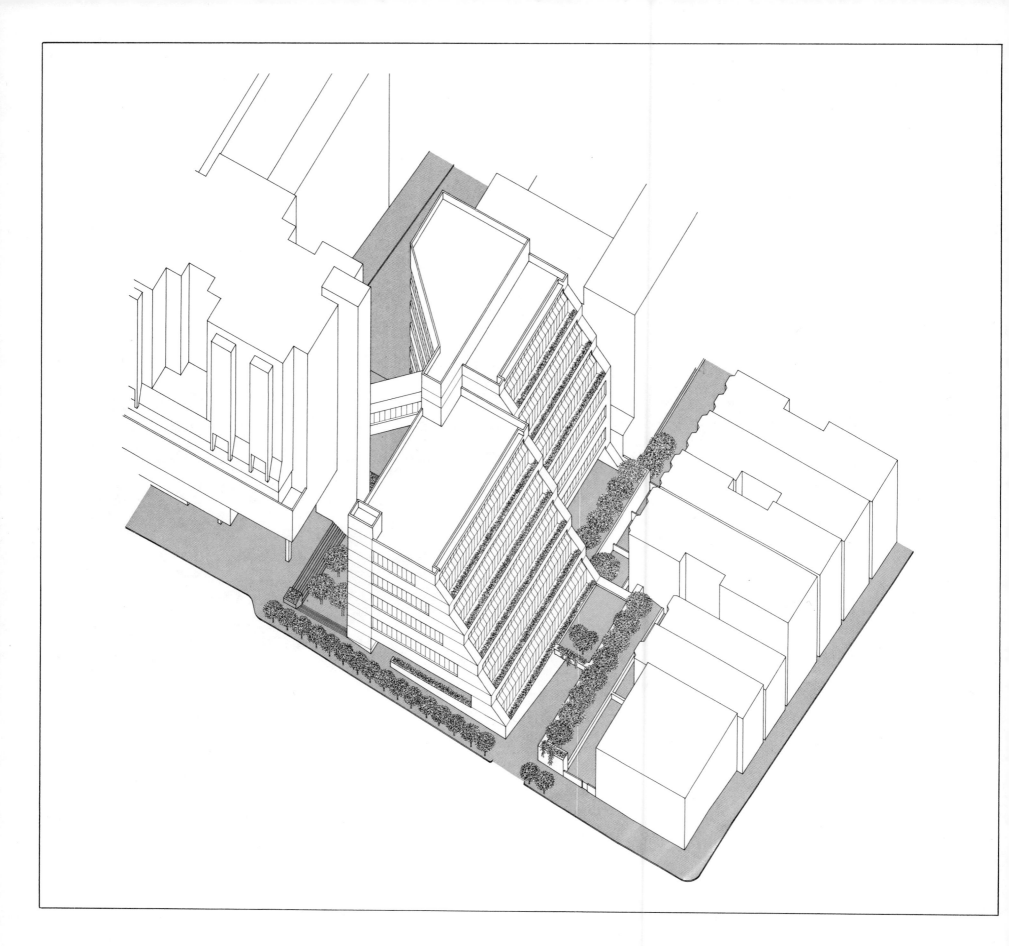

Roger Owen Boyer

Office Building, Pacific Medical Center

Roger Owen Boyer, Carl A. Scholz Architects & Planners

635 MADISON AVENUE   NEW YORK, N.Y. 10022   TELEPHONE 212 PLAZA 8-1766

MARCEL BREUER AND ASSOCIATES, ARCHITECTS

MARCEL BREUER, FAIA
HERBERT BECKHARD, AIA
ROBERT F. GATJE, AIA
HAMILTON P. SMITH, AIA

TICIAN PAPACHRISTOU, AIA

EUROPEAN OFFICE   48 RUE CHAPON PARIS 3   TELEPHONE TURBIGO 14-58

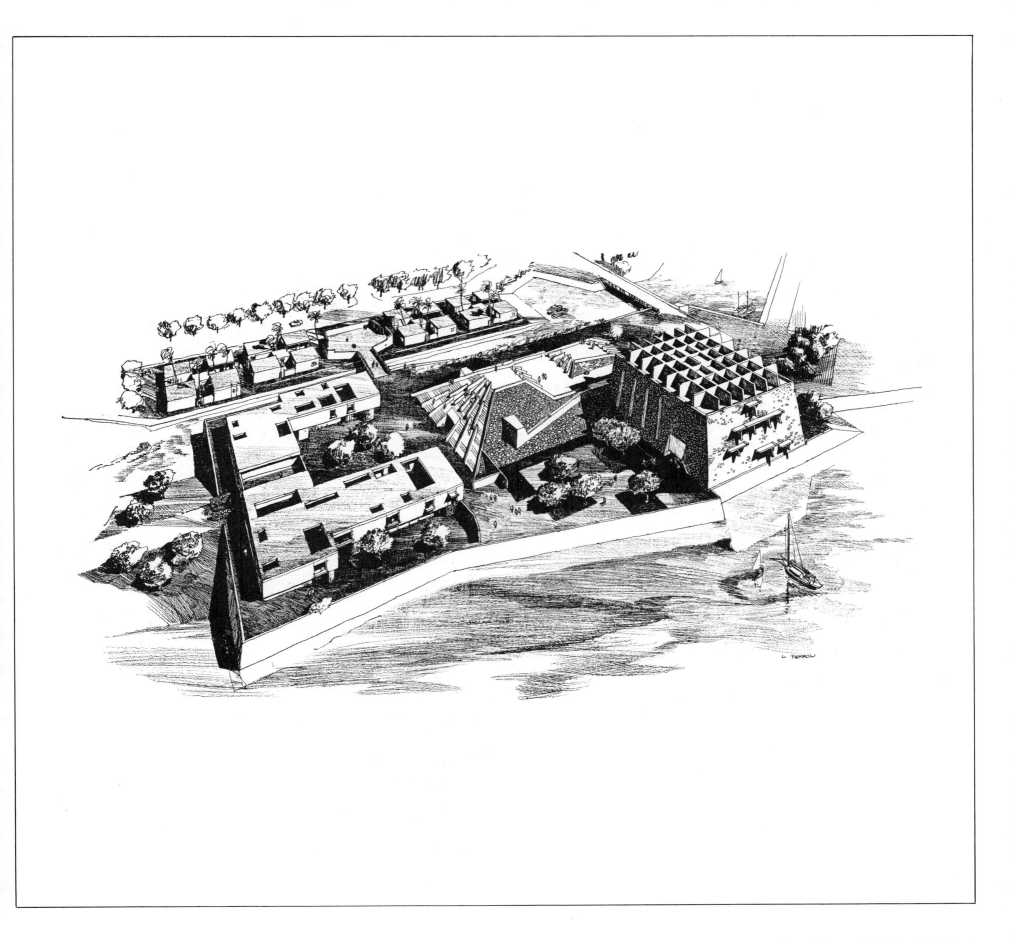

Larry Perron (Lutz Associates)

Interama

Marcel Breuer with Herbert Beckhard

Mark deNalovy-Rozvadovski

60 State Street, Boston

Marcel Breuer with Herbert Beckhard

Mark deNalovy-Rozvadovski

60 State Street, Boston

Marcel Breuer with Herbert Beckhard

Larry Perron (Lutz Associates)

Bayonne, France "Z.U.P." Project

Marcel Breuer & Associates, Architects

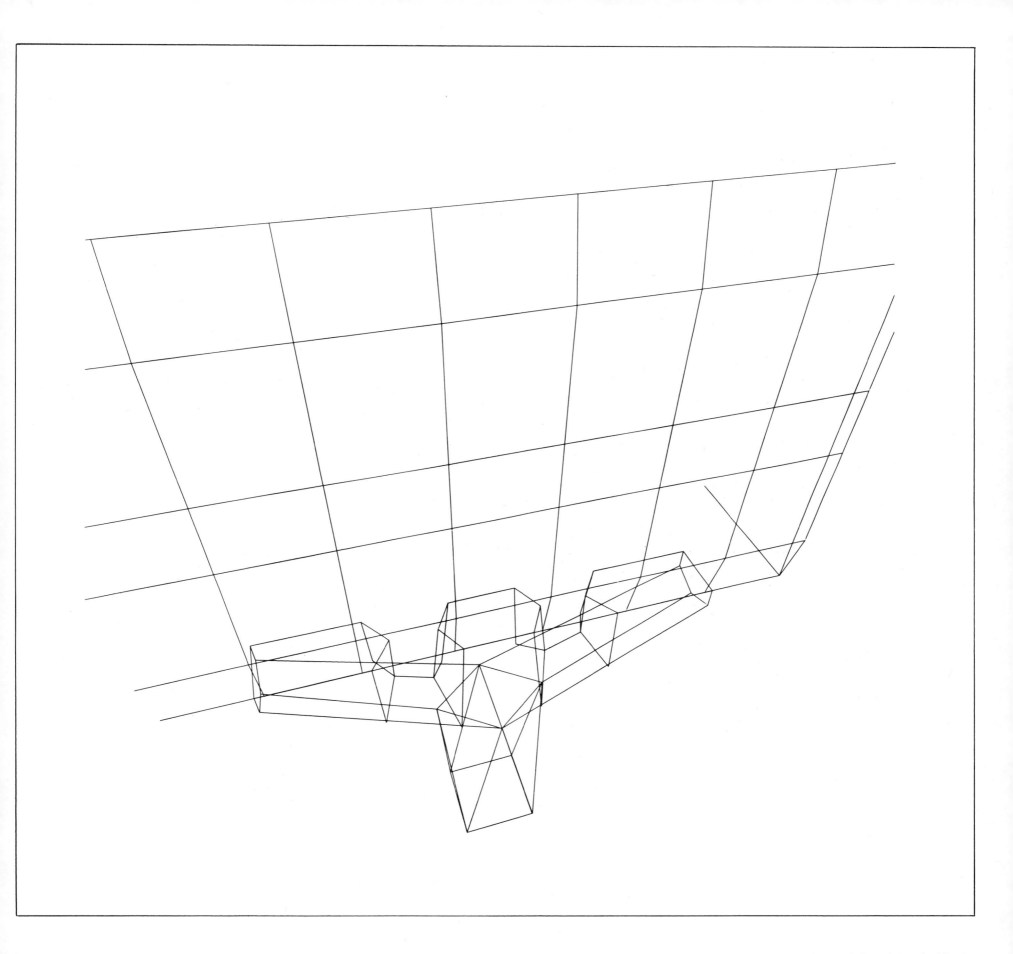

The Plotter, Computer Drawings

IBM—France Research Center

Marcel Breuer & Associates, Architects

Architecture & Planning
Musto Plaza 350 *Pacific Avenue*
San Francisco 94111
Telephone 415 781-1526
Henrik Bull FAIA
John Louis Field AIA
Daniel G Volkmann AIA
Sherwood Stockwell AIA

BULL
FIELD
VOLKMANN
STOCKWELL

Associates:

Robert E Allen

Henry C Bruce

Robert E Kindorf

Steven Y Kodama

David L Paoli

James K. M. Cheng

Russian Hill Property Study

Bull, Field, Volkmann, Stockwell

James K. M. Cheng

Emeryville Marina Development

Bull, Field, Volkmann, Stockwell

James K. M. Cheng

Emeryville Marina Development

Bull, Field, Volkmann, Stockwell

James K. M. Cheng

Pinecrest Lake Resort

Bull, Field, Volkmann, Stockwell

Serge Bicking

North Star at Tahoe

Bull, Field, Volkmann, Stockwell

BURKE KOBER NICOLAIS ARCHULETA

2601 WILSHIRE BOULEVARD, LOS ANGELES, CALIFORNIA 90057 / (213) 386-7534 ·278 POST STREET, SAN FRANCISCO, CALIFORNIA 94108 / (415) 391-1080

ARCHITECTURE   ENGINEERING   STORE PLANNING   INTERIOR DESIGN

Charles Toke

Columbus Mall

Burke, Kober, Nicolais, Archuleta

H. J. Nicolais

Warner Center, Woodland Hills

Burke, Kober, Nicolais, Archuleta

Charles Toke

Northridge Fashion Center, Northridge, California

Burke, Kober, Nicolais, Archuleta

Jon Jarde

ISI Building Addition, San Francisco

Burke, Kober, Nicolais, Archuleta

H. J. Nicolais

Chevy Chase Fire Station and Library

Burke, Kober, Nicolais, Archuleta

CALLISTER

AND

PAYNE

1865 MAR WEST • TIBURON, CALIFORNIA 94920

POST OFFICE BOX 377 • 415-435-4513

CHARLES WARREN CALLISTER
JOHN M. PAYNE, ARCHITECT

James Bischoff

The Exchange

Terry Stephens

Stowe, Vermont *(Detail)*

Callister and Payne

Terry Stephens

Stowe, Vermont

Callister and Payne

James Bischoff

Ayer Road Apartments

Callister and Payne

Richard Whitaker

Recreational Facility

Callister and Payne

Cambridge Seven Associates, Inc.

1000 Massachusetts Avenue
Cambridge, Massachusetts 02138
(617) 492-7000

830 Third Avenue
New York, New York 10022
(212) PLaza 2-1194

Louis J. Bakanowsky
Ivan Chermayeff
Peter Chermayeff
Paul E. Dietrich
Thomas H. Geismar
Terry Rankine
Charles Redmon
Erling Falck
William K. Goodwin, Jr.
Ernest S. Barbee
Philip M. Briggs
Benjamin C. Moore
Andrew Bartholomew
Charles A. Russell

P. Stephenson Oles

Boston Arts Complex, The Hingeblock, Boston, Mass.

Cambridge Seven Associates

Charles Redmon

Boston Arts Complex, The Hingeblock, Boston, Mass. *(Detail)*

Cambridge Seven Associates

Charles Redmon

Boston Arts Complex, The Hingeblock, Boston, Mass.

Cambridge Seven Associates

CAUDILL ROWLETT SCOTT
ARCHITECTS PLANNERS ENGINEERS
1111 WEST LOOP SOUTH
P.O. BOX 22427
HOUSTON TEXAS 77027
CABLE: CROSCOT HOUSTON
713-621-9600

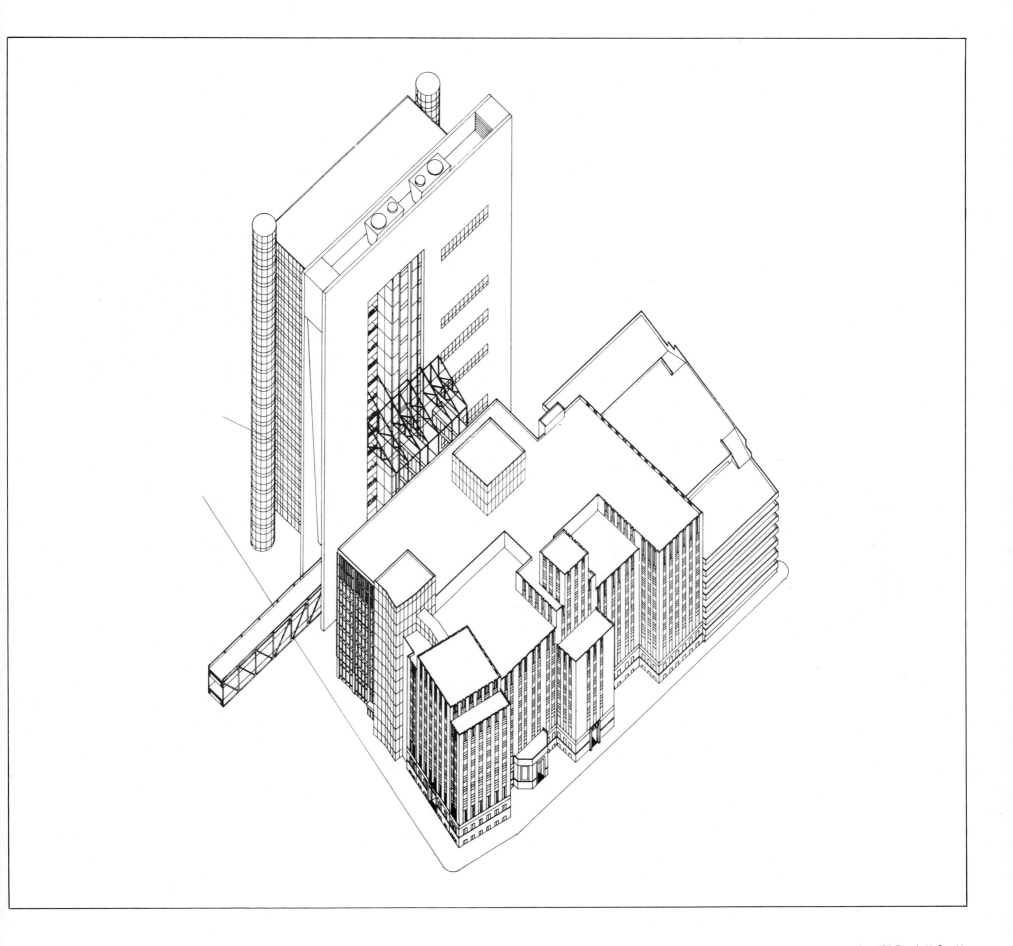

Carl Landow

Manhattan Community College

Caudill Rowlett Scott

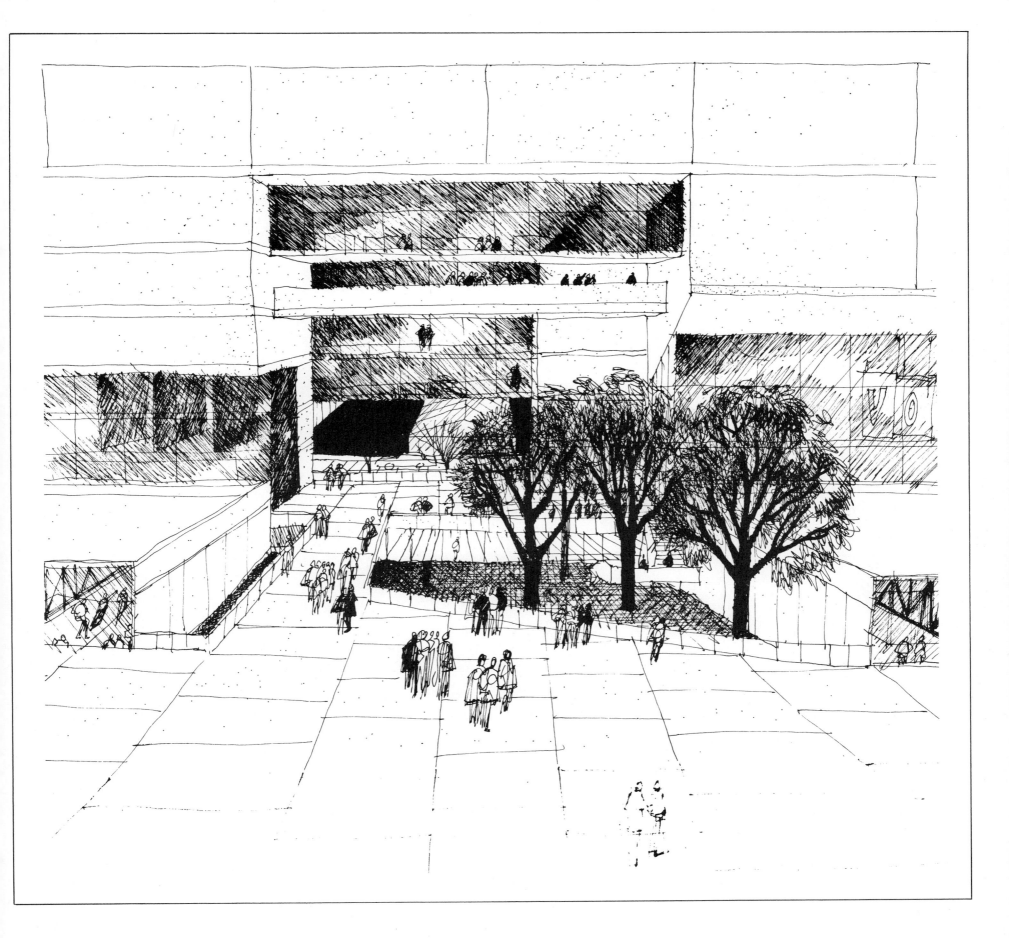

Carl Landow   Manhattan Community College   Caudill Rowlett Scott

Richard Payne

Baltimore Mental Health Center

Caudill Rowlett Scott

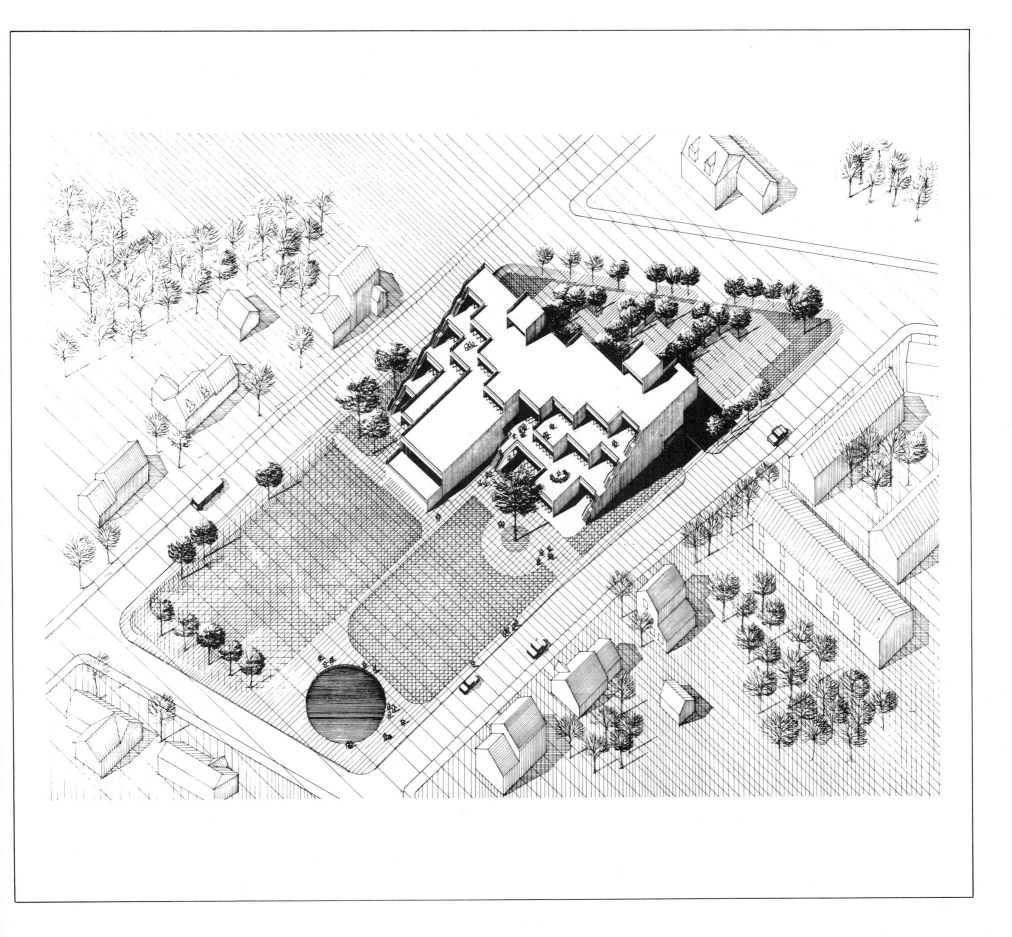

Peter Gumpez

Maple Hill School

Caudill Rowlett Scott

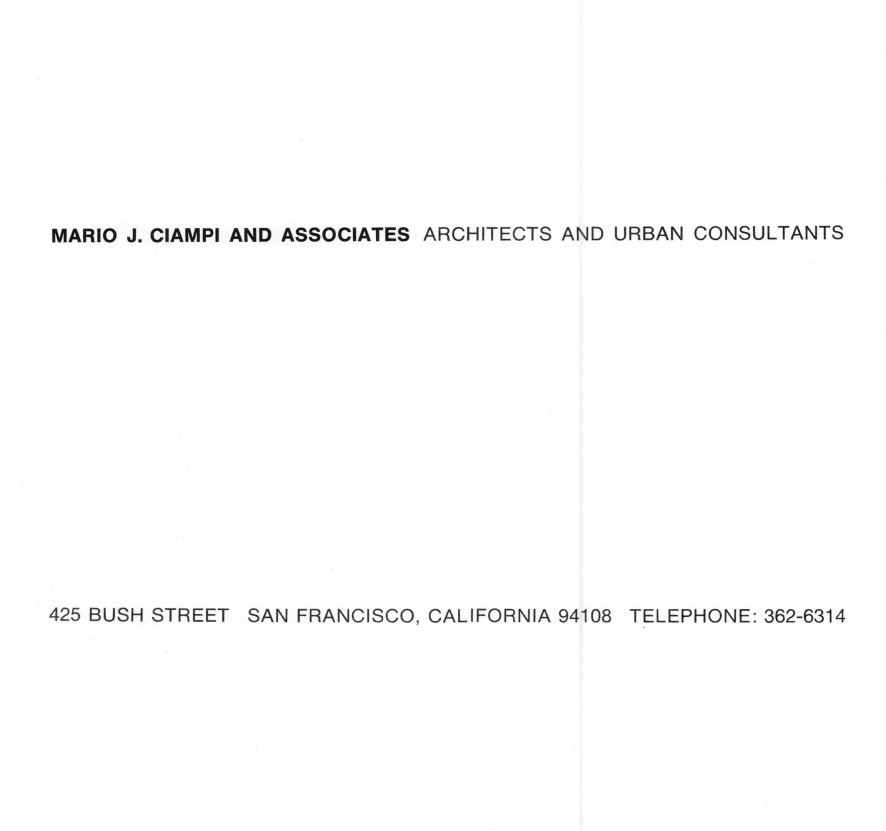

MARIO J. CIAMPI AND ASSOCIATES ARCHITECTS AND URBAN CONSULTANTS

425 BUSH STREET   SAN FRANCISCO, CALIFORNIA 94108   TELEPHONE: 362-6314

Richard L. Jorash and Ronald E. Wagner   University Art Museum   Mario Ciampi & Associates

Richard L. Jorash and Ronald E. Wagner

University Art Museum, Berkeley

Mario Ciampi & Associates

Richard L. Jorash and Ronald E. Wagner   University Art Museum, Berkeley   Mario Ciampi & Associates

ARCHITECTS
CONKLIN&ROSSANT

251 PARK AVENUE SOUTH, NEW YORK, NEW YORK 10010 (212) 777-2120

WILLIAM J CONKLIN AIA   JAMES S. ROSSANT AIA   RAYMOND BOLTON AIA   WALTER P. BOGNER AIA

James S. Rossant
Lake Anne Village
Conklin & Rossant Architects

James S. Rossant

Lake Anne Village

Conklin & Rossant Architects

James S. Rossant
Lake Anne Village
Conklin & Rossant Architects

James S. Rossant

Battery Park City, New York

Conklin & Rossant Architects

James S. Rossant The Lower Manhattan Plan Conklin & Rossant Architects

James S. Rossant

Town Center Concept, Reston

Conklin & Rossant Architects

James S. Rossant

New Town Concept

Conklin & Rossant Architects

CORLETT AND SPACKMAN • ARCHITECTS

121 SECOND STREET • SAN FRANCISCO 94105 • TELEPHONE YUKON 2-1838

WILLIAM CORLETT • FAIA
WENDELL R. SPACKMAN • AIA
PETER H. SKAER • ASSOCIATE
WILBUR STEELE ROGERS

MEMBERS AMERICAN INSTITUTE OF ARCHITECTS

Ernest Burden

Berkeley High School Cafeteria

Corlett & Spackman Architects

Anne Knorr

1960 Winter Olympics, Spectator's Center, Squaw Valley

Corlett & Spackman Architects

Anne Knorr   1960 Winter Olympics, Athletes' Lounge, Squaw Valley   Corlett & Spackman Architects

JOHN   H.   CROWTHER,   A.I.A.   -   ARCHITECT

10 SOUTH FULLERTON AVE.   •   MONTCLAIR, N. J. 07042   •   744-8788

Thomas K. Dahlquist

Academic Building, Saint Peter's College

John Hassan Crowther, Architect

DAMAZ & WEIGEL

ARCHITECTS & PLANNERS   1010 THIRD AVENUE   NEW YORK, N. Y. 10021   TE 8-6033

PAUL F. DAMAZ AIA   H. BOURKE WEIGEL AIA

Gregory Ihnatowicz

Hallets Cove Development

Damaz & Weigel Architects & Planners

Helmut Jacoby

Student Union, New York State University

Damaz & Weigel Architects & Planners

Helmut Jacoby   Fine Arts Building, New York State University   Damaz & Weigel Architects & Planners

DMJM

DANIEL, MANN, JOHNSON, & MENDENHALL

PHILLIP J. DANIEL
ARTHUR E. MANN
S. KENNETH JOHNSON
IRVAN F. MENDENHALL
T. K. KUTAY
DAVID R. MILLER
SVEN B. SVENDSEN
ALBERT A. DORMAN
STANLEY M. SMITH

PLANNING § ARCHITECTURE § ENGINEERING § SYSTEMS § ECONOMICS
ONE PARK PLAZA · 3250 WILSHIRE BOULEVARD · LOS ANGELES, CALIFORNIA 90010 · (213) 381-3663 · CABLE: DIMJIM LOS ANGELES

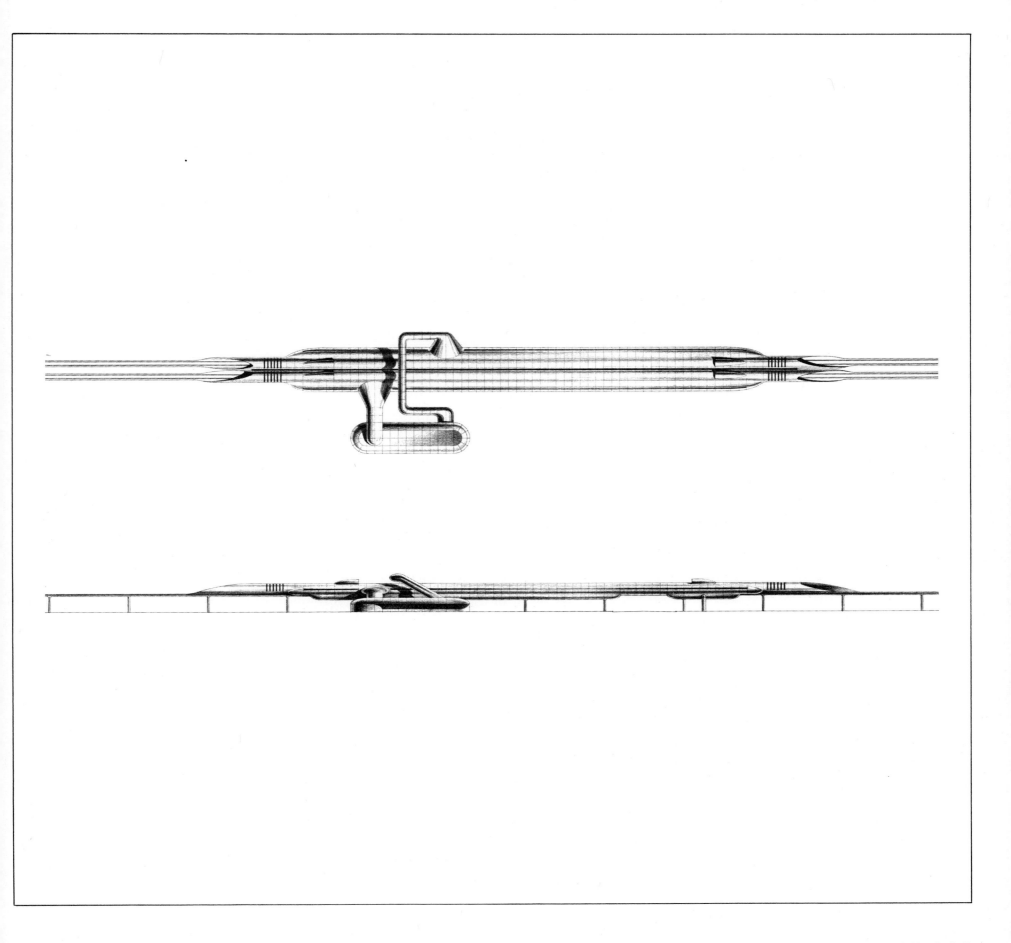

P. J. Jacobson | Los Angeles Rapid Transit Station | Daniel, Mann, Johnson & Mendenhall

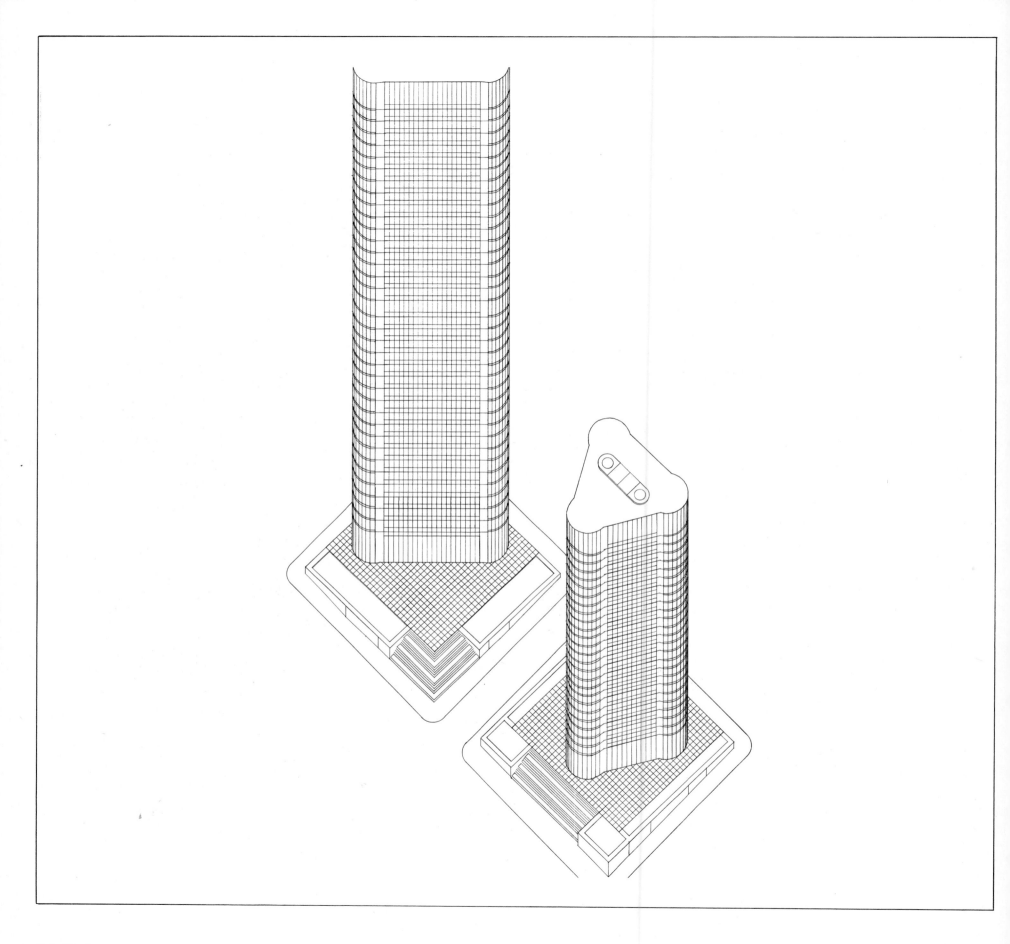

R. L. Tipping

Portland Plaza, Office-Apartment Complex

Daniel, Mann, Johnson & Mendenhall

A. J. Lumsden   Sunset Mountain Park   Daniel, Mann, Johnson & Mendenhall

Leavitt Dudley

Sepulveda Water Reclamation Project

Daniel, Mann, Johnson & Mendenhall

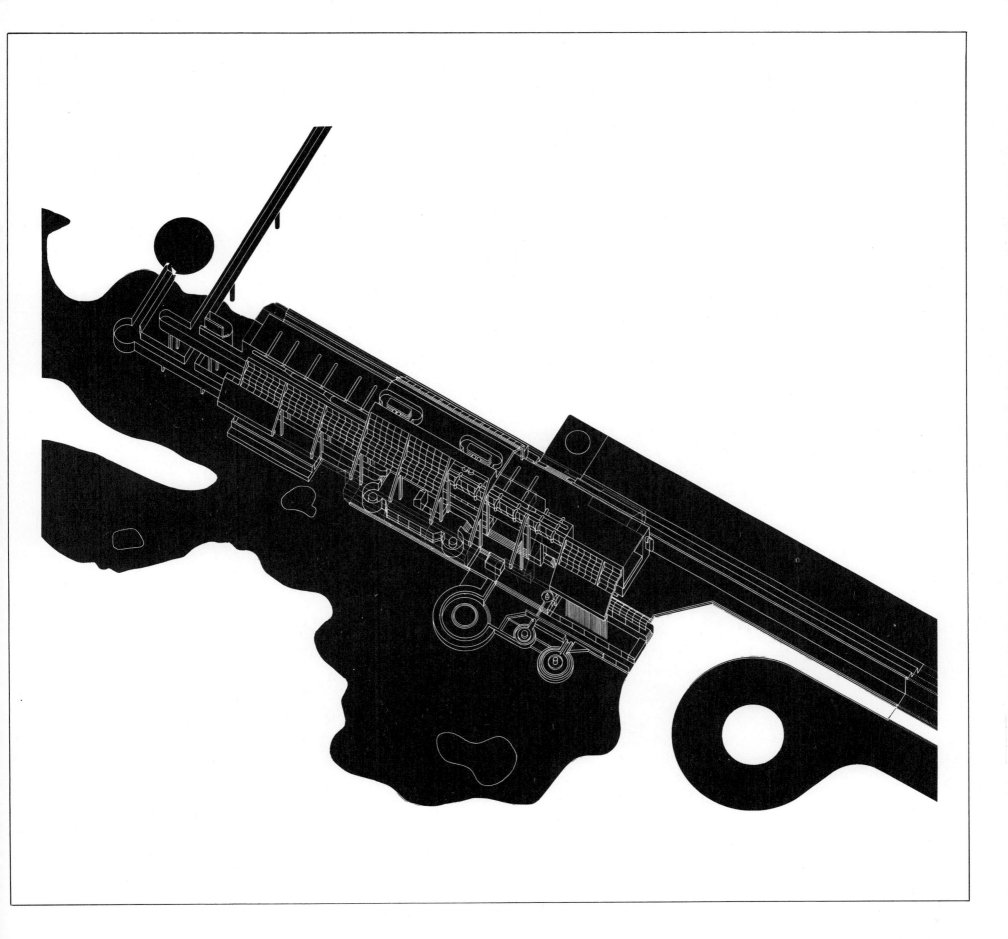

Engelbert Zobl

Sepulveda Water Reclamation Project

Daniel, Mann, Johnson & Mendenhall

Carlos Diniz Associates

Beverly Hills Hotel

Daniel, Mann, Johnson & Mendenhall

Carlos Diniz Associates

Beverly Hills Hotel

Daniel, Mann, Johnson & Mendenhall

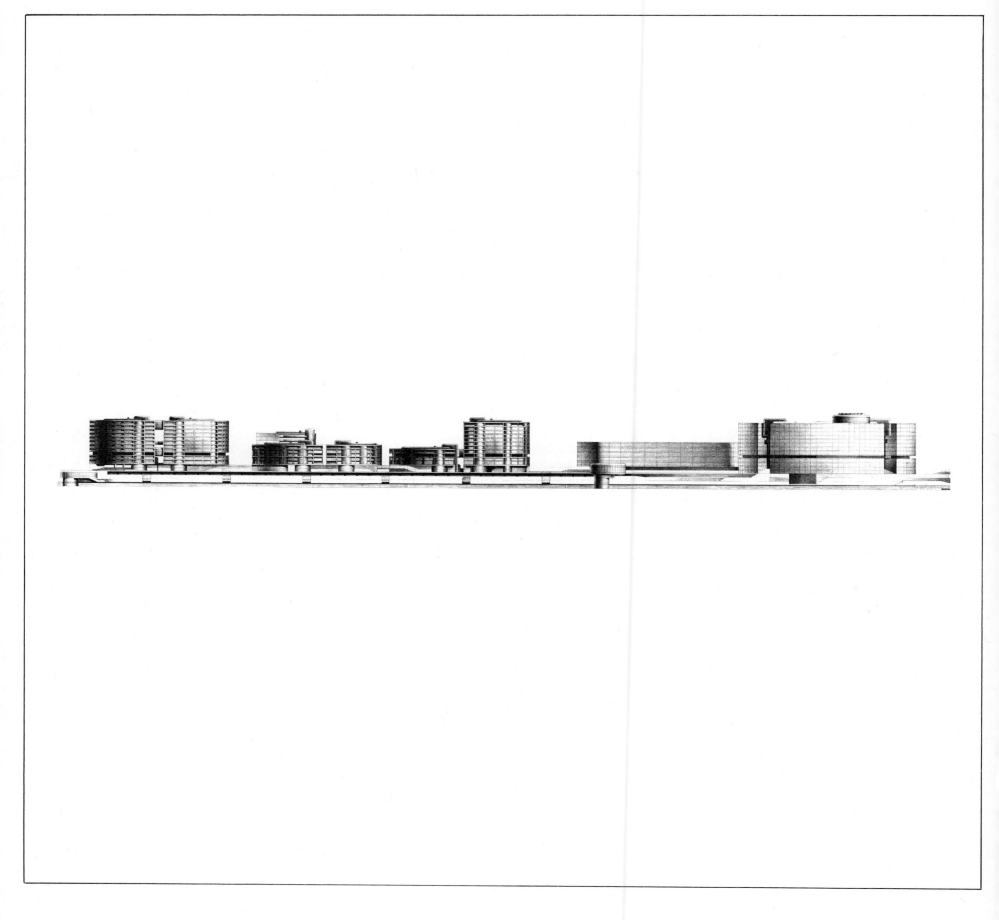

P. J. Jacobson

Marina City

Daniel, Mann, Johnson & Mendenhall

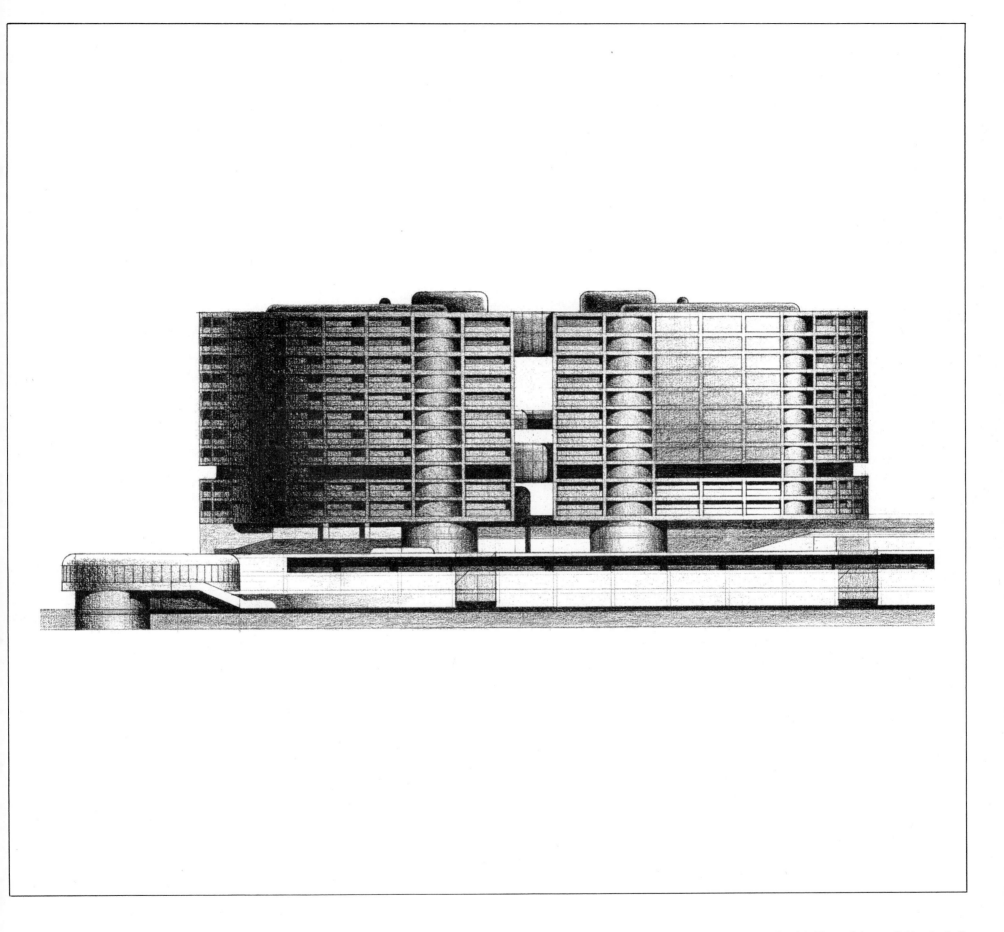

P. J. Jacobson

Marina City *(Detail)*

Daniel, Mann, Johnson & Mendenhall

147

DE MARS AND WELLS

ARCHITECTS • 2161 Shattuck Avenue, Berkeley, California 94704, Phone 841-7190

Vernon DeMars, FAIA   *Architect*
John G. Wells, AIA   *Architect*

Edward J. Bennett   *Architect*
Robert D. Hill   *Architect*

Thomas Aidala   Zellerbach Hall   DeMars and Wells Architects

Thomas Aidala

Zellerbach Playhouse, U. C. Berkeley

DeMars and Wells Architects

Thomas Aidala

Lobby of Zellerbach Hall

DeMars and Wells Architects

Donald Reay

Redevelopment of C.B.D.

DeMars and Wells Architects with Donald Reay

Jack Sidener   Cross Keys, Baltimore   DeMars and Wells Architects

Desmond-Miremont-Burks Architect-Engineers

703 LAUREL STREET - BATON ROUGE. LA. 70802
409 WEST MORRIS STREET - HAMMOND. LA. 70401

MEMBER AMERICAN INSTITUTE OF ARCHITECTS
343-0093   345-2280

JOHN DESMOND, F.A.I.A. - - - - ARCHITECT
L. E. MIREMONT, P.E. - - - - - ENGINEER
WM. C. BURKS, A.I.A. - - - - - ARCHITECT
ANDREW GASAWAY, A.I.A., A.I.P. - ARCHITECT-PLANNER
L. W. BOND - - - - - FIELD SUPERVISOR

John Desmond   Chicago   Desmond-Miremont-Burks, Architects-Engineers

John Desmond

Atlanta, Georgia

Desmond-Miremont-Burks, Architects-Engineers

John Desmond

The Hermitage, Historical Building, Burnside

Desmond-Miremont-Burks, Architects-Engineers

Wm. C. Burks

St. Alberts Catholic Student Center

Desmond-Miremont-Burks, Architects-Engineers

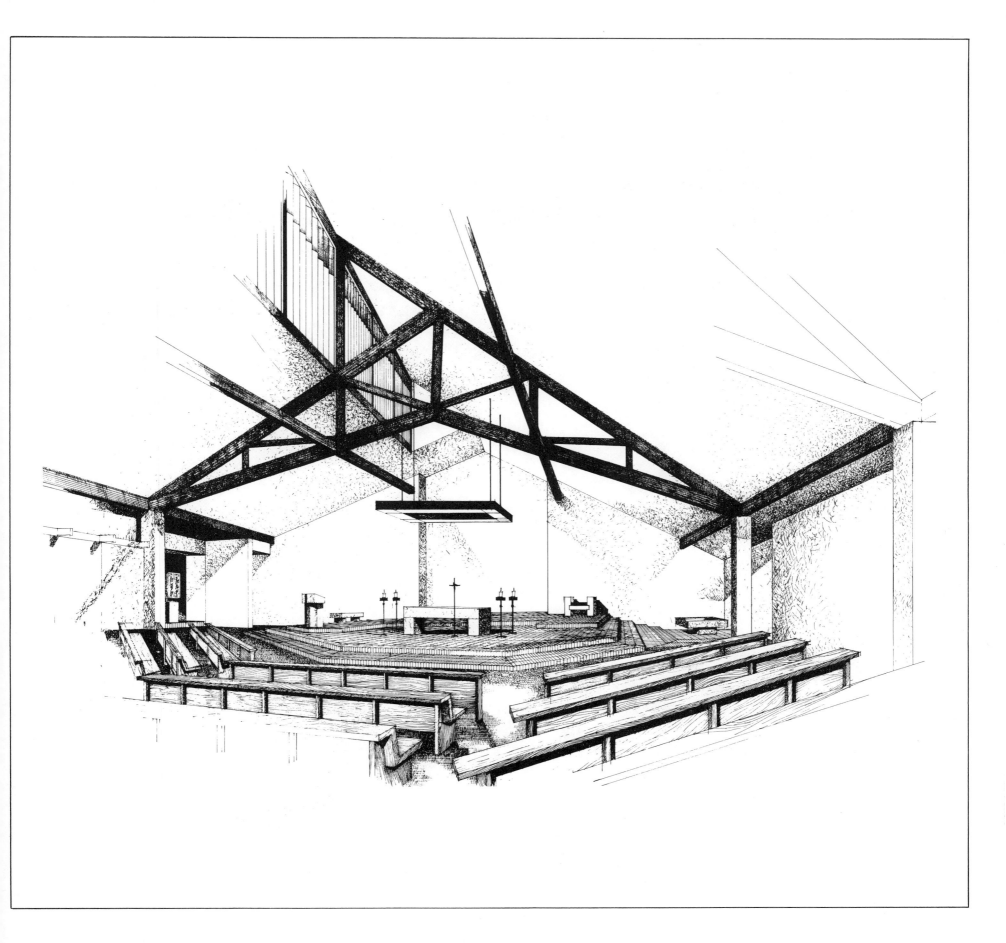

James Greene Campbell

Mater Dolorosa Church

Desmond-Miremont-Burks, Architects-Engineers

John Desmond

Stone Village, Blanchland Northumberland, England

Desmond-Miremont-Burks, Architects-Engineers

John Desmond

Rancho Nosara, Costa Vista

Desmond-Miremont-Burks, Architects-Engineers

DORMAN/MUNSELLE ASSOCIATES ARCHITECTURE & PLANNING

RICHARD DORMAN F.A.I.A.   PETER MUNSELLE A.I.A.
113 NORTH SAN VICENTE BOULEVARD, BEVERLY HILLS, CALIFORNIA 90211/TELEPHONE: (213) 651-2810 / MEMBERS AMERICAN INSTITUTE OF ARCHITECTS

Richard Dorman

Island Apartments

Dorman/Munselle Associates

Pete Munselle

Island Apartments

Dorman/Munselle Associates

Richard Dorman

Proposed Country Club

Dorman/Munselle Associates

Richard Dorman

Office Building

Dorman/Munselle Associates

167

Dworsky

Daniel L. Dworsky F. A. I. A.
Architect and Associates
1017 N. La Cienega Boulevard
Los Angeles, California 90069
Telephone 655-5300

T. N. Echternach

Equitable Savings Buildings

Daniel Dworsky and Associates

The Chrysler Building, University of Michigan *(Detail)*

Daniel Dworsky and Associates

Andrew Cyga   The Chrysler Building, University of Michigan   Daniel Dworsky and Associates

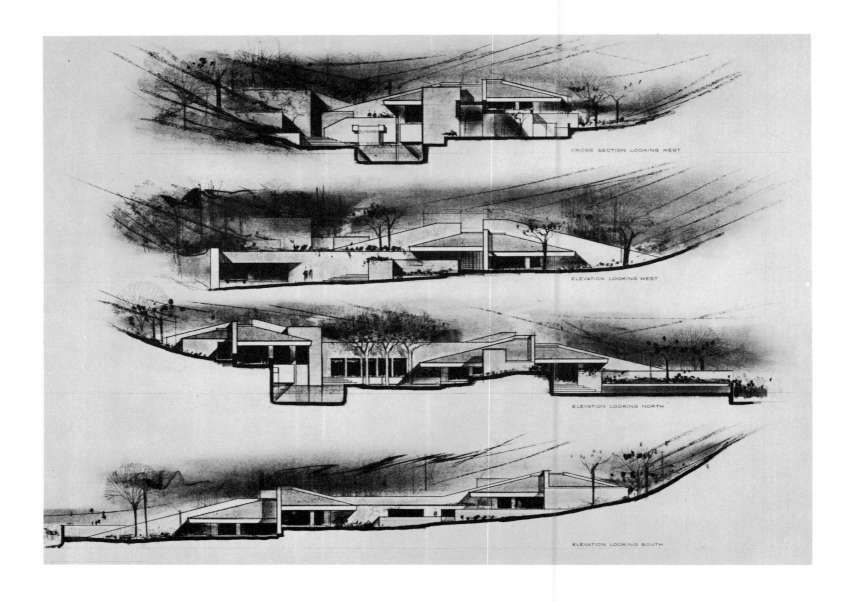

CROSS SECTION LOOKING WEST

ELEVATION LOOKING WEST

ELEVATION LOOKING NORTH

ELEVATION LOOKING SOUTH

Daniel L. Dworsky   Residence for Mr. Joseph Drown   Daniel Dworsky and Associates

Daniel L. Dworsky

Residence for Mr. Joseph Drown *(Detail)*

Daniel Dworsky and Associates

ECKBO
DEAN
AUSTIN &
WILLIAMS

Landscape Architecture, Urban Design, Environmental Planning   San Francisco, Los Angeles and Honolulu
7440 North Figueroa Street, Los Angeles, California 90041   Telephone (213) 254-9257

Don Woodruff

Frank G. Bonnelli Regional Park

Eckbo, Dean, Austin & Williams

THE EGGERS PARTNERSHIP

ARCHITECTS AND PLANNERS
100 PARK AVENUE, NEW YORK, NEW YORK 10017 • TELEPHONE 212-725-2100

DAVID L. EGGERS   AIA
C. GATES BECKWITH   AIA
GUSTAVE R. KEANE   FAIA
FRANK W. MUNZER   AIA
RICHARD M POTT   AIA
R. JACKSON SMITH   AIA
THEODORE J. YOUNG   FAIA

RICHARD F. EGGERS   NSID

ROBERT L. BIEN   AIA
JOSEPH A. CAPANO   AIA
E. ALLEN DENNISON   AIA
JOHN B. HAYDEN   AIA
BERNWARD U. KURTZ   AIA
PAUL LAMPL   AIA
J. J. McFADDEN, JR.   FASCE
PETER G. MOORE   AIA
ALLEN C. PARRETTE   AIA
ROBERT H. WELZ   AIA
ELIOT B. WILLAUER   AIA

E. A. Jimenez

Morri Sonia Housing Project

O. Figueroa

Nassau Community College

The Eggers Partnership

Nassau Community College

ELS

Elbasani/Logan/Severin
Architects
Urban Design Consultants

2315 Prince Street
Berkeley
California 94705
Telephone: (415) 549-2929

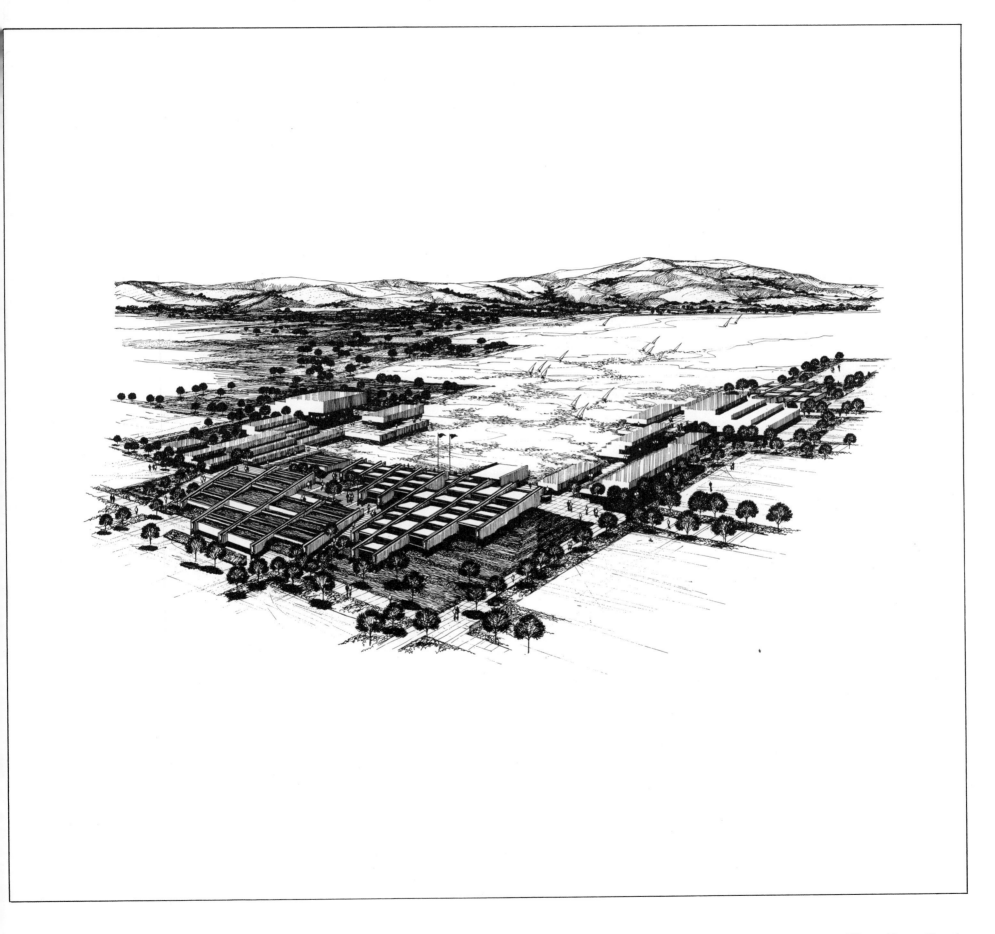

Jacques de Brer

Fremont Civic Cultural Center, Fremont Competition

Elbasani/Logan/Severin

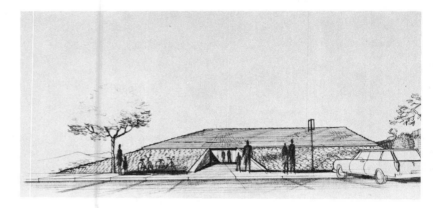

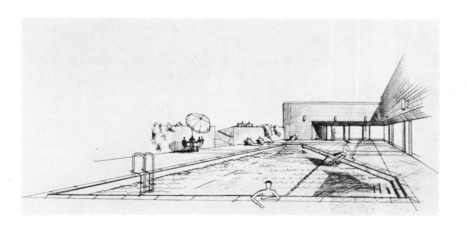

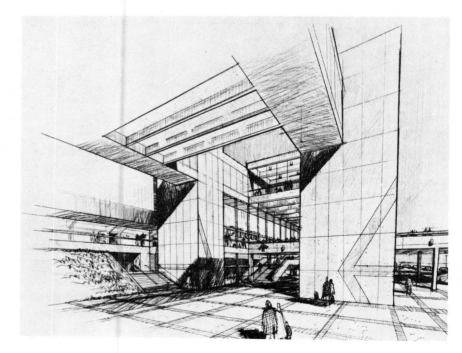

George R. Duncan

Golden West Savings Building, Moraga, California

Elbasani/Logan/Severin

Michael Severin

Boome County Arena, Binghamton, N.Y.

Elbasani/Logan/Severin

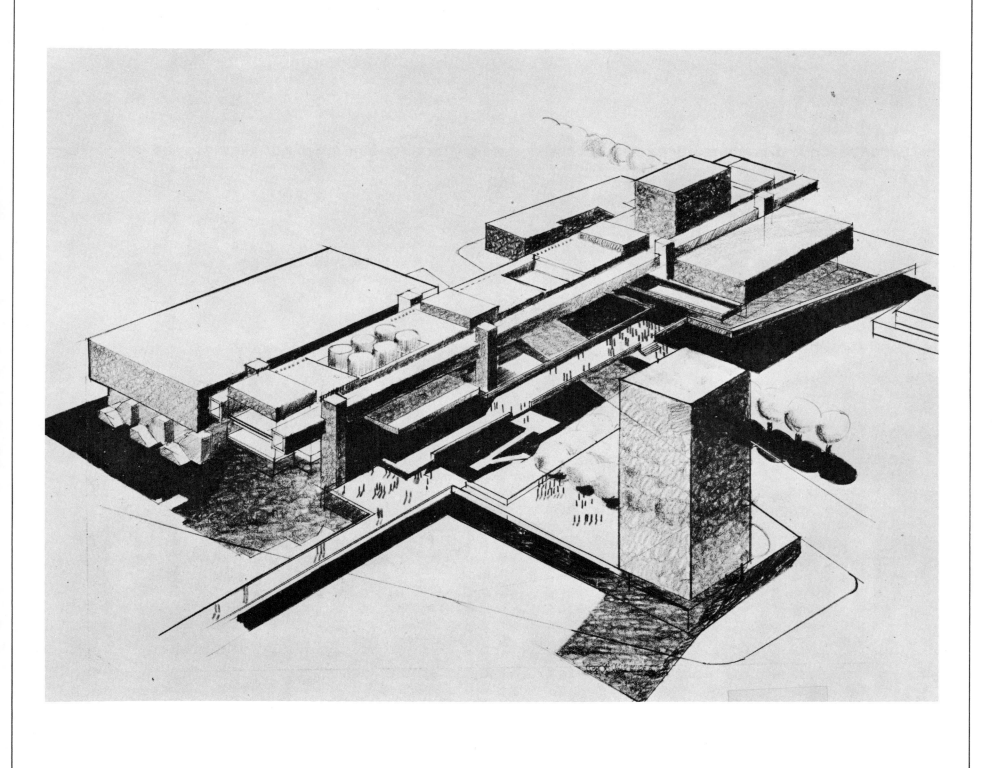

Michael Severin

Boome County Arena & Theater, Binghamton, N.Y.

Elbasani/Logan/Severin

CRAIG ELLWOOD ASSOCIATES | ARCHITECTURE & RELATED DESIGN | 1107 S. ROBERTSON BOULEVARD, LOS ANGELES 90035 | TEL: (213) 273-6614

ASSOCIATES | JAMES TYLER | ROBERT BACON | ARCHITECTS

James Tyler

Xerox Data Systems

Craig Ellwood Associates

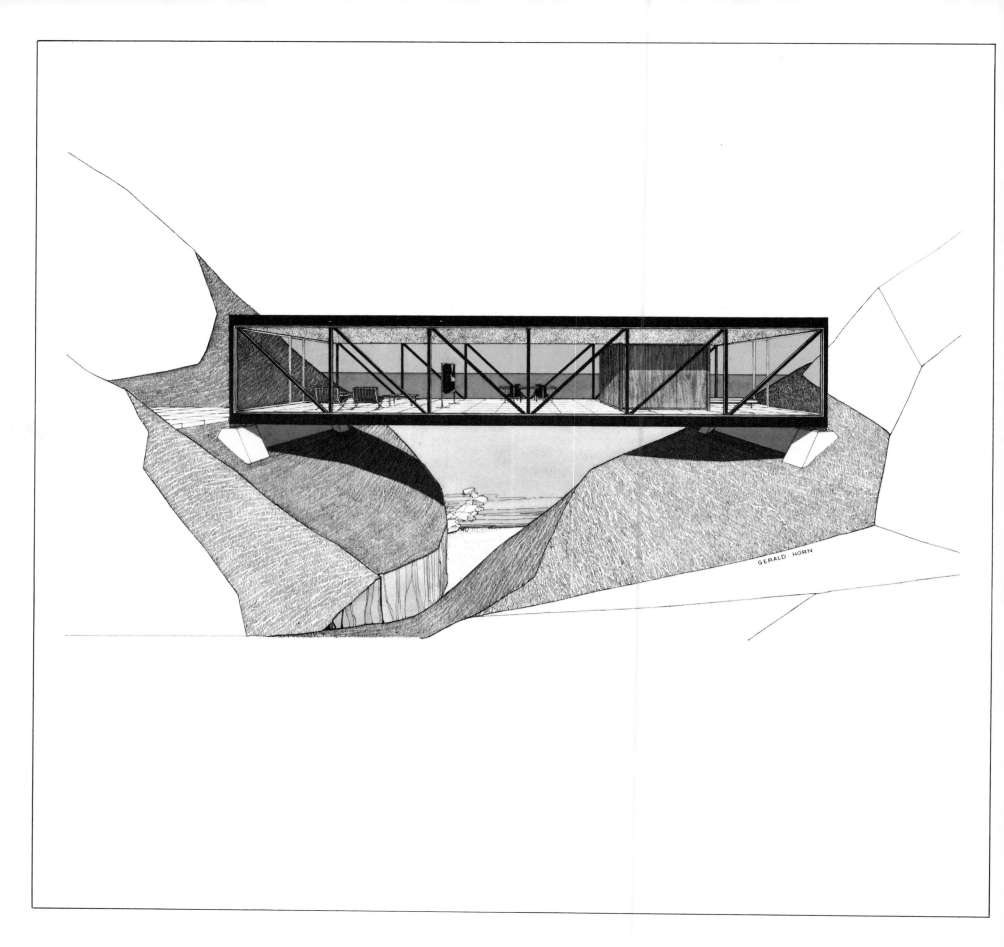

Gerald Horn

Weekend House Project

Craig Ellwood Associates

Gerald Horn   Weekend House Project   Craig Ellwood Associates

Michael Gould

Bridge House

Craig Ellwood Associates

James Tyler

Huntington Beach Exhibition Hall

Craig Ellwood Associates

environmental planning associates

333 fayetteville street   suite 904   raleigh, north carolina 27601   phone (919) 832-2226

Brian Shawcroft

Pan American Health Organization Competition

Environmental Planning Associates

Brian Shawcroft

Environmental Planning Associates

Brian Shawcroft

High Rise, View From City Hall

Environmental Planning Associates

Esherick Homsey Dodge and Davis   Architects and Planners

120 Green Street
San Francisco, California 94111
(415) 421-1924

Joseph Esherick FAIA
George Homsey AIA
Peter Dodge AIA
Charles Davis AIA

Associates
William Simpson AIA
Laura Davenport

Gerald K. Lee

St. Thomas, U.S. Virgin Islands Resort

Esherick, Homsey, Dodge and Davis

197

Gerald K. Lee

St. Thomas, U.S. Virgin Islands Resort

Esherick, Homsey, Dodge and Davis

198

Gerald K. Lee

St. Thomas, U.S. Virgin Islands Resort

Esherick, Homsey, Dodge and Davis

Gerald K. Lee

Town and Fourt Village, St. Louis

Esherick, Homsey, Dodge and Davis

Gerald K. Lee
Lewis D. Sibio

Praia Grande, Algarve, Portugal

Esherick, Homsey, Dodge and Davis

Ferendino
Grafton
Spillis
Candela

architects
engineers
planners

SENIOR PARTNERS

Andrew J. Ferendino, FAIA
Edward G. Grafton, AIA
Peter J. Spillis, AIA
Hilario F. Candela, AIA
Aristides Martinez, PE

PARTNERS

W. Pinson Whiddon, AIA
Ernest C. Norlin, CSI
Jose M. Corbato, AIA
Jorge L. Delgado, AIA
Jose Feito, AIA
Alberto Otero
J. Bruce Spencer, AIA
Louis Lamperty, PE

ASSOCIATE PARTNERS

Rafael J. Portuondo, AIA
E. Monroe Davenport, CSI
Ricardo S. Gomez, PE
Efraim B. Oliver
Henry C. Alexander, Jr., AIA
Grayson G. Welty

INTERIOR DESIGN

Dean K. Newberry

P.O. BOX 567
ST. THOMAS,
VIRGIN ISLANDS
00801
809/774-2688

7600
GEORGIA AVE., N.W.
WASHINGTON, D.C.
20012
202/882-1900

**800
DOUGLAS ENTRANCE
CORAL GABLES
FLORIDA 33134
305/444-4691**

Efraim Oliver

University of Miami, Mailman Center

Ferendino, Grafton, Spillis & Candela

Efraim Oliver

Miami-Dade Junior College

Ferendino, Grafton, Spillis & Candela

Efraim Oliver   Miami-Dade Junior College   Ferendino, Grafton, Spillis & Candela

Operation Headstart, Portable Units

Ferendino, Grafton, Spillis & Candela

Efraim Oliver

Miami Beach First National Bank

Ferendino, Grafton, Spillis & Candela

FITCH LAROCCA CARINGTON JONES Architects Planners 351 East Ohio Street Chicago 60611 Illinois 312/527 2474

Michael Gelick

Thornton Community College

Fitch Larocca Carington Jones

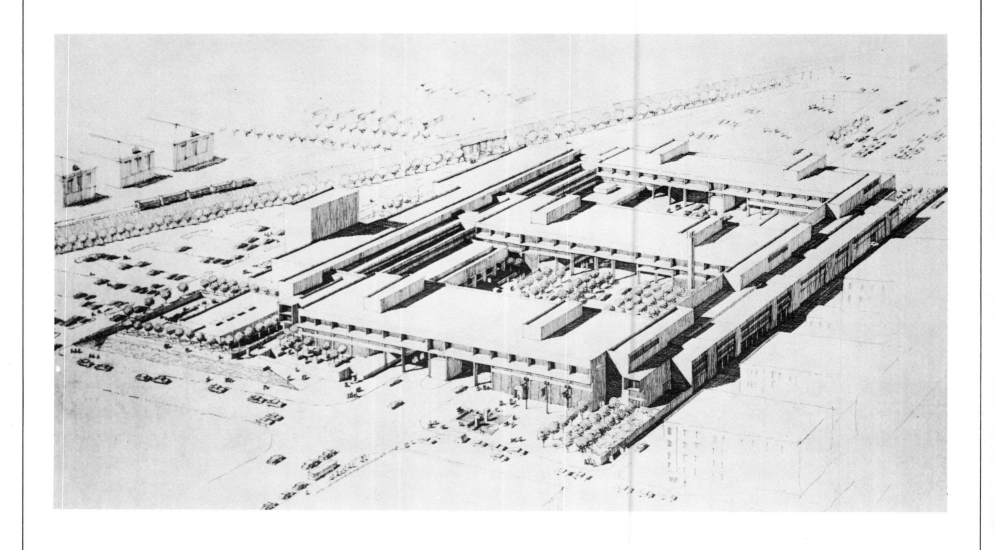

R. W. Carington

Kennedy King College

Fitch Larocca Carington Jones

R. W. Carington

Kennedy King College

Fitch Larocca Carington Jones

211

EARL R. FLANSBURGH AND ASSOCIATES, INC. ARCHITECTS AIA ■ 14 STORY STREET ■ CAMBRIDGE, MASSACHUSETTS 02138 ■ 617 876-6440

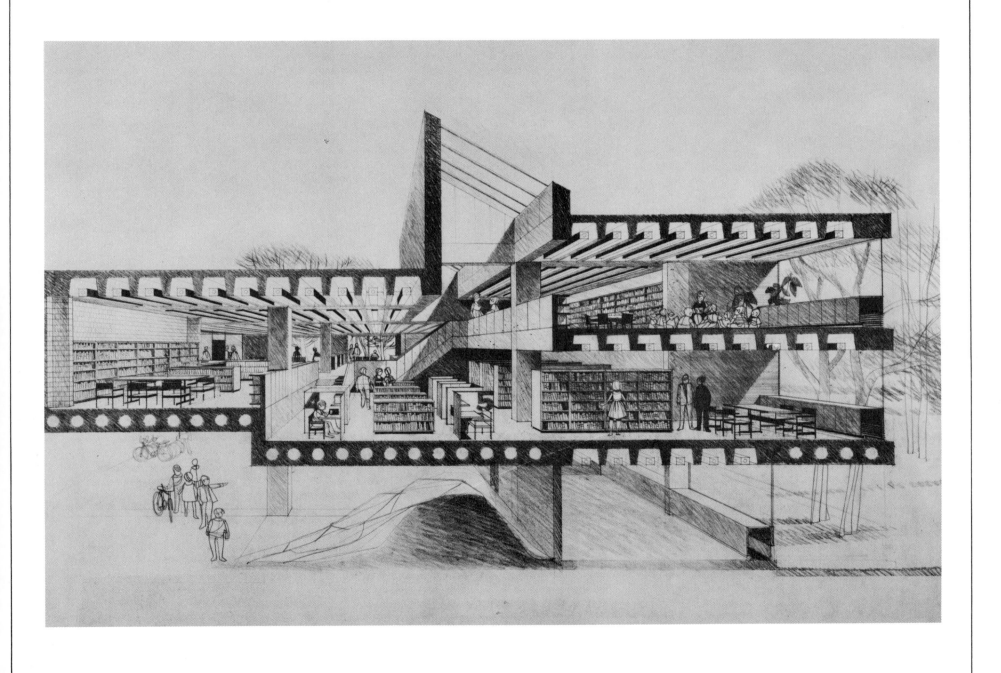

Donald A. Reed

Park School of Brookline

Earl R. Flansburgh & Associates

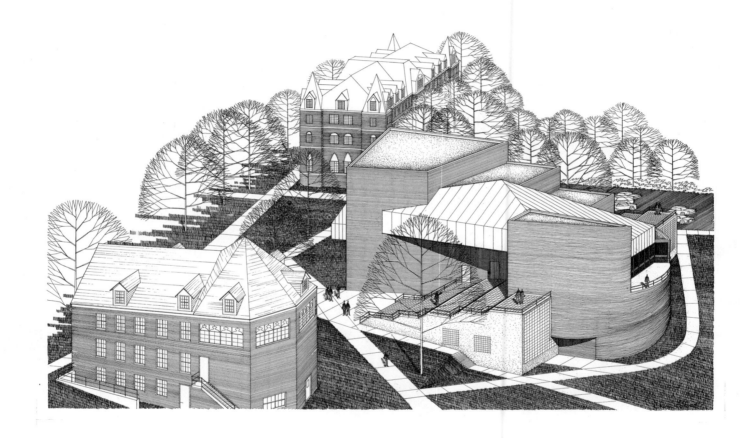

Tufts University Drama Center

Earl R. Flansburgh & Associates

R. Christian Schmitt

Cambridge Office Building

Earl R. Flansburgh & Associates

Donald A. Reed

The Park School of Brookline

Earl R. Flansburgh & Associates

Donald A. Reed

The Park School of Brookline

Earl R. Flansburgh & Associates

FROST ASSOCIATES ARCHITECTS THIRTY EAST FORTY SECOND STREET
NEW YORK NEW YORK 10017 AREA CODE 212 687-7870

FREDERICK G FROST JR FAIA   CARL J CARLSON AIA   NEMBHARD N CULIN AIA   RACHELLE R BENNETT AIA
A CORWIN FROST AIA   CARL FELTZ AIA   GEORGE J SCHWARZ AIA   ALAN B GOLDSAMT AIA

Kenneth Sailor

Martin Luther King High School

Michael Bobrick

Gaylord Hospital

Frost Associates

Kenneth Sailor

Psychology Building, University of Connecticut

Frost Associates

Kenneth Sailor

Howe Avenue Nursing Home *(Detail)*

Frost Associates

Kenneth Sailor

Howe Avenue Nursing Home

Frost Associates

HARLAN H. GEORGESCO

ARCHITECT   A. I. A.

century city   •   gateway west bldg. suite 946

los angeles, california, 90067 — tel. 277-0055

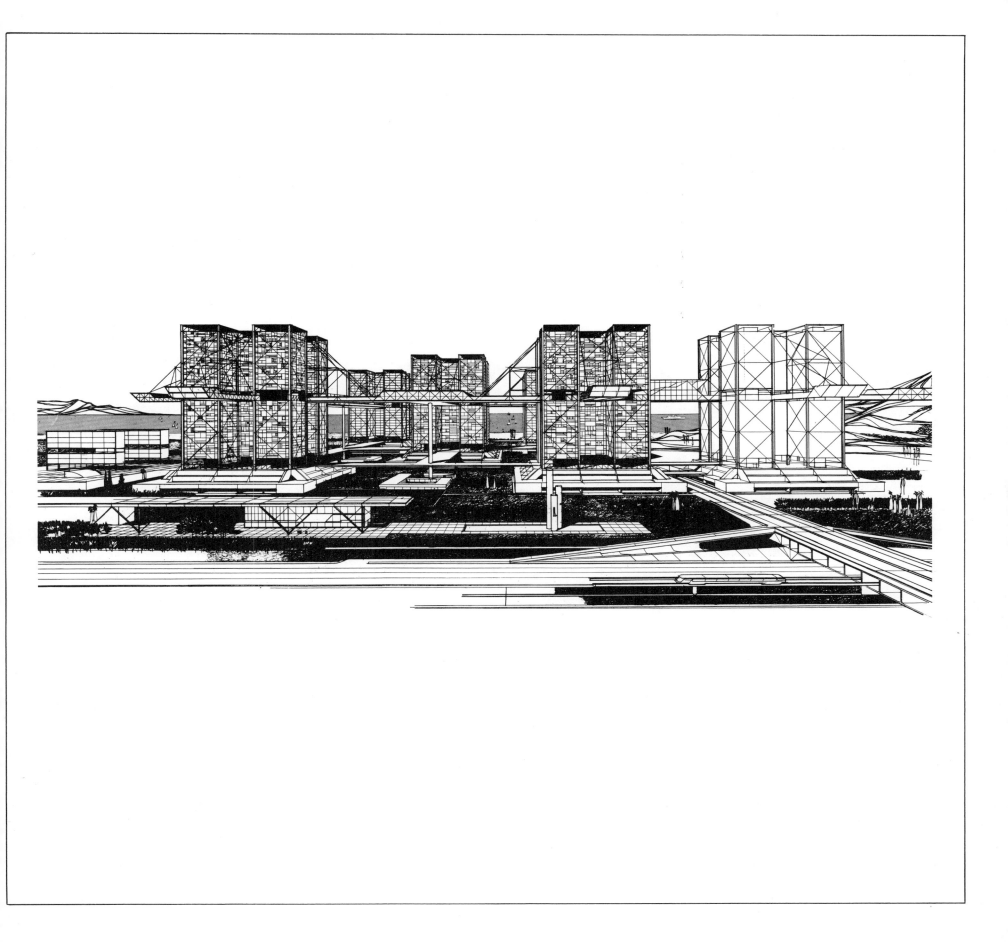

Harlan H. Georgesco

Proposed Urban Renewal Development

Harlan H. Georgesco, Architect

Harlan H. Georgesco

Shopping Center, Urban Renewal Development

Harlan H. Georgesco, Architect

Harlan H. Georgesco

H. H. Georgesco Residence

Harlan H. Georgesco, Architect

Residence for Dr. and Mrs. Hyman

BERTRAND   GOLDBERG   ASSOCIATES

ARCHITECTS   ENGINEERS

MARINA   CITY
CHICAGO   60610
CABLE: ARCHITECT
▶ 312   321-1200

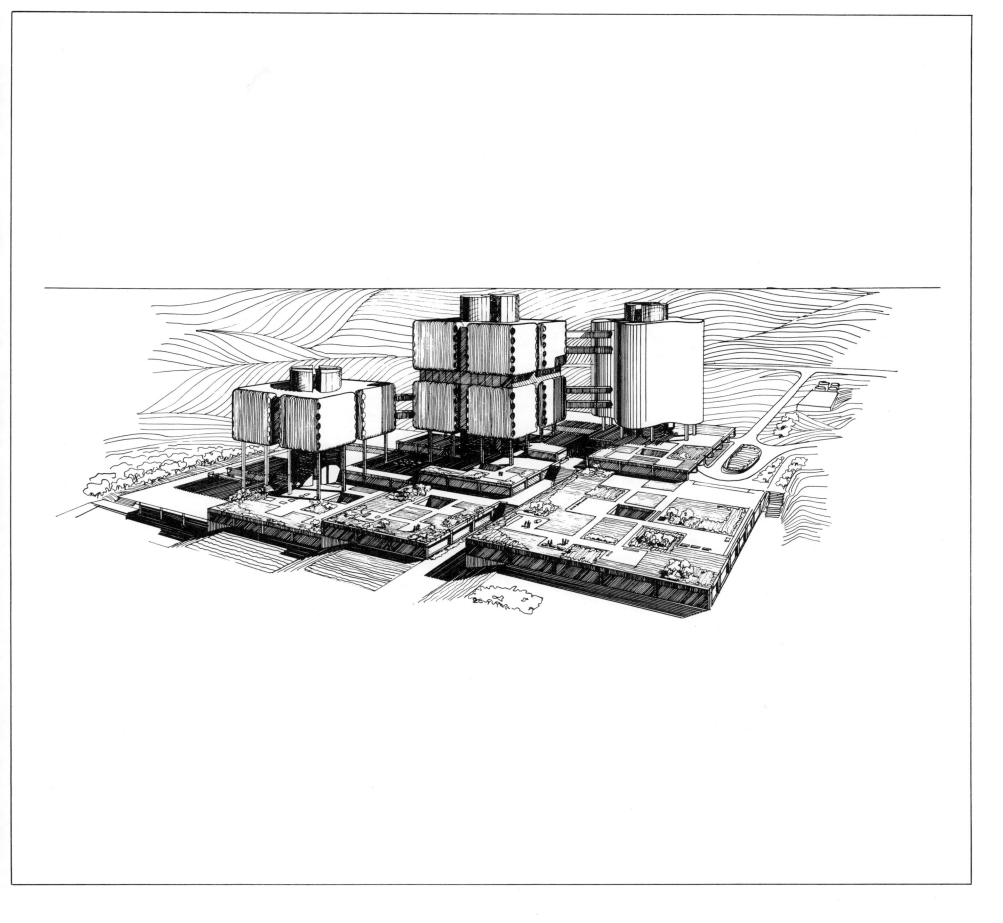

Zloigniew Cianciara

Health Sciences Center

Bertrand Goldberg Associates, Architects

231

George Adams

Women's Hospital and Maternity Center of Chicago

Bertrand Goldberg Associates, Architects

Dale Byrd   The Affiliated Hospitals Center, Boston   Bertrand Goldberg Associates, Architects

MARVIN E. GOODY, JOHN M. CLANCY & ASSOCIATES, INC., ARCHITECTS AIA
136 BOYLSTON STREET   BOSTON   MASSACHUSETTS   02116   (617) LIBERTY 2-6569

MARVIN E. GOODY
JOHN M. CLANCY
ROBERT J. PELLETIER
JOAN E. GOODY

Austris Vitols

Prefabricated Concrete Modular

Marvin E. Goody, John M. Clancy & Associates

235

Austris Vitols

Jewish Family and Children's Service

Marvin E. Goody, John M. Clancy & Associates

Austris Vitols

Jewish Family and Children's Service

Marvin E. Goody, John M. Clancy & Associates

GRUEN ASSOCIATES

ARCHITECTURE · PLANNING · ENGINEERING

KARL VAN LEUVEN, AIA
EDGARDO CONTINI, F. ASCE
BEN H. SOUTHLAND, AIA
HERMAN GUTTMAN, AIA
BEDA ZWICKER, AIA
CESAR PELLI, AIA
DANIEL M. BRANIGAN, AIA
WILLIAM H. DAHL, AIA
ABBOTT HARLE, AIA

LOS ANGELES · NEW YORK · WASHINGTON   6330 San Vicente Boulevard, Los Angeles, California 90048 Tel (213) 937-4270

Barry Zauss

Office Building Study

Gruen Associates

239

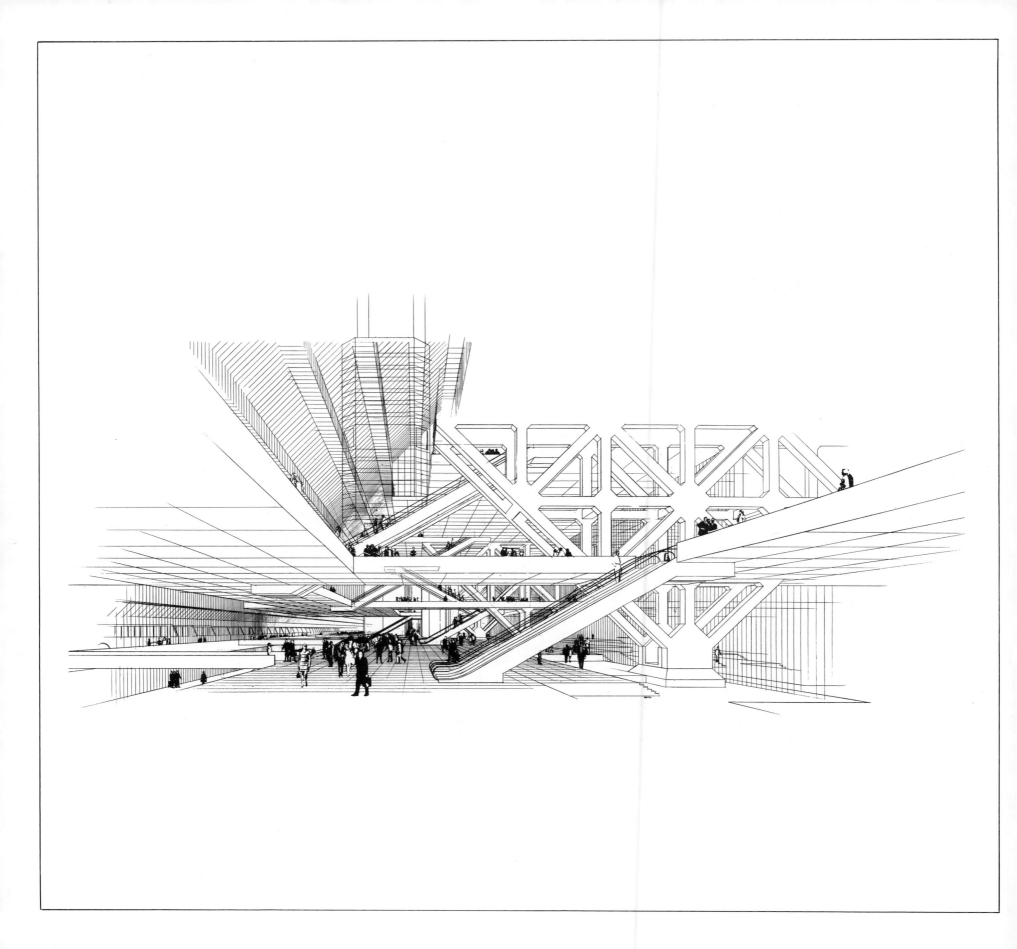

Barry Zauss

UN City Competition, Vienna

Gruen Associates

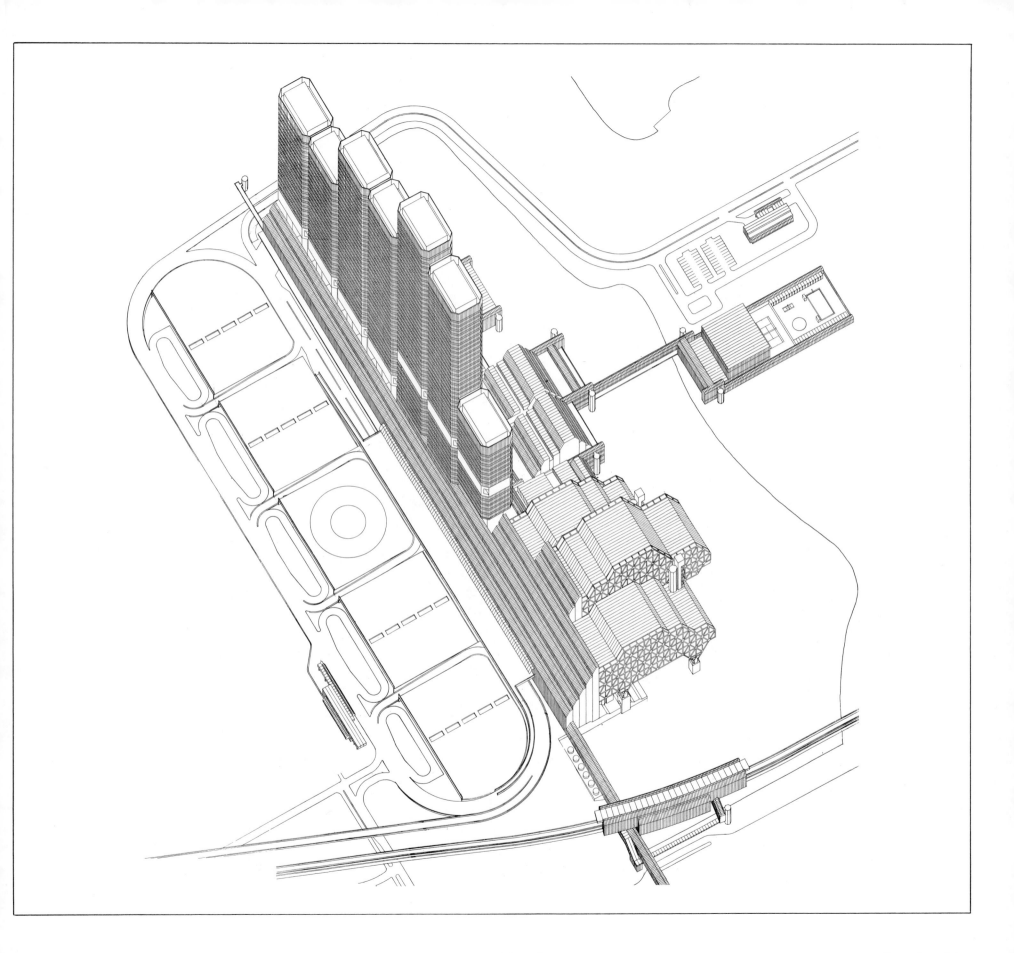

Doug Meyer   UN City Competition, Vienna   Gruen Associates

Ben Althen

Boston Mall

Gruen Associates

Ernest Burden

Lancaster Square

Gruen Associates

Cesar Pelli, Roylance L. Bird Jr., Arthur Golding,
and Constantine Theordoresco

San Bernardino City Hall

Gruen Associates

Barry Zauss

San Bernardino Cultural Center

Gruen Associates

**GRUZEN &
PARTNERS**
FORMERLY
KELLY & GRUZEN

A R C H I T E C T S
P L A N N E R S
E N G I N E E R S

1 7 0 0 B R O A D W A Y
N E W Y O R K N Y 1 0 0 1 9
(AREA 212) 582 7040

24 COMMERCE STREET
N E W A R K N J 0 7 1 0 2
(AREA 201) 643 1944

Brian Burr

Frawley Plaza

Gruzen & Partners

Boston Parcel and Office Building

Helmut Jacoby

Police Headquarters, Manhattan Civic Center

Gruzen & Partners

Larry Perron

S.E. Loop/Rochester New Tolin

Gruzen & Partners

Ernest Burden

Foley Square Courthouse

Gruzen & Partners

Larry Merek

Landsay-Bushwick

Gruzen & Partners

Mark DeNalovy-Rozvadovski   Kissena II Elderly Apartments   Gruzen & Partners

540 Madison Avenue
New York, N.Y. 10022
PLaza 2-6760 Cable: Hannerly

PARTNERS
Albert Kennerly AIA
Lloyd H. Slomanson AIA
Ian H. Smith ARIBA AIA

ASSOCIATES
I. E. Drescher AIA
Manuel Tavarez
Eugene M. Sewell AIA

FOUNDER
William Hamby AIA

Hamby,Kennerly,Slomanson & Smith Architects

David Morgan   Science Building, Stevens Institute of Technology   Hamby, Kennerly, Slomanson & Smith, Architects

T. Morgan

710 Fifth Avenue Office Building

Hamby, Kennerly, Slomanson & Smith, Architects

David Morgan

710 Fifth Avenue Office Building

Hamby, Kennerly, Slomanson & Smith, Architects

HARRISON & ABRAMOVITZ
ARCHITECTS

630 FIFTH AVENUE, NEW YORK, N. Y. 10020

WALLACE K. HARRISON
MAX ABRAMOVITZ
———
CHARLES H. ABBE
MICHAEL M. HARRIS
BRADFORD N. CLARK
JAMES A. KINGSLAND
———
JOSEPH T. AUSSEM
WALTER R. COLVIN
JOHN R. HAYES
CARL W. HOLMES
JAMES M. SNOW, JR.

Tad Leski

A Study for New Houses and Office
Development, Norwalk, Conn.

Harrison & Abramovitz Architects

Max Balassiano

Celanese Building

Harrison & Abramovitz Architects

Max Balassiano · Celanese Building Arcade—Interior · Harrison & Abramovitz Architects

marvin hatami and associates
marvin hatami aia architect

**architecture
urban design and planning**

975 grant street
denver colorado 80203
area code 303. 222-2648

Marvin Hatami

University Arts Center

Marvin Hatami & Associates

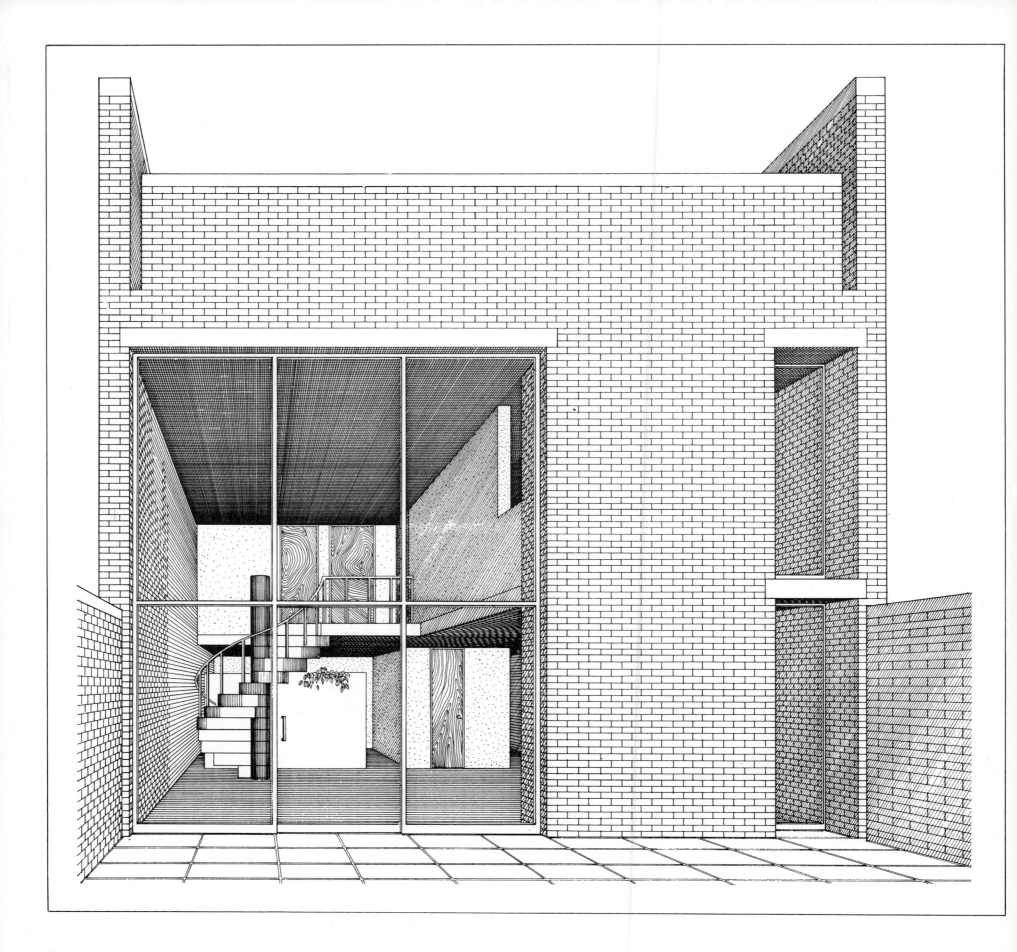

Marvin Hatami

Residential Development

Marvin Hatami & Associates

Martin Hatami

Town House

h+k

Hellmuth, Obata & Kassabaum Inc., Architects

315 North Ninth Street, St. Louis, Missouri 63101
Telephone: 314-421-0343   Cable: HOKASOC

Offices in: Belleville, Ill., San Francisco, Calif., Washington, D.C., Dallas, Texas, Anchorage, Alaska

Jack Barkley

Lambert—St. Louis Airport

Hellmuth, Obata & Kassabaum, Inc. Architects

Jack Barkley

North Park Office Building, Dallas

Hellmuth, Obata & Kassabaum, Inc. Architects

Jack Barkley

First National Bank Building

Hellmuth, Obata & Kassabaum, Inc. Architects

Jack Barkley

Equitable Building, St. Louis

Hellmuth, Obata & Kassabaum, Inc. Architects

Jack Barkley   St. Louis Skyline   Hellmuth, Obata & Kassabaum, Inc. Architects

Jack Barkley

Lake St. Louis Development, Missouri

Hellmuth, Obata & Kassabaum, Inc. Architects

Jack Barkley   National Museum of Transport, St. Louis   Hellmuth, Obata & Kassabaum, Inc. Architects

Jack Barkley

Orlando Post Office, Florida

Hellmuth, Obata & Kassabaum, Inc. Architects

274

Jack Barkley

Sunyab Health Science Faculty, Buffalo

Hellmuth, Obata & Kassabaum, Inc. Architects

HERTZKA & KNOWLES
ARCHITECTS A. I. A.

TWENTY-FIVE MAIN STREET   .   SAN FRANCISCO, CALIFORNIA 94105   .   (415) 421-5891

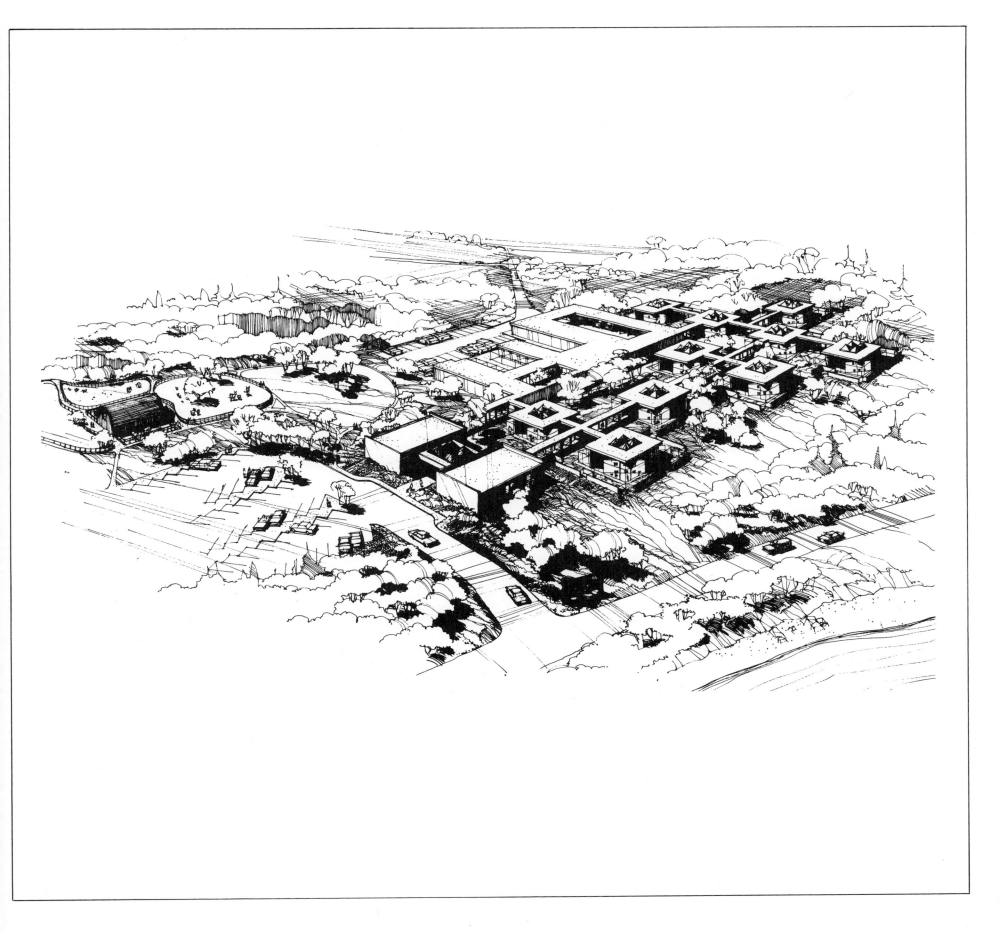

Dennis McCollough

Peninsula Humane Society

Hertzka & Knowles, Architects

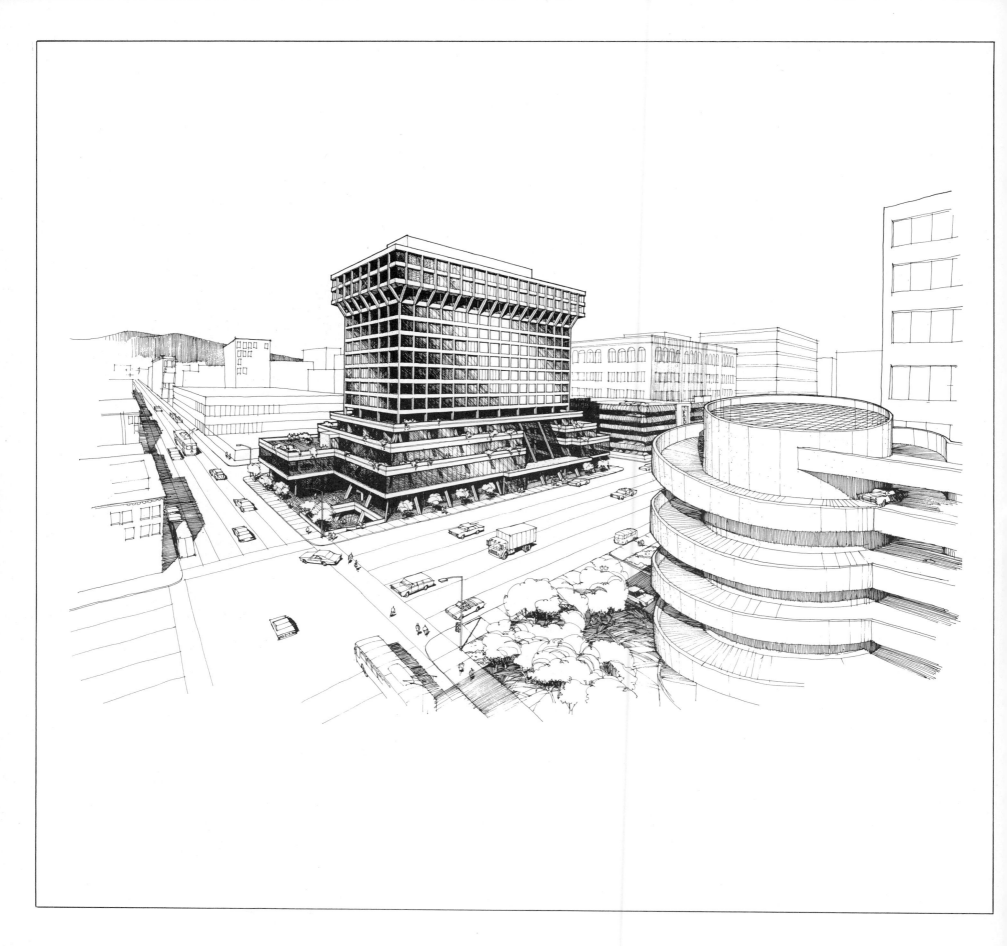

Dennis McCollough

Office Building, Yerba Buena Redevelopment

Hertzka & Knowles, Architects

George Hanna

16th and 24th Street Mission Stations

Hertzka & Knowles, Architects

Honnold, Reibsamen & Rex ARCHITECTS

P. K. REIBSAMEN, A. I. A.
PARTNER

9026 MELROSE AVENUE
LOS ANGELES, CALIFORNIA 90069
(213) 272-0929, 271-5271

Carlos Diniz Associates

Solar Observatory

Honnold, Reibsamen and Rex

Carlos Diniz Associates

Art Center College

Honnold, Reibsamen and Rex

Carlos Diniz

Art Center College, Los Angeles

Honnold, Reibsamen and Rex

MELROSE

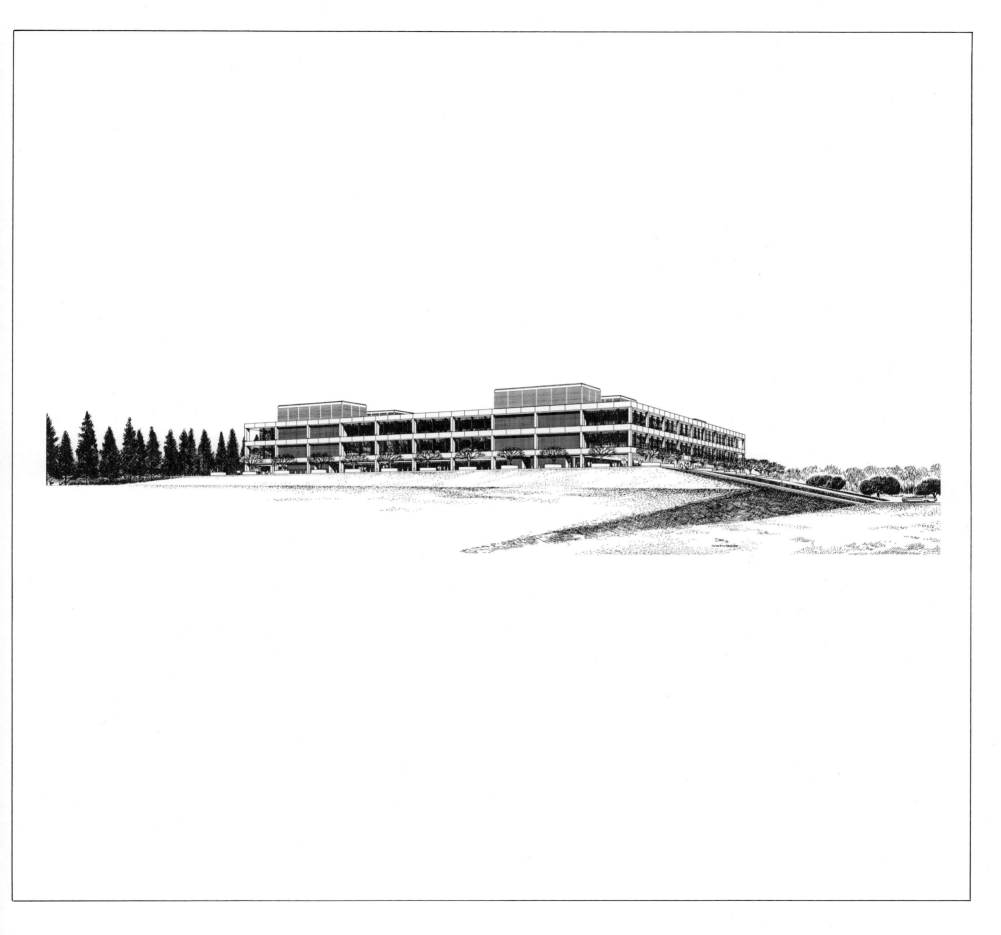

Carlos Diniz Associates

Southwest College

Honnold, Reibsamen and Rex

HUNTER RICE AND ENGELBRECHT   615 BANKERS TRUST BUILDING DES MOINES IOWA 50309 AC 515 283 2748

Mark C. Engelbrecht

Housing Development for the Elderly, Des Moines, Iowa

Hunter, Rice & Engelbrecht

287

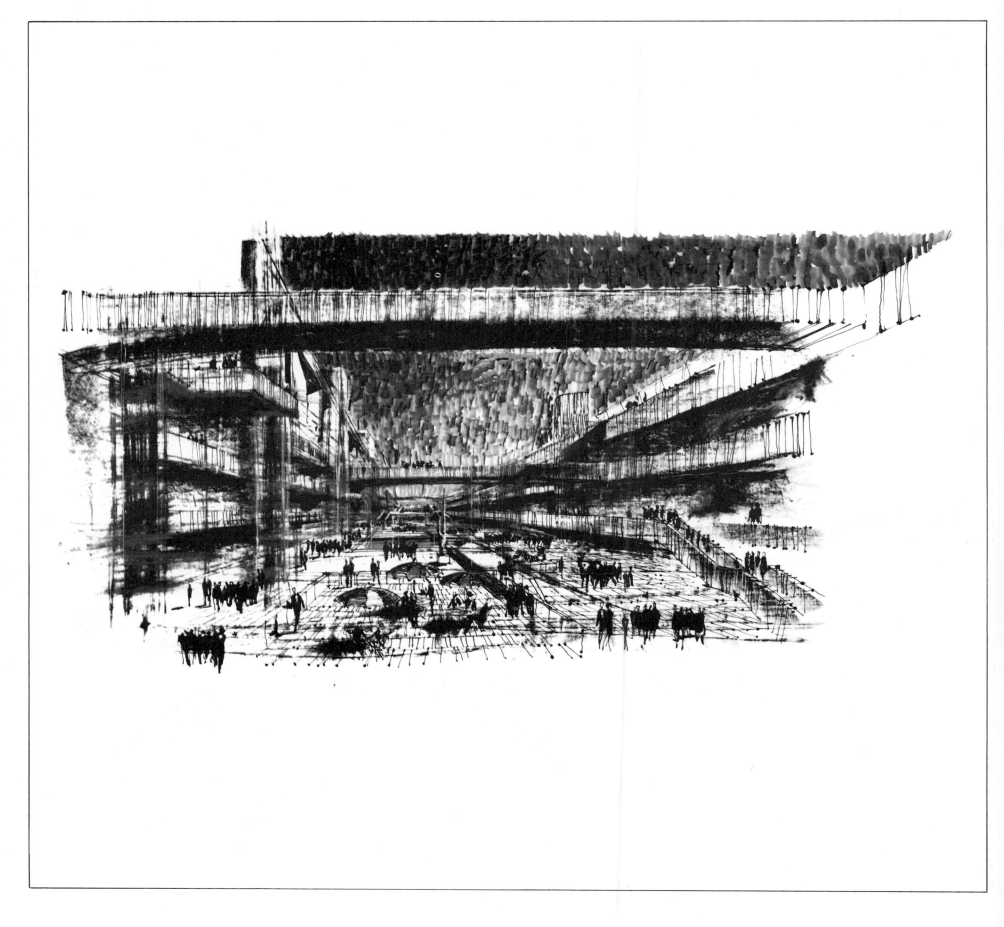

Tadeus M. Janowski

Birmingham-Jefferson Civic Center Competition

Hunter, Rice & Engelbrecht

288

Tadeus M. Janowski

St. Mary's Church, Winnipeg, Manitoba, Canada

Hunter, Rice & Engelbrecht

HUYGENS AND TAPPÉ INC.

ARCHITECTS AND PLANNERS   462 BOYLSTON STREET BOSTON MASS. 02116 536-5451

MEMBER, AMERICAN INSTITUTE OF ARCHITECTS, AMERICAN INSTITUTE OF PLANNERS

Remmert W. Huygens

Concert Hall and Library, Longy School of Music

Huygens & Tappé Inc.

Terry A. Crackenbill

Town Beach in Sharon, Massachusetts

Huygens & Tappé Inc. with Moriele & Gary

Remmert W. Huygens   Keane House   Huygens & Tappé Inc.

Remmert W. Huygens

Huygen's Chalet, Switzerland

Huygens & Tappé Inc.

Remmert W. Huygens

Banking and Parking Garage

Huygens & Tappé Inc.

JOHN M. JOHANSEN F.A.I.A.

401 EAST THIRTY SEVENTH STREET, NEW YORK, NEW YORK 10016/ 212 889-2560

ASSOCIATES

ASHOK M. BHAVNANI
THADDEUS HANSER
MICHAEL HOLLANDER

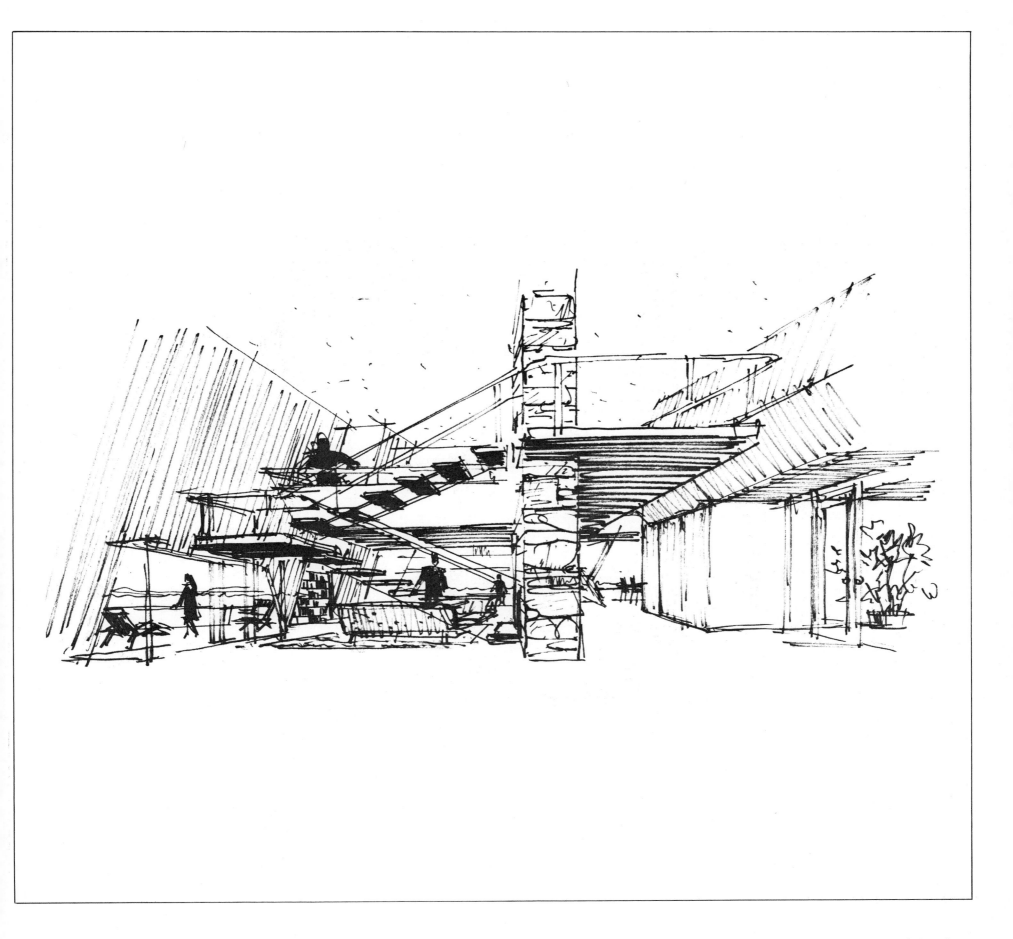

John M. Johansen

Guest House

John M. Johansen & Associates

John M. Johansen

Leap Frog Housing

John M. Johansen & Associates

John M. Johansen   Leap Frog Housing   John M. Johansen & Associates

Johnson, Johnson & Roy/inc.
Landscape Architects

303 N. Main Street
Ann Arbor, Michigan 48104
313 662 4457

William J. Johnson / Carl D. Johnson / Clarence Roy
James E. Christman / Elwood J. Holman
Richard Macias / Philip B. Wargelin

Carl D. Johnson

Louisville Mall

Johnson, Johnson & Roy Inc.

Carl D. Johnson

Sketches, Detroit Institute of Technology

Johnson, Johnson & Roy Inc.

Donald F. Hilderbrandt

Johnson, Johnson & Roy Inc.

Sandra Hansen

Pedestrian Alley Sketch, DeKalb, Urban Renewal

Johnson, Johnson & Roy Inc.

Carl D. Johnson

Louisville Mall

Johnson, Johnson & Roy Inc.

Philip Johnson & John Burgee, Architects

375 PARK AVENUE NEW YORK N Y 10022 PLAZA 1- 7440

Ronald Love

The Harbor Town Square Long Island Development

Philip Johnson & John Burge Architects

Ronald Love

Glass-Roofed Arcade Long Island Development

Philip Johnson & John Burge Architects

Ronald Love

Long Island Development

Philip Johnson & John Burge Architects

JOHNSTON • CAMPANELLA • MURAKAMI • BRUMMITT AND COMPANY

ARCHITECTS - CONSULTANTS - PLANNERS 830 N. RIVERSIDE DRIVE, RENTON, WASHINGTON 98055 (206) 255-1476

PARTNERS: DAVID A. JOHNSTON, A.I.A. • FELIX M. CAMPANELLA, A.I.A. • TERRY T. MURAKAMI, R.A. • ROBERT S. BURNS, C.S.I. • CHARLES W. BRUMMITT, A.I.A.

Felix Campanella   Arlington Senior High School   Johnston, Campanella, Murakami, Brummitt and Company

311

Felix Campanella

Renton City Library

Johnston, Campanella, Murakami, Brummitt and Company

Chuck Brummitt   Tolt Senior High School   Johnston, Campanella, Murakami, Brummitt and Company

A. QUINCY JONES, F.A.I.A., AND ASSOCIATES, ARCHITECTS, INC.

ARCHITECTS & SITE PLANNERS   12248 SANTA MONICA BOULEVARD   LOS ANGELES CALIFORNIA 90025   (213) 272-8208 826-0881

ASSOCIATE ARCHITECTS: EMIEL BECSKY · KAZ NOMURA · LOUIS J. LIETS · JOHN E. THOMAN · WILLIAM G. LAFFIN · DONALD C. PICKEN

A. Quincy Jones

Travel Sketch, San Juan Capistrano Mission

A. Quincy Jones & Associates

A. Quincy Jones

Travel Sketch, Wool Market, Marrakech, Morocco

A. Quincy Jones & Associates

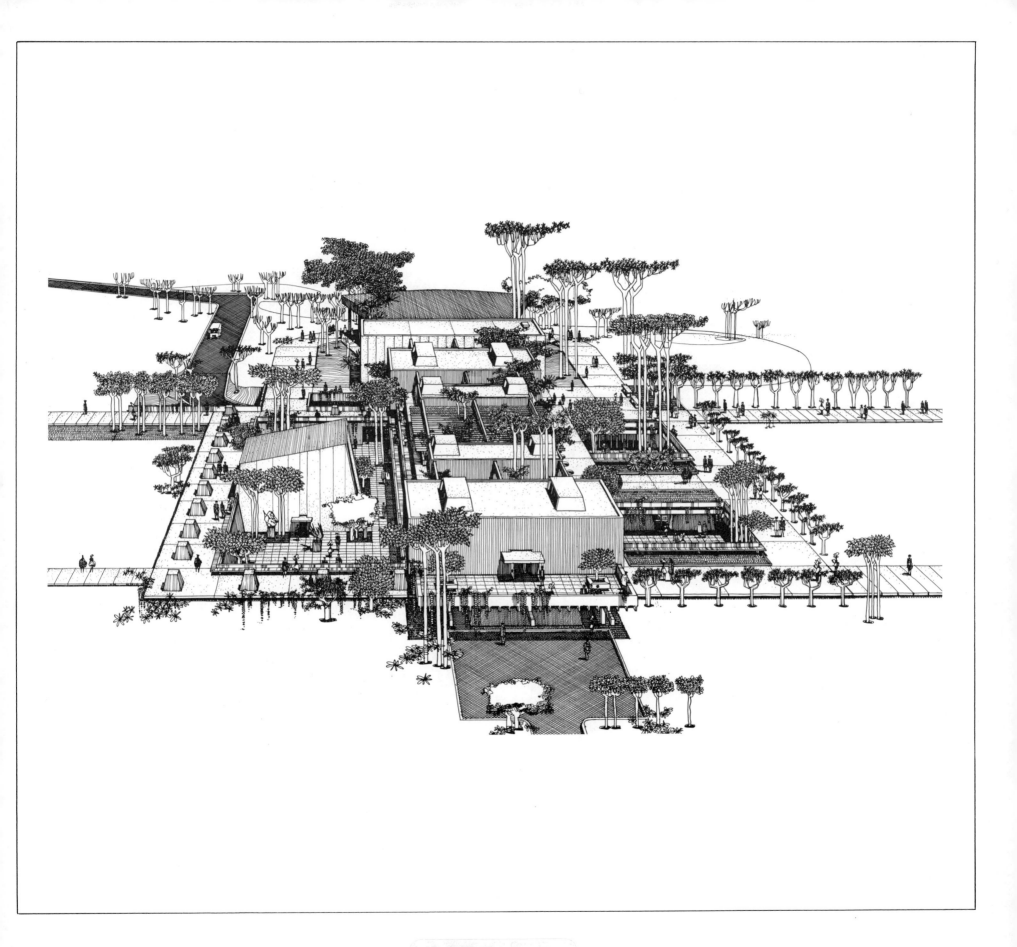

Kaz Nomura

A. Quincy Jones & Associates

WALKING EXPERIENCE

TEACHING

EXHIBITION

Kaz Nomura

Calif. State College, Dominguez Hills

A. Quincy Jones & Associates

Univ. of Calif., San Diego, Mandeville Center—Humanities Bldg.

A. Quincy Jones & Associates

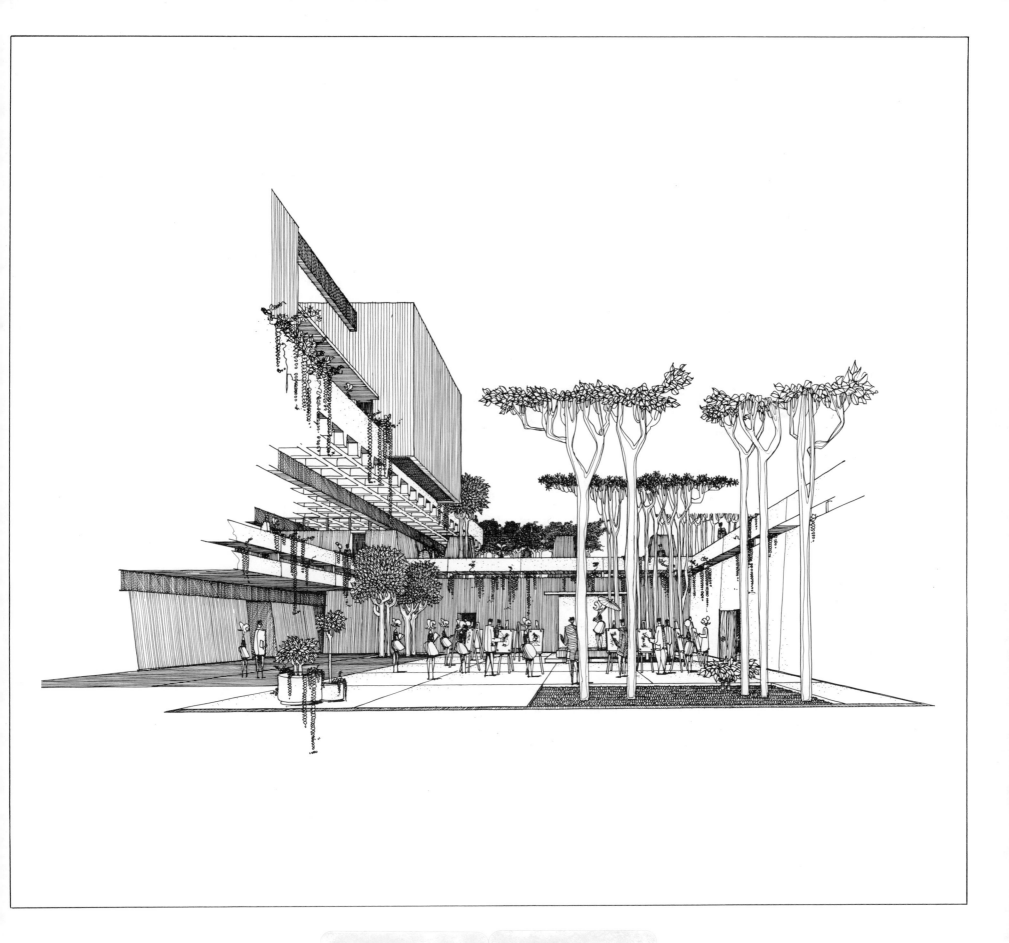

Kaz Nomura

Univ. of Calif., San Diego, Mandeville Center – Humanities Bldg.

A. Quincy Jones & Associates

Hospital for Palo Alto Medical Research Foundation

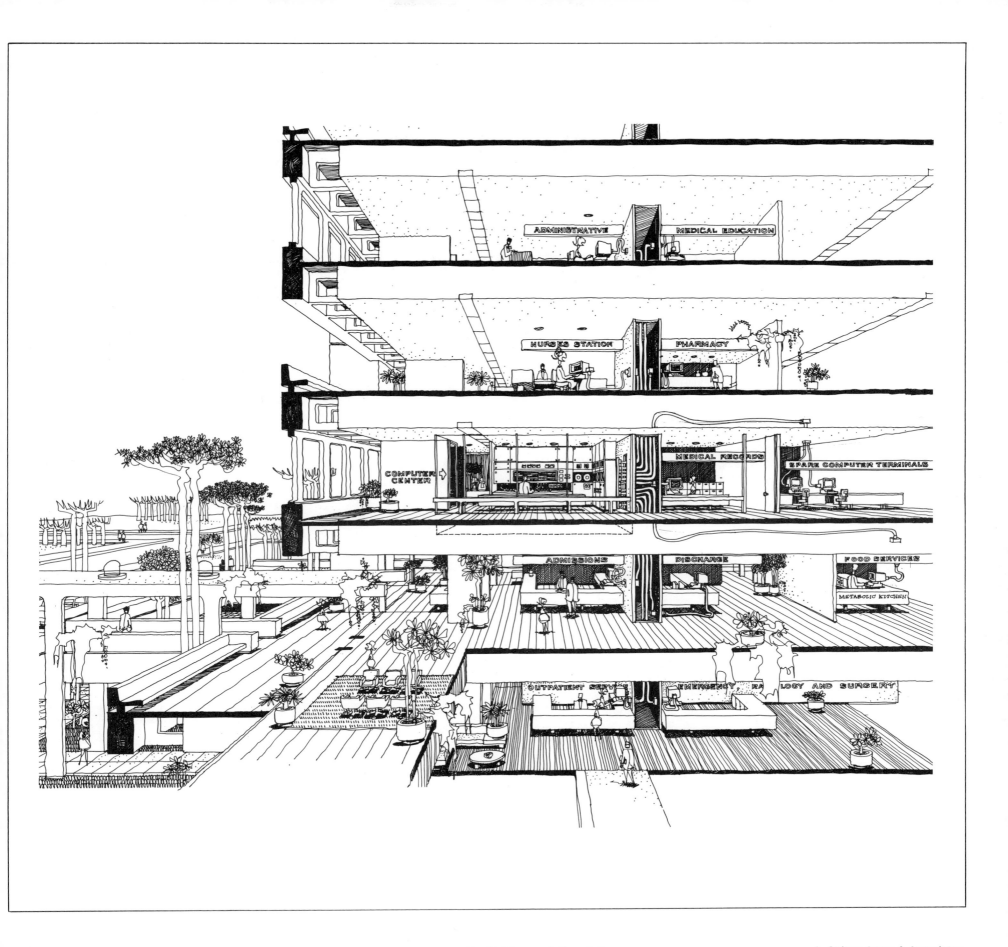

Kaz Nomura

Hospital for Palo Alto Medical Research Foundation

A. Quincy Jones & Associates

KAHN KAPPE LOTERY ARCHITECTS PLANNERS

501 SANTA MONICA BOULEVARD   SANTA MONICA, CALIFORNIA 90401   TELEPHONE 451-5494

HERBERT KAHN AIA   RAYMOND KAPPE FAIA   REX LOTERY AIA   ASSOCIATE   CLELIO BOCCATO

William Simonium

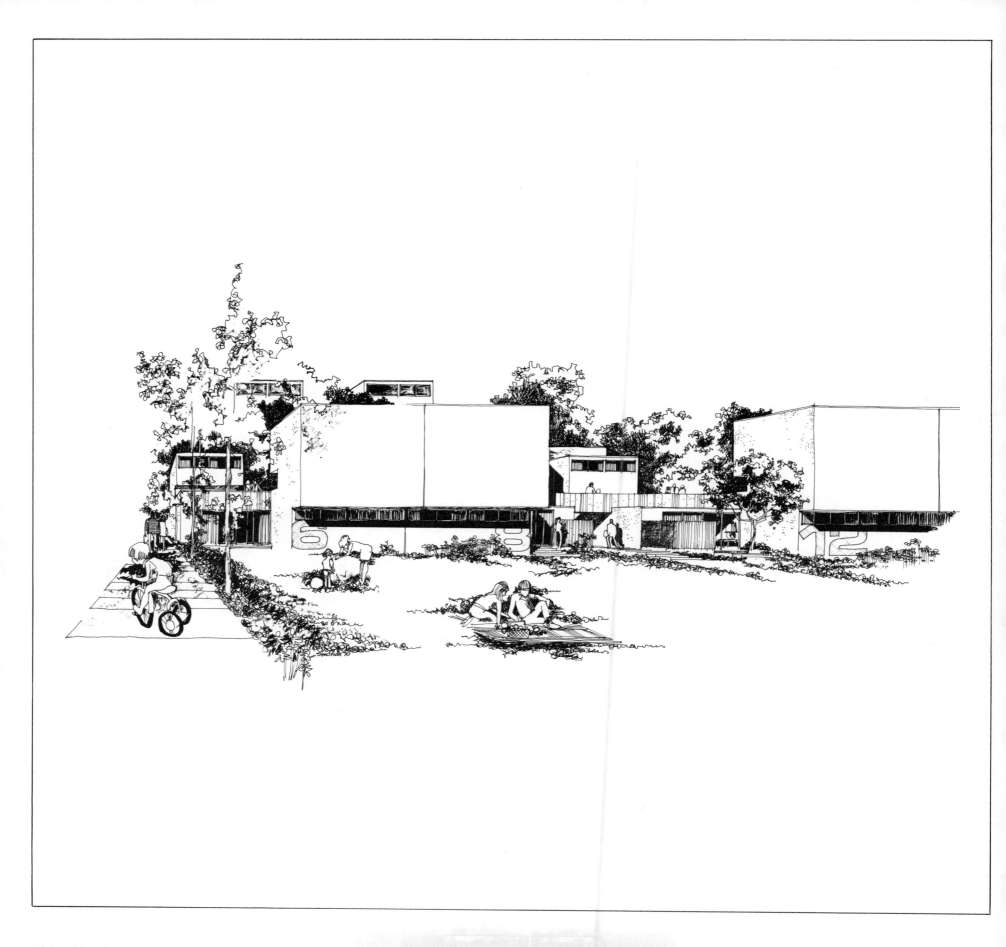

Student Housing

William Simonium

Student Housing, Cal Poly, San Luis Obispo

Kahn, Kappe, Lottery

William Simonium

Kahn, Kappe, Lottery

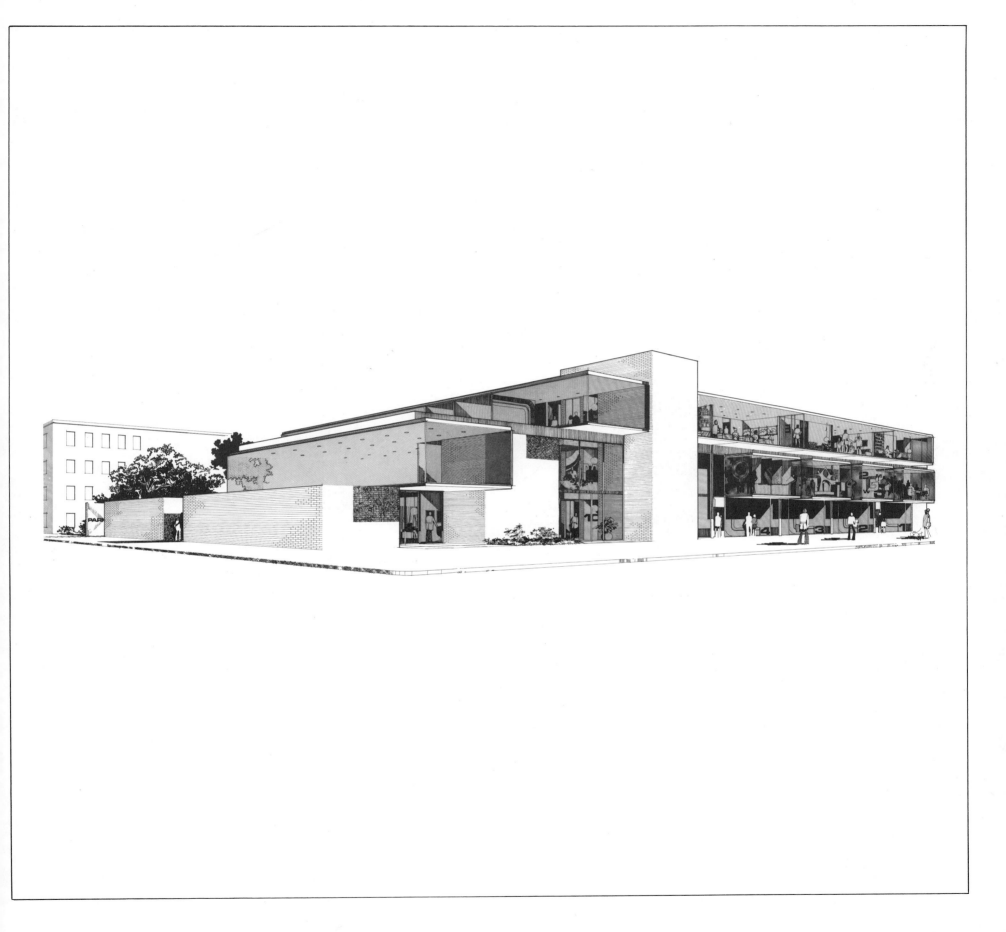

KALLMANN & McKINNELL, ARCHITECTS   127 TREMONT STREET BOSTON MASSACHUSETTS 02108   617-482-5745

GERHARD MICHAEL KALLMANN AIA ARIBA NOEL MICHAEL McKINNELL AIA HENRY A. WOOD AIA JEFFREY W. BROWN AIA

Noel Michael McKinnell

Boston City Mall

Kallman, McKinnell & Knowles Campbell,
Aldrich & Nulty LeMessurier Associates, Inc.

KAMNITZER/MARKS & PARTNERS 1627 PONTIUS AVENUE, LOS ANGELES, CALIFORNIA 90025 TELEPHONE (213) 477-5511/879-2972

PETER KAMNITZER *american institute of planners*
BORIS MARKS *american institute of architects*
FRED K. LAPPIN

Louie Gadel

McArthur Beach, Venice, Florida

Kamnitzer/Marks & Partners

John Reinwald

Canaan Close, New Canaan, Conn.

Kamnitzer/Marks & Partners

Greg Chazanas

Fred Lappin

Brookside Village, Redondo Beach, California

Kamnitzer/Marks & Partners

Fred Lappin

Brookside Village, Redondo Beach, California

Kamnitzer/Marks & Partners

Kemper & Associates Suite 920, 1801 Avenue of the Stars, Century City, Los Angeles, Calif. 90067, (213) 277-1110, 277-6621

Planning / Architecture / Engineering

William H. Cufflin

Transamerica Branch Office

Kemper & Associates

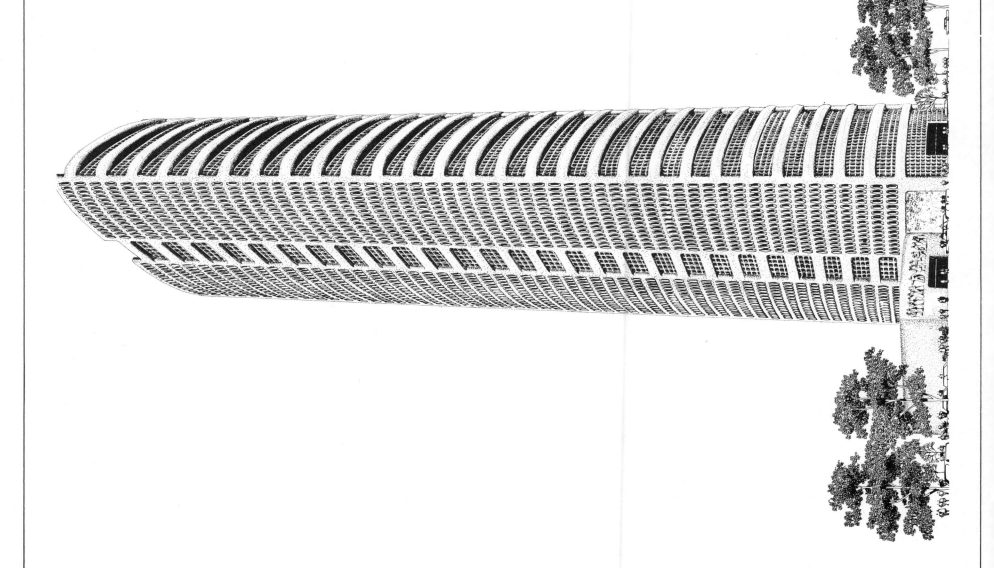

Ben Althen

Peugeot Building, Buenos Aires Competition

Kemper & Associates

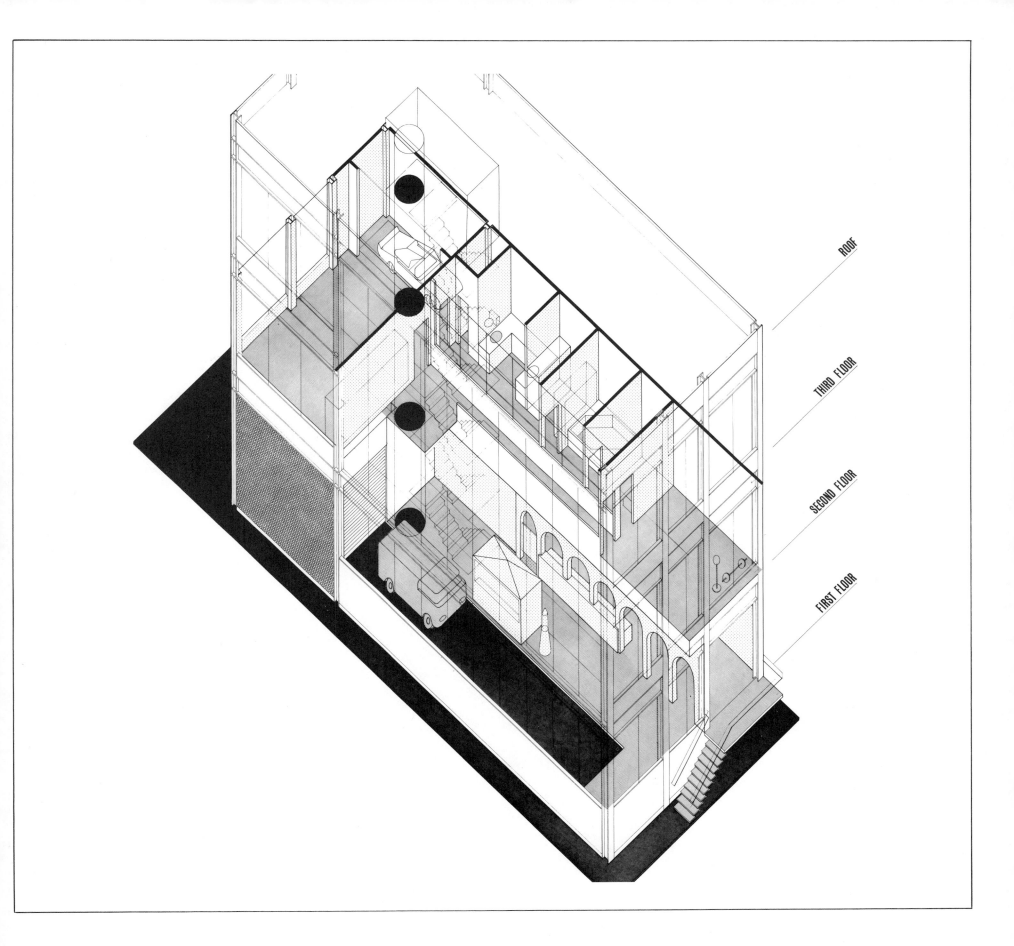

ROOF

THIRD FLOOR

SECOND FLOOR

FIRST FLOOR

Constantine Theodorescu   Runyan Residence   Kemper & Associates

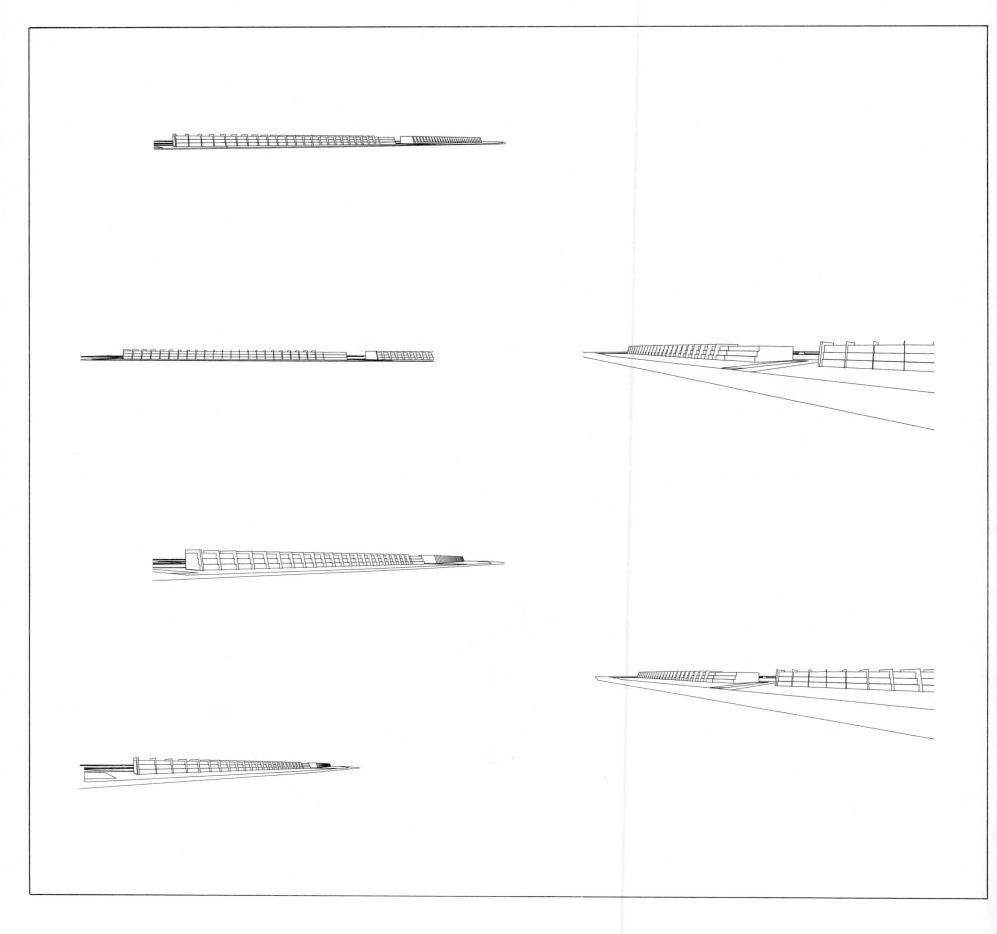

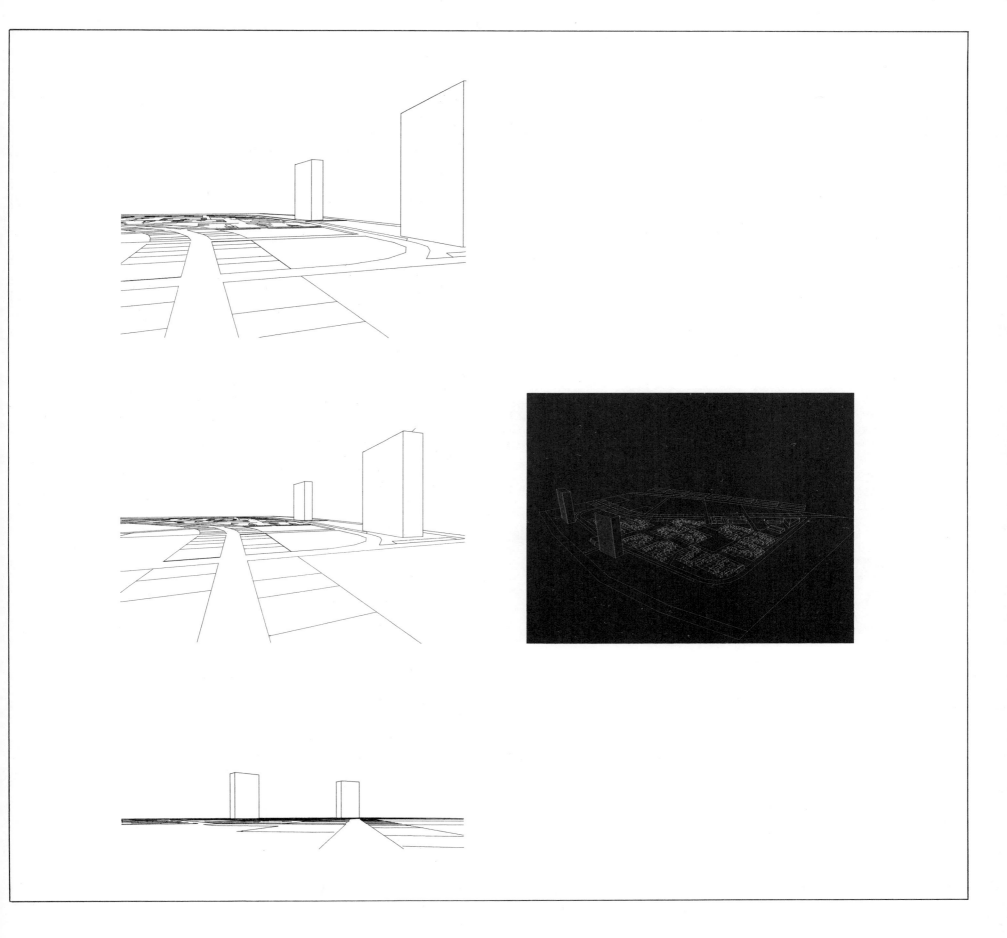

Digital Enterprises, Sol DePicciotto, and Sam Mori   Bahia Kino Development, Mexico   Kemper & Associates

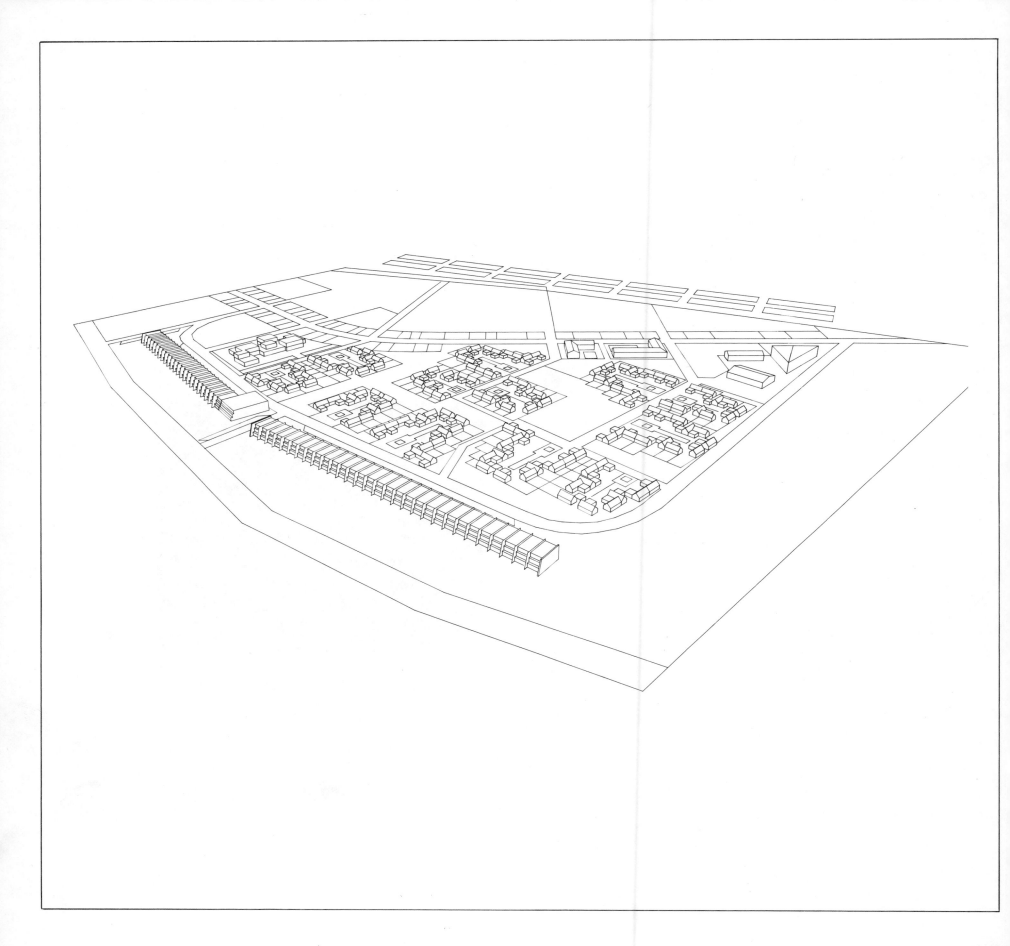

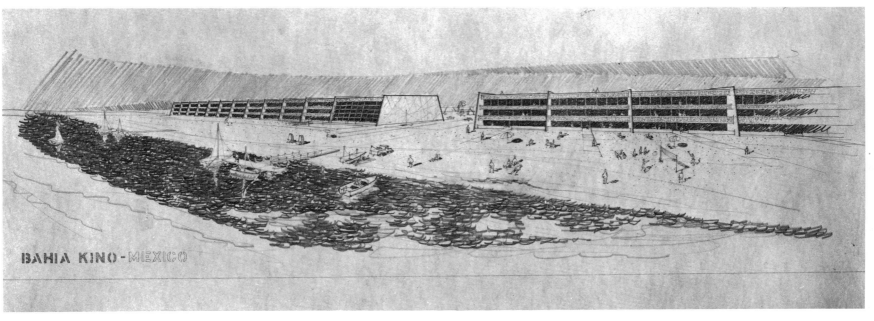

Alfred M. Kemper   Bahia Kino Development, Mexico   Kemper & Associates

KING
&
KING

ARCHITECTS   420 EAST GENESEE STREET, SYRACUSE, NEW YORK 13202

HARRY A. KING AIA
F. CURTIS KING AIA
RUSSELL A. KING AIA
FRED R. FRANK AIA
MORRIS M. GAMBLE AIA
WENDELL W. HOONE AIA
ROBERT W. SECOR AIA

DAVID E. CHASE
DONALD A. SHERMAN

Helmut Jacoby

Ernest Stevenson Bird Library, Syracuse, New York

King & King

PIERRE KOENIG A. I. A. ARCHITECT

12221 DOROTHY ST., LOS ANGELES, CALIF. 90049 - TEL. 826-1414

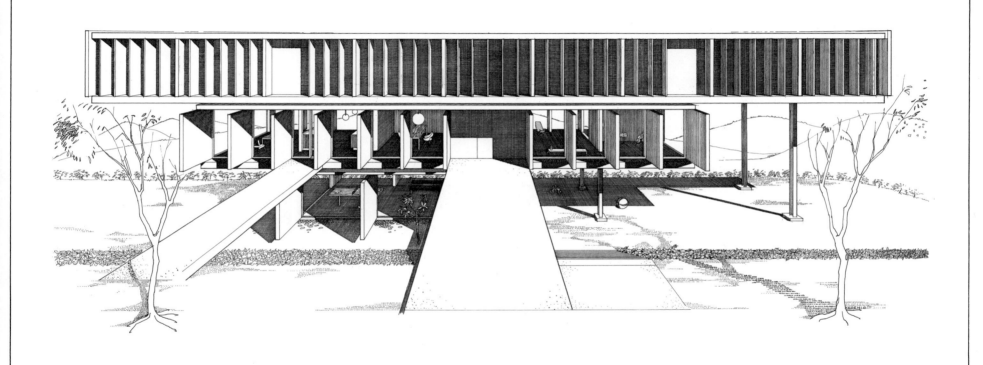

Pierre Koenig

Iwata Residence

Pierre Koenig

351

Pierre Koenig

Islamic Mosque

Pierre Koenig

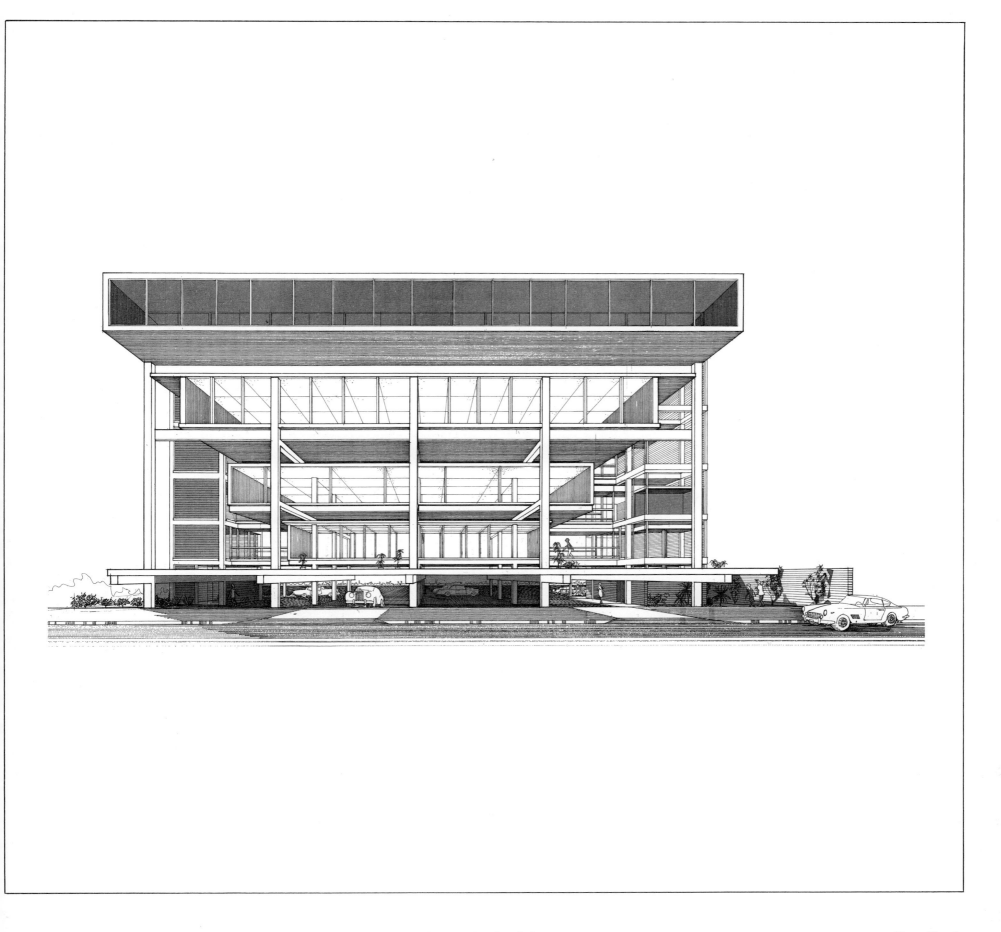

Pierre Koenig

Franklyn Medical Bldg.

Pierre Koenig

ERNEST J. KUMP ASSOCIATES

325 LYTTON AVENUE, PALO ALTO, CALIFORNIA 94301

TELEPHONE (415) 324-2561

ARCHITECTS

PALO ALTO, CALIFORNIA   SAN FRANCISCO, CALIFORNIA

Hiko Takeda

Marine Station Stanford Univ.

Ernest J. Kump Associates

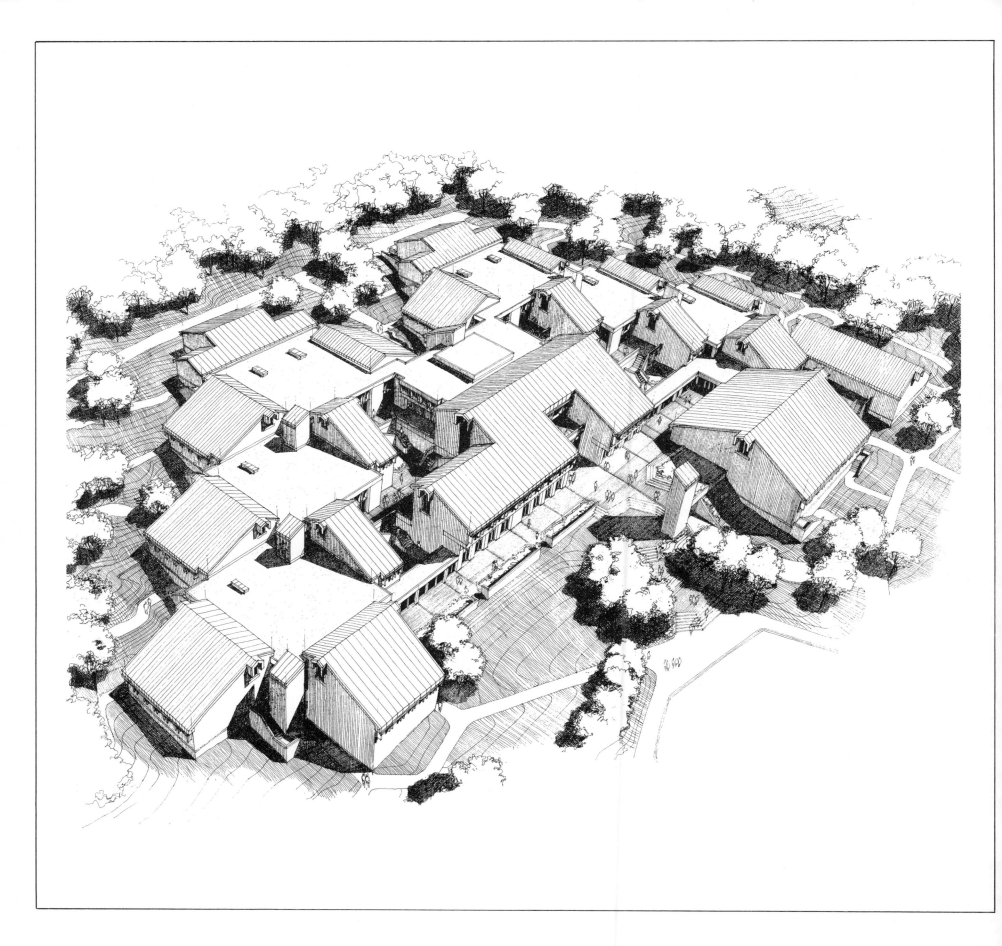

Robert B. Sprague

Community College (Greenfield)

Ernest J. Kump Associates

Hiko Takeda

Community College (Court)

Ernest J. Kump Associates

LANGDON & WILSON
ARCHITECTS

ROBERT E. LANGDON JR. A.I.A.
ERNEST C. WILSON JR. A.I.A.

HANS MUMPER A.I.A.

3345 WILSHIRE BOULEVARD   380-9930   LOS ANGELES, CALIFORNIA 90005

Walter Greub

Proposed Office Building, Downtown Los Angeles

Langdon & Wilson

Walter Greub

City Center Mall, San Diego

Langdon & Wilson

Walter Greub

Proposed Warehouse Facility, Los Angeles

Langdon & Wilson

MORRIS LAPIDUS ASSOCIATES

ARCHITECTS

MORRIS LAPIDUS, AIA
ALAN H. LAPIDUS, AIA
JOHN A. BOWSTEAD, AIA
DONALD J. SEIDLER, AIA
ROBERT M. SWEDROE, AIA
WARREN C. WUERTZ, AIA

———————

LEO KOMARIN

———————

ALAN D. ASCHNER
CONTROLLER

1688 MERIDIAN AVENUE · MIAMI BEACH FLORIDA 33139 · JEFFERSON 8-4331

641 LEXINGTON AVENUE, NEW YORK, N. Y. 10022 · PLAZA 3-4570

Hugo Alpazar

City in the Sky

Morris Lapidus Associates

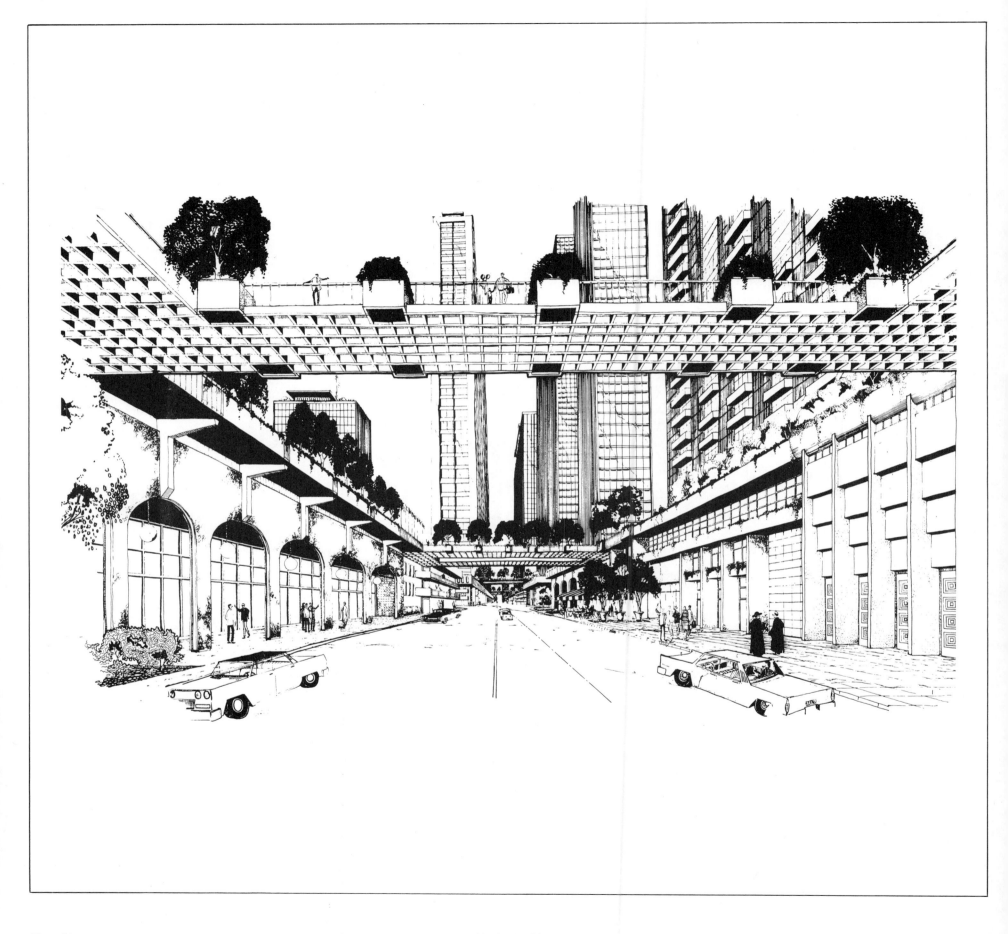

Hugo Alpazar

City in the Sky

Morris Lapidus Associates

Morris Lapidus

Sterling Foresthouse

Morris Lapidus Associates

Hugo Alpazar

Proposed Apartment House

Morris Lapidus Associates

7046 HOLLYWOOD BOULEVARD
LOS ANGELES CALIFORNIA 90028
(2 1 3)   4 6 2   2 3 7 3

JOHN LAUTNER
ARCHITECT, F.A.I.A.

VIEW FROM NORTH

SECTION B-B

Angela Zar

Rancho Del Valle, Crippled Children's Society

John Lautner

VIEW OF MRS HOPE'S BEDROOM & GARDEN
FROM OPEN UPPER TERRACE

DRAWN BY
GORDON SMALL

John Lautner
F.A.I.A. ARCHITECT

Hope Residence

Angela Zar   Arango Residence   John Lautner

Robert B. Liles, Inc.... **ARCHITECT AND ENGINEER**

Telephone 981-4040

840 BATTERY STREET
SAN FRANCISCO, CALIF. 94111

John G. Merrill

Pearlridge Mall, Honolulu

Robert B. Liles

LOMAX-ASSOCIATES-ARCHITECTS

JERROLD E. LOMAX A.I.A.   **DONALD N. MILLS A.I.A.**   **RICHARD SCHOEN A.I.A.**

2300 WESTWOOD BOULEVARD,   LOS ANGELES, CALIFORNIA 90064   474-1569/879-1244

Jerrold E. Lomax

Lacerte & Wilbur Office Building

Lomax Associates

Doctor's Residence Building

Philo John Jacobson

Miller Desk Co.

Lomax Associates with Philo John Jacobson

Charles Luckman Associates 9220 Sunset Blvd., Los Angeles, Calif. 90069, CRestview 4-7755

Planning / Architecture / Engineering / Los Angeles / Phoenix / Boston / New York

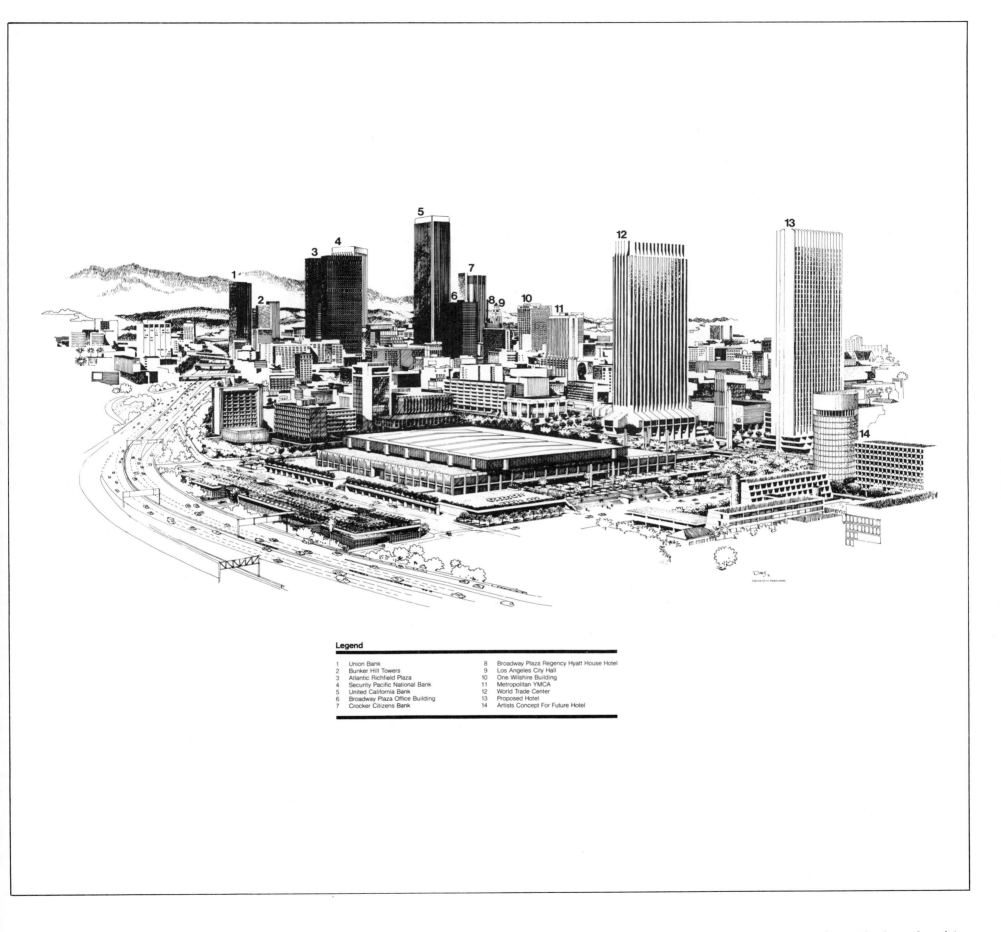

Legend

1	Union Bank	8	Broadway Plaza Regency Hyatt House Hotel
2	Bunker Hill Towers	9	Los Angeles City Hall
3	Atlantic Richfield Plaza	10	One Wilshire Building
4	Security Pacific National Bank	11	Metropolitan YMCA
5	United California Bank	12	World Trade Center
6	Broadway Plaza Office Building	13	Proposed Hotel
7	Crocker Citizens Bank	14	Artists Concept For Future Hotel

Carlos Diniz Associates   Los Angeles Skyline 1981   Charles Luckman Associates

Carlos Diniz Associates

Broadway Plaza, Shopping Mall, Los Angeles, California

Charles Luckman Associates

Carlos Diniz Associates

Hyatt Regency Hotel, Los Angeles, California

Charles Luckman Associates

Carlos Diniz Associates

Broadway Plaza, Shopping Mall, Los Angeles, California

Charles Luckman Associates

**Marquis and Stoller
Architects and Planners**

737 Beach Street
San Francisco, Calif. 94109
(415) 776-2644

Robert B. Marquis FAIA
Claude Stoller FAIA
Peter Winkelstein AIA
Peter Kämpf AIA
David Evan Glasser AIA

Robert N. Goldfeder AIA
Julian F. Knox AIA
Phyllis Martin-Vegue AID

New York Office:
157 East 35th Street
New York, N.Y. 10016
(212) 683-4435

Hon-Ming Ng

Bay Towers

Marquis & Stoller

385

Albert C. Martin and Associates

Planning | Architecture | Engineering

Union Bank Square | Box 60147 | Fifth and Figueroa Street | Los Angeles, California 90060 | Tel. 213 683-1900

Val Thornton   Warner Ranch   Albert C. Martin & Associates

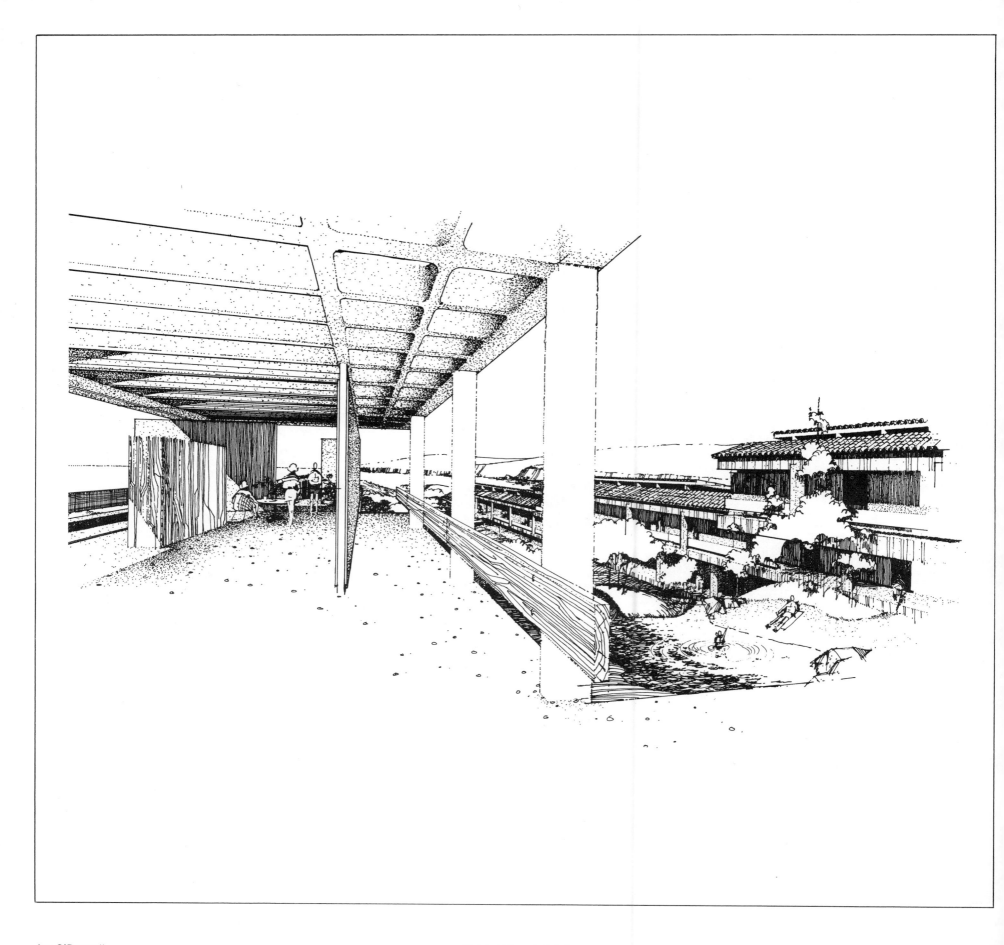

Joe O'Donnell

Mokolai Resort Hotel

Albert C. Martin & Associates

Dan Nicholl

Denver Metropolitan College

Albert C. Martin & Associates

Dan Nicholl

Denver Metropolitan State College

Albert C. Martin & Associates

Dan Nicholl

Denver Metropolitan State College

Albert C. Martin & Associates

CARL MASTON
ARCHITECT
Fellow American Institute of Architects

2811 Cahuenga Boulevard   •   Los Angeles, California 90068   •   (213) 851-2275

Louis Angelikis

School of Environmental Design, Cal Poly, Pomona

Carl Maston

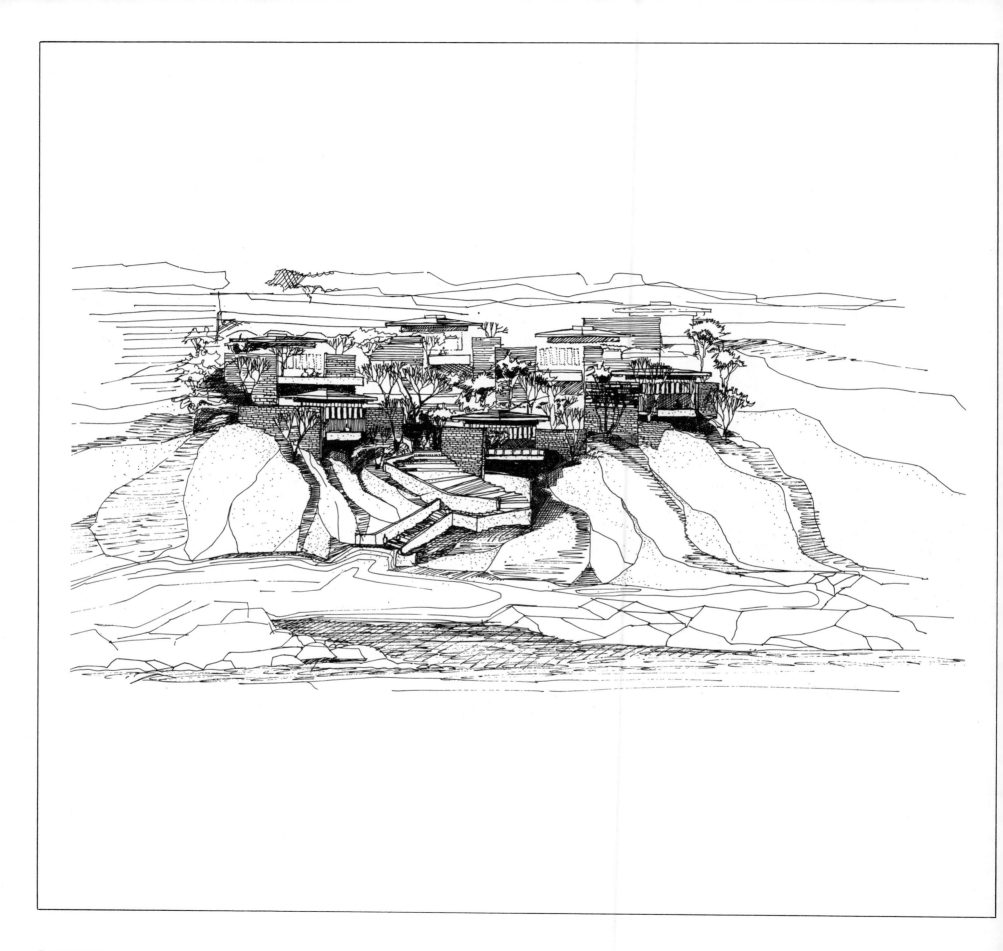

Edward Niles

Condominiums, Laguna Beach, Calif.

Carl Maston

Mel For

Architects Office Building

Carl Maston

MAYER AND KANNER ARCHITECTS A.I.A.

I. HERMAN KANNER, A.I.A., 1945–1953

ROBERT J. MAYER, A.I.A., I.S.P.
CHARLES G. KANNER, A.I.A.

ASSOCIATE ARCHITECT
TOM HOSHIZAKI

1740 WESTWOOD BOULEVARD, LOS ANGELES, CALIFORNIA 90024   TELEPHONE 474-3541 • 879-9222

Charles Kanner

Wilshire/Beverly Glen Apartments

Mayer & Kanner

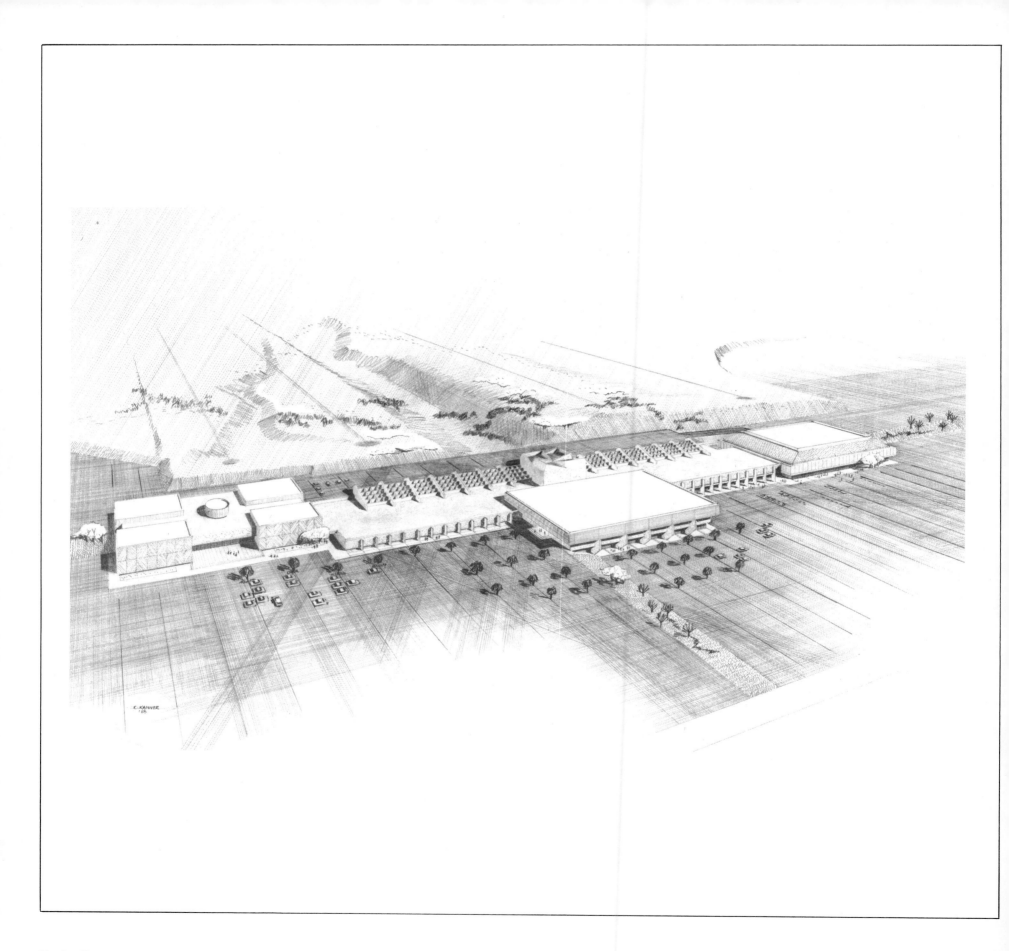

Charles Kanner

Richmond Mall Shopping Center

Mayer & Kanner

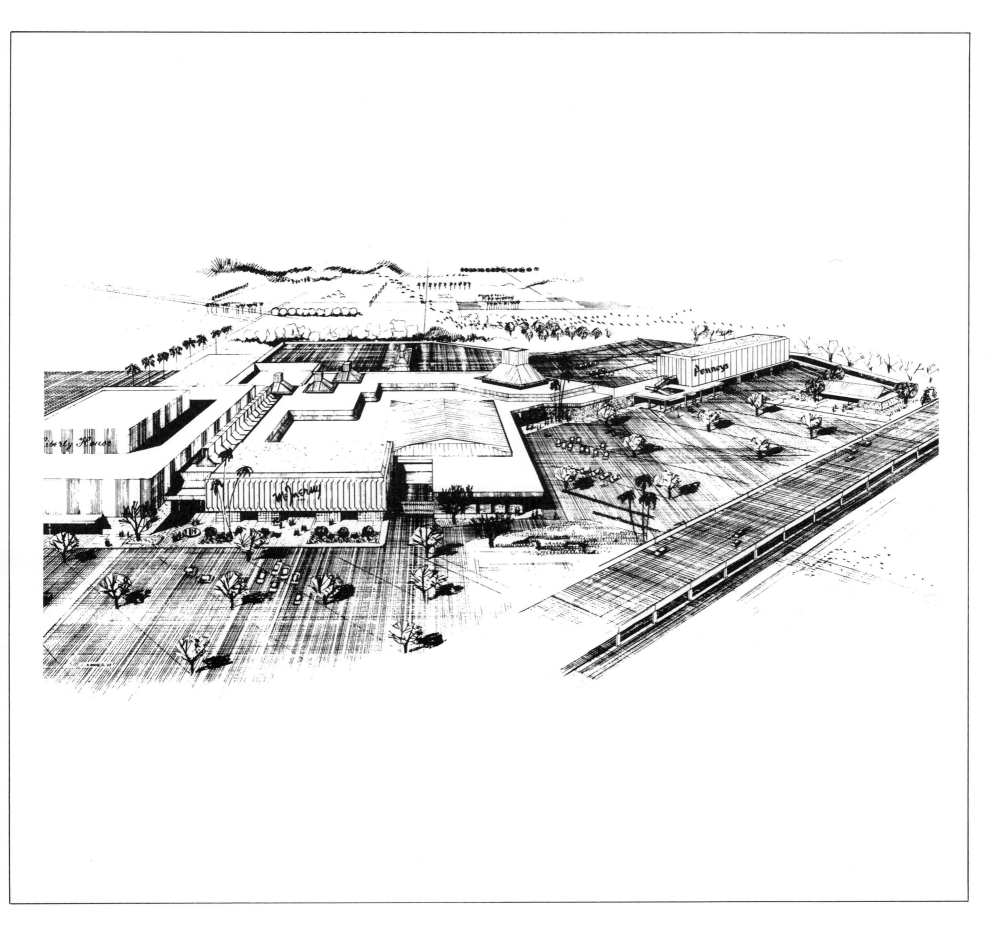

Charles Kanner

Kahala Mall

Mayer & Kanner

Richard Meier Architect AIA Associates Murray Emslie Gerald Gurland Carl Meinhardt   136 East 57 Street New York New York 10022 Telephone 593 1170

Richard Meier & Associates Architects

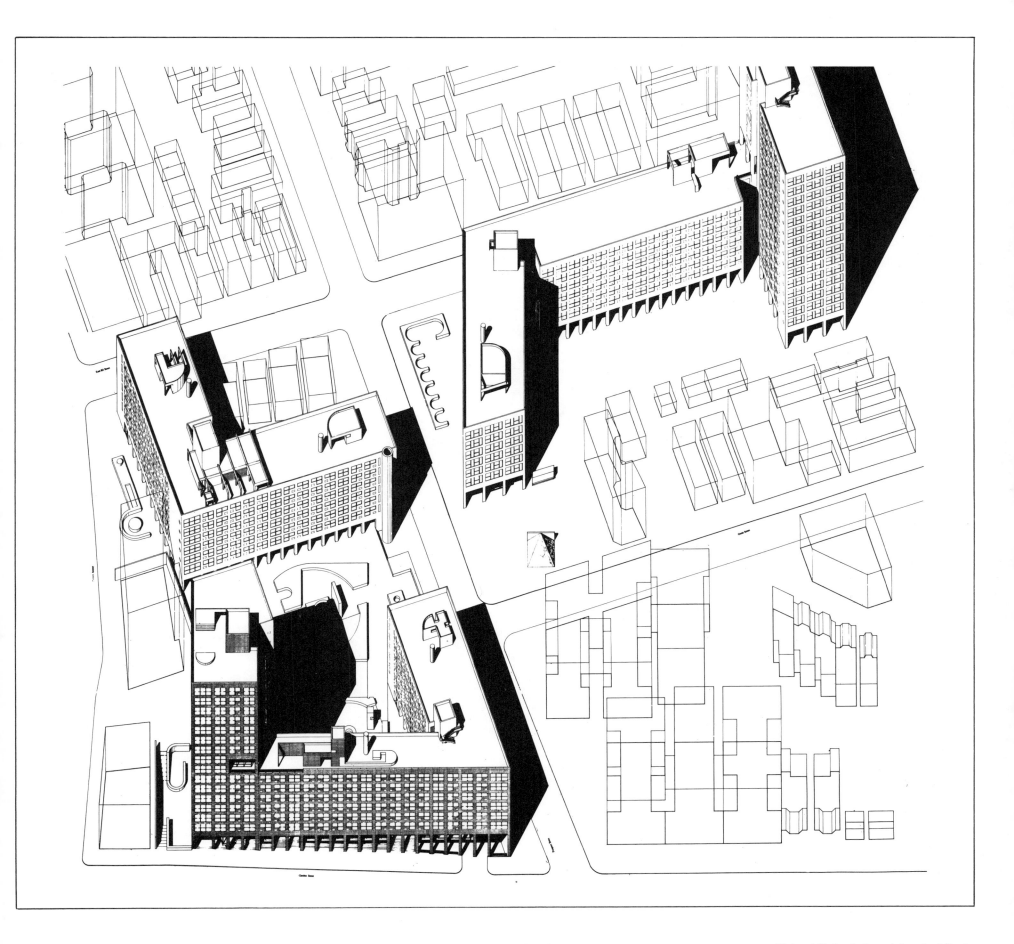

W. Rainey

Housing—Twin Parks Northeast

Richard Meier & Associates, Architects

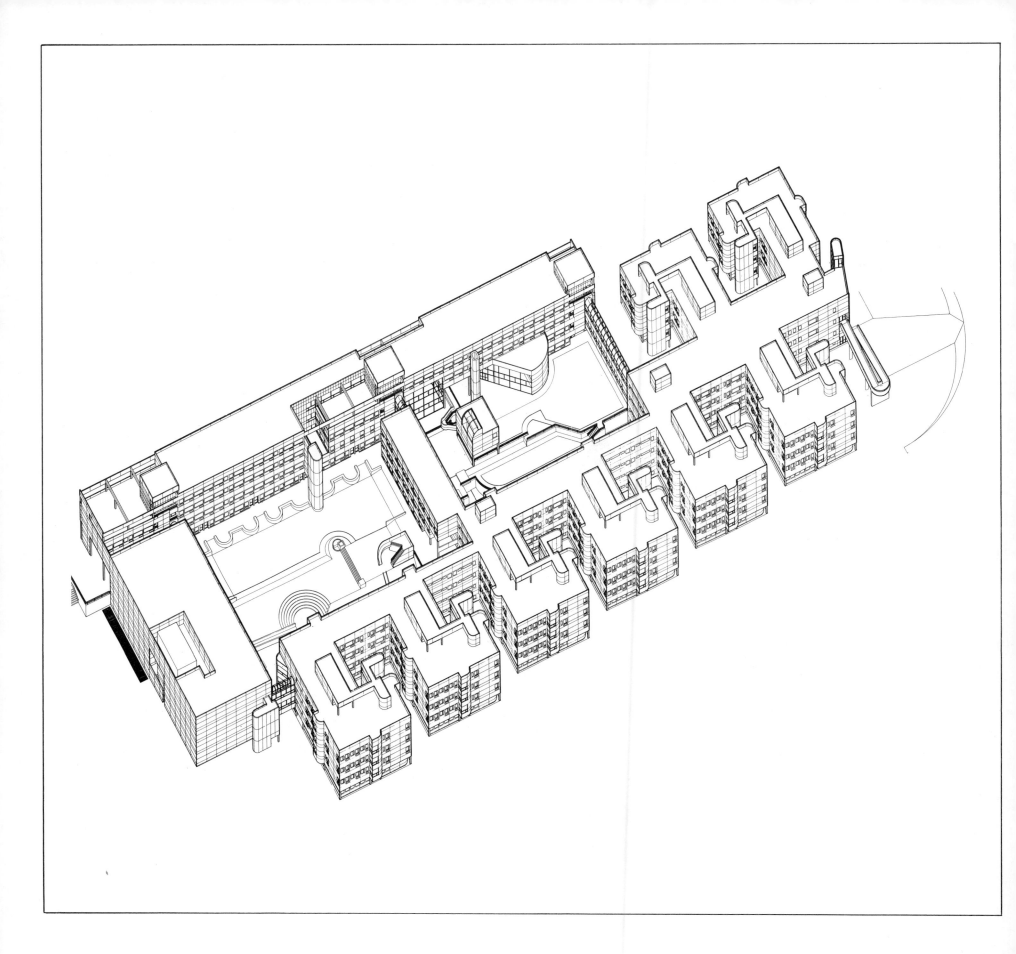

Bronx State School

Richard Meier & Associates, Architects

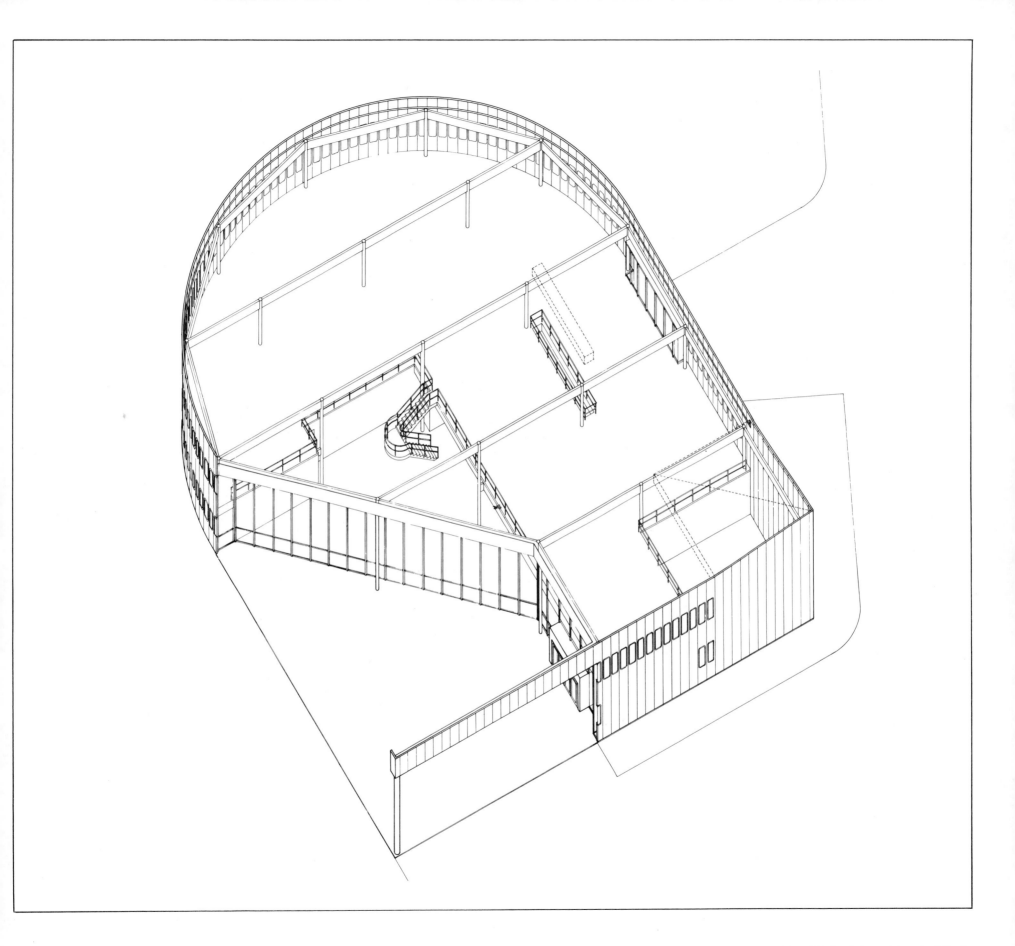

Charles-Michael Industrial
Industrial Building, Fairfield, New Jersey

Richard Meier & Associates, Architects

Mitchell/Giurgola Associates Architects
1316 Arch Street   Philadelphia   Pennsylvania 19107
215/561-1600

Ehrman B. Mitchell, Jr. FAIA
Romaldo Giurgola AIA

R. M. Kliment AIA
Fred L. Foote AIA

Rollin R. La France AIA
C. William Fox AIA
John Q. Lawson AIA
G. Daniel Perry AIA

Romaldo Giurgola

William Penn High School

Mitchell/Giurgola Associates, Architects

Adult Learning Research Center

Mitchell/Giurgola Associates, Architects

Romaldo Giurgola

Robert Whitehead Theater

Mitchell/Giurgola Associates, Architects

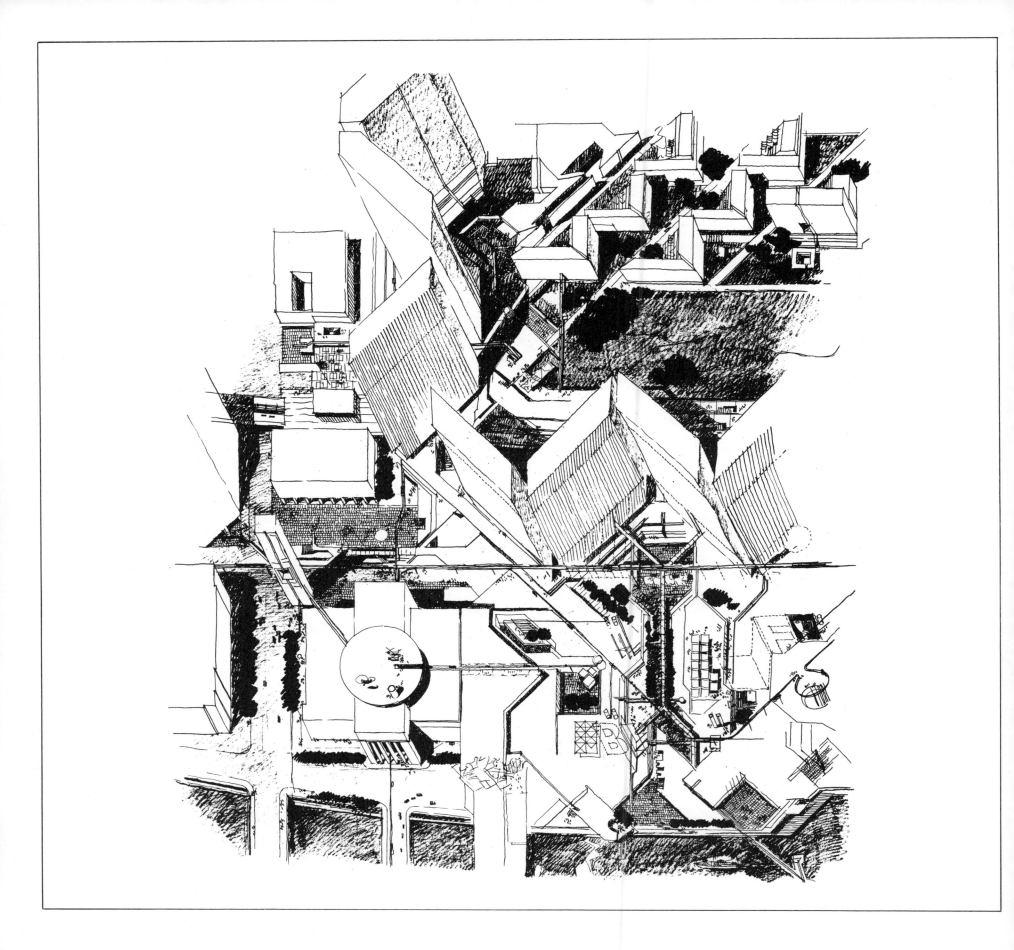

Romaldo Giurgola

Philadelphia Bicentennial

Mitchell/Giurgola Associates, Architects

Romaldo Giurgola

Townhouses, Williamsburg

Mitchell/Giurgola Associates, Architects

413

MLTW/Turnbull Associates

Architects & Planners

Pier 1½
The Embarcadero
San Francisco
California 94111
Telephone: 415-986-3642

William Turnbull, Jr.,
Architect, A.I.A.

Robert Simpson,
Architect

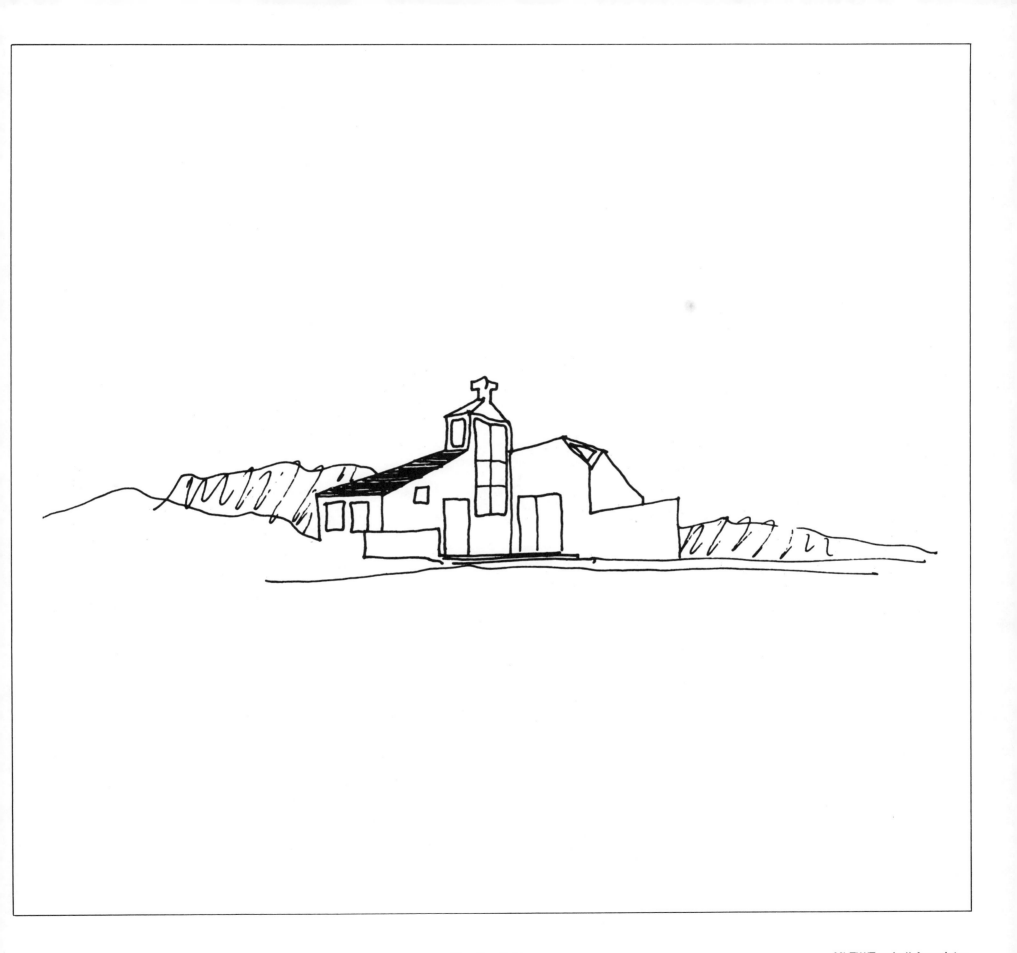

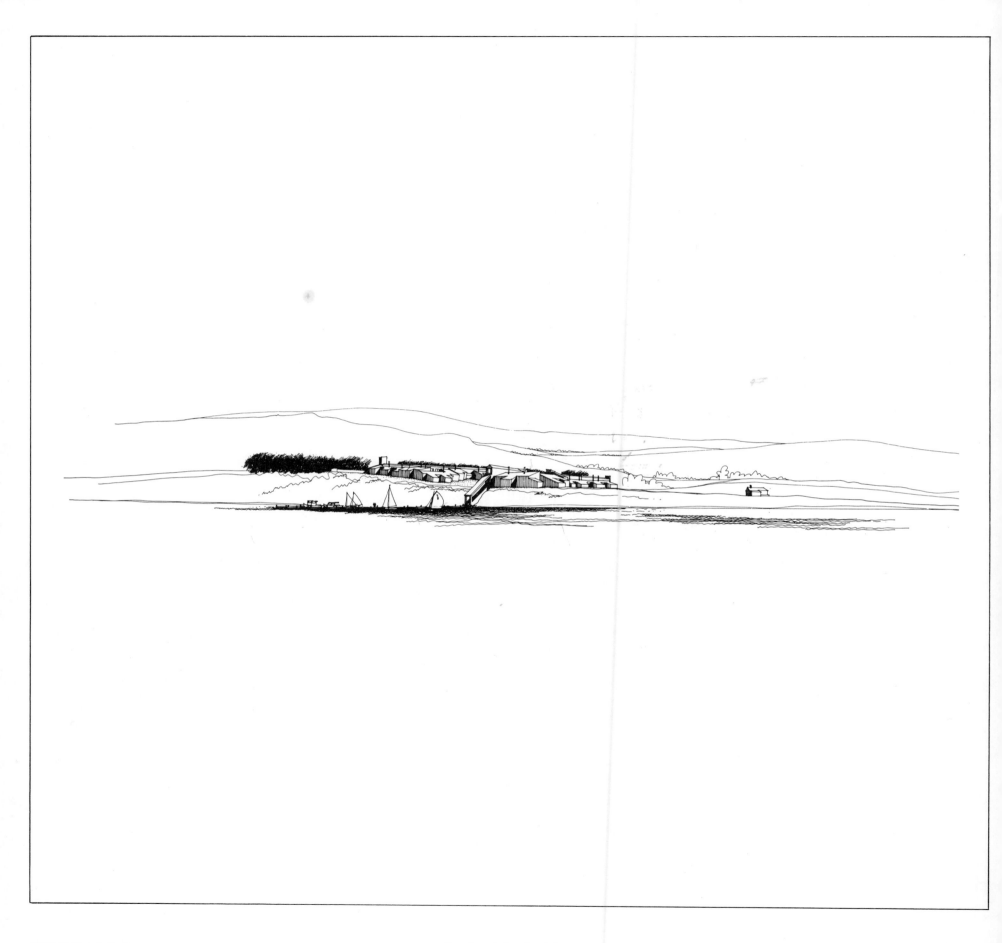

William Turnbull, Jr.

Bay Ranch Condominiums

MLTW/Turnbull Associates

VIEW SOUTH

William Turnbull, Jr.   Sea Ranch Condominiums   MLTW/Turnbull Associates

Golden West Savings & Loan

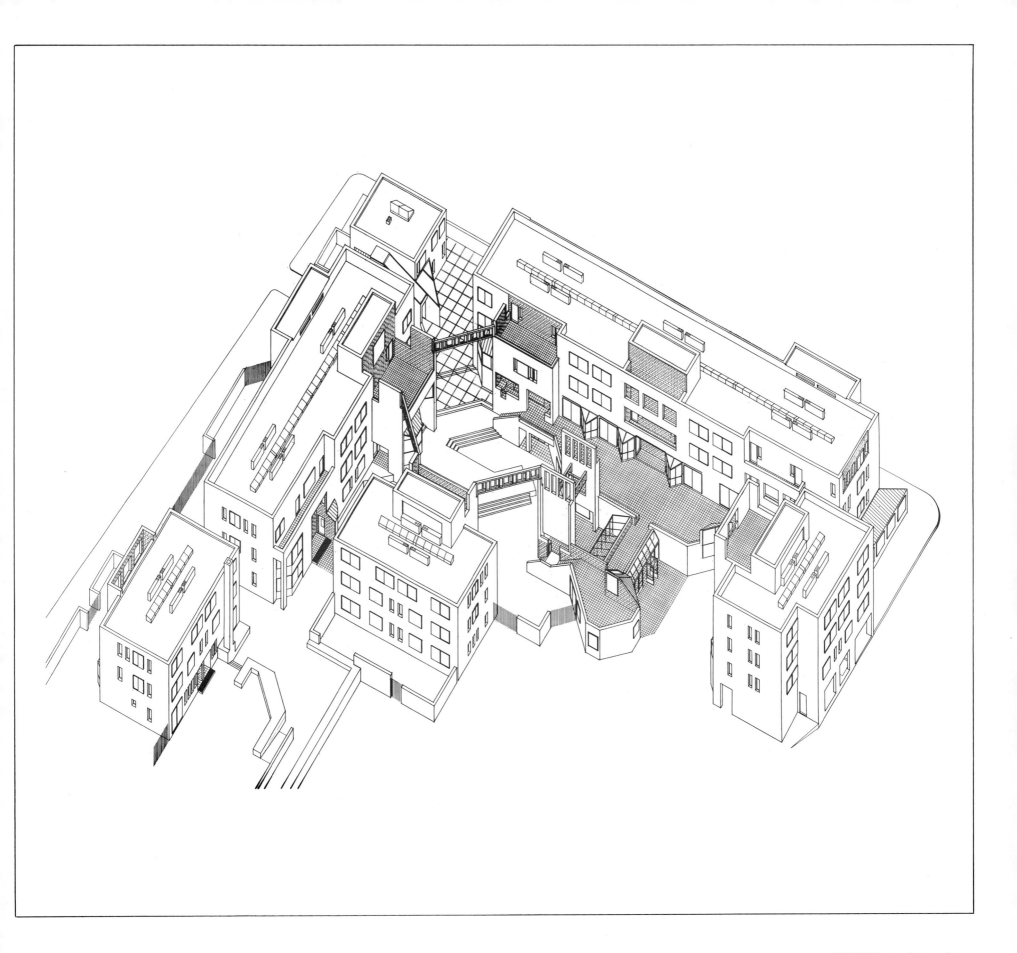

Pembroke Dormitory, Brown University

William Morgan Architect

1800 Universal Marion Building / Jacksonville, Florida 32202 / Telephone 904/356-4195

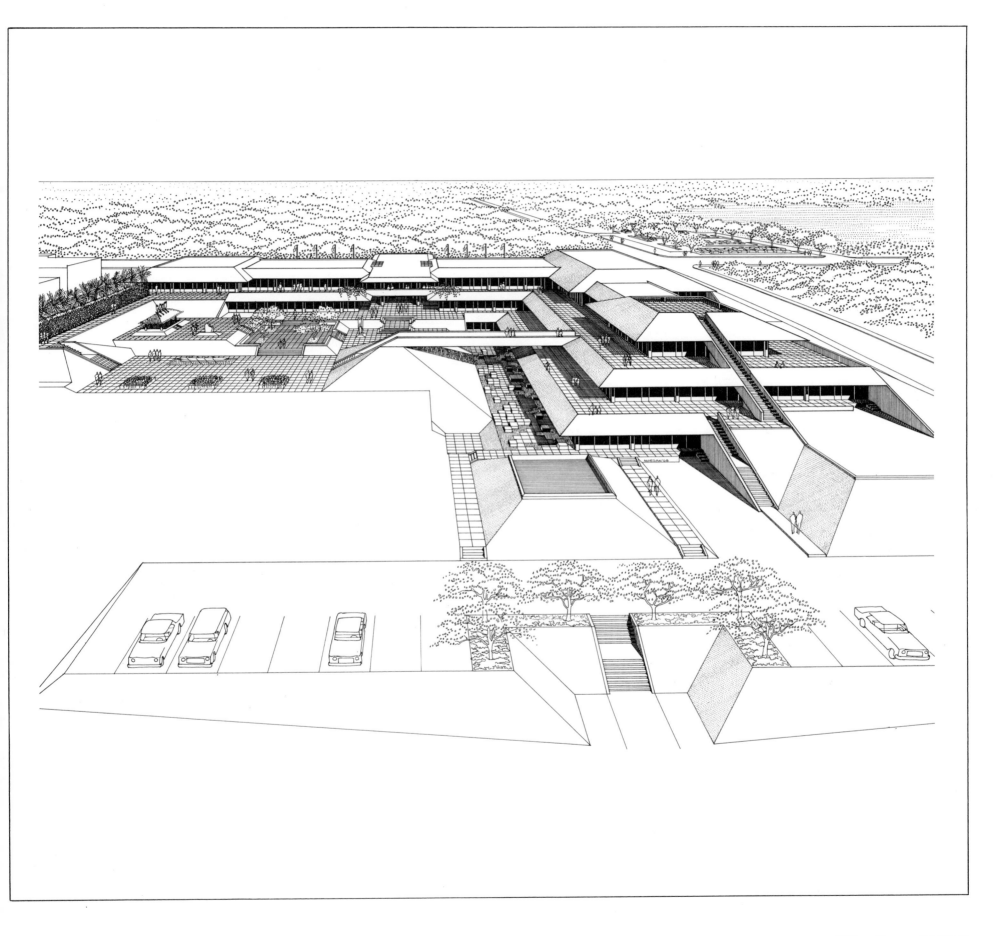

William Morgan

Florida State Museum

William Morgan, Architect

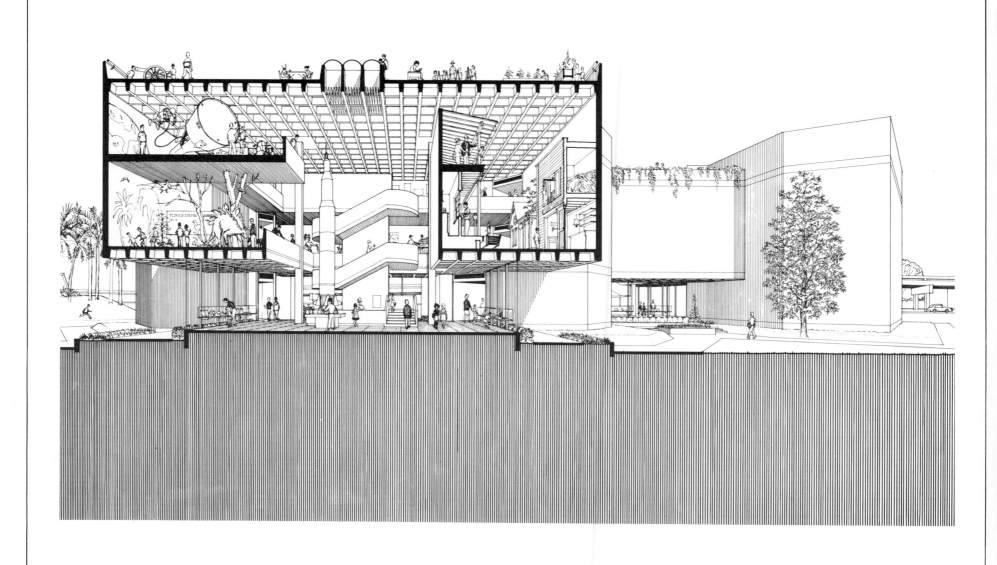

Robert D. Woolverton

Jacksonville Children's Museum

William Morgan, Architect

John Byal

Place by the Sea

William Morgan, Architect

William Morgan

Four-Level House

William Morgan, Architect

William Morgan

Interpod Tower I

William Morgan, Architect

MORGANELLI-HEUMANN AND ASSOCIATES

347 SOUTH OGDEN DRIVE, LOS ANGELES, CALIFORNIA 90036 (213) 937-6330

ARCHITECTURE ∎ PLANNING ∎ INTERIOR DESIGN

LOS ANGELES   SAN FRANCISCO   DAN MORGANELLI, A.I.A.   NEW YORK   PITTSBURGH

Ben Althen

The Hecht Co.

Morganelli-Heumann and Associates

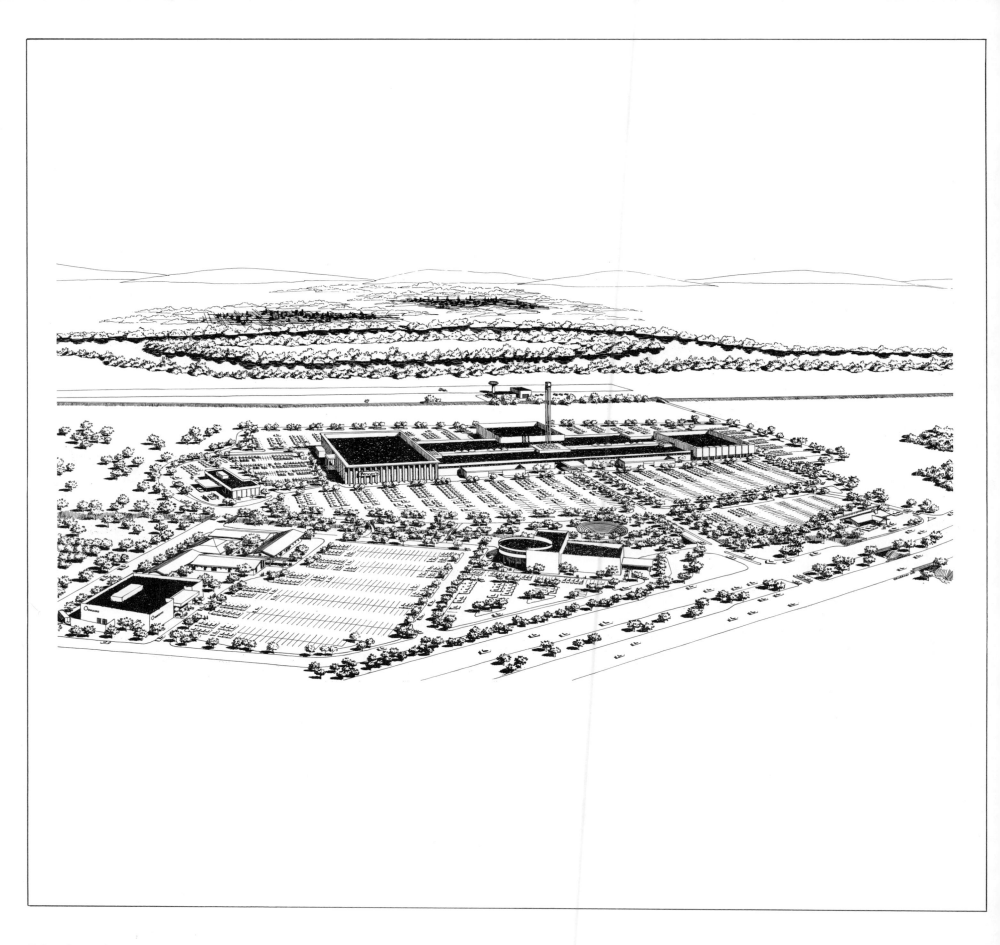

Grand Central Mall, Parkersburg

Morganelli-Heumann and Associates

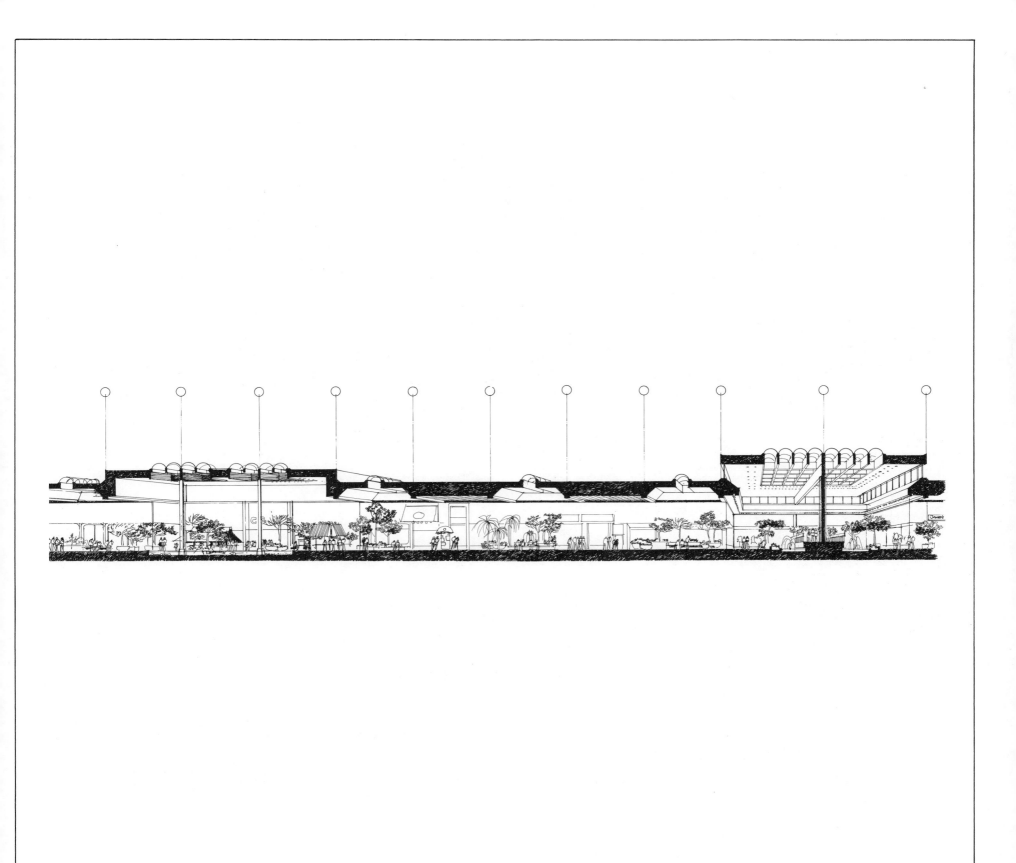

Keith H. Rockwood

Interior Sketches

Morganelli-Heumann and Associates

Naramore Bain Brady & Johanson

Architects Engineers Planners 904 Seventh Avenue Seattle, Washington 98104 (206) 622-7600 Offices: Honolulu, Anchorage
Partners: Floyd A. Naramore, FAIA William J. Bain, FAIA Clifton J. Brady, 1963 Perry B. Johanson, FAIA William Bain, Jr., AIA
Robert A. Floren, AIA David Hoedemaker, AIA James O. Jonassen, AIA Melvin J. Larson, AIA Herbert K. C. Luke, AIA Robert J. Pope, AIA
Eric C. Rising, AIA Robert R. Sowder, AIA Donald A. Winkelmann, AIA Business Manager: Harry G. Widener, Jr., CPA

Larry Segedin

Municipal Office Building

Naramore, Bain, Brady & Johanson

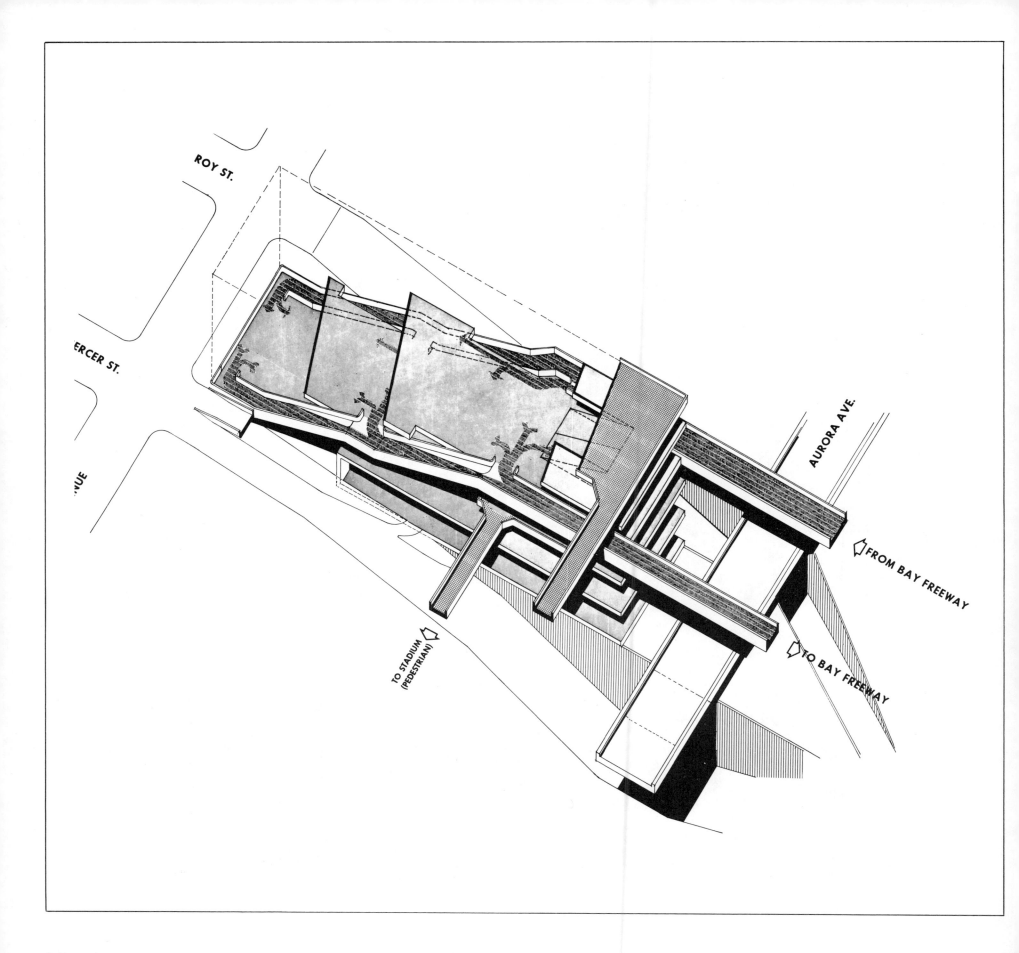

ROY ST.

ERCER ST.

AURORA AVE.

FROM BAY FREEWAY

TO BAY FREEWAY

TO STADIUM
(PEDESTRIAN)

Seattle Center Parking Garage

Naramore, Bain, Brady & Johanson

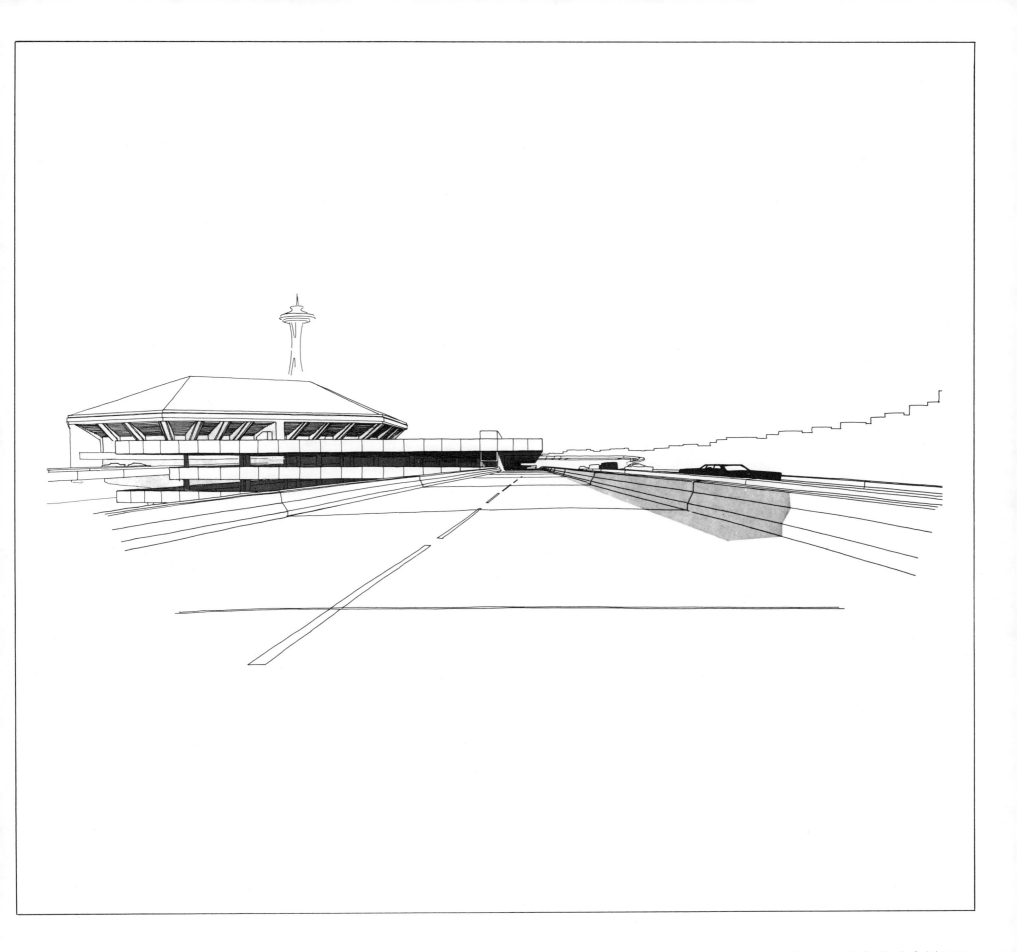

Dale V. Cox

Seattle Center Parking Garage

Naramore, Bain, Brady & Johanson

435

Carlos Diniz Associates

King County Stadium, Seattle

Naramore, Bain, Brady & Johanson

436

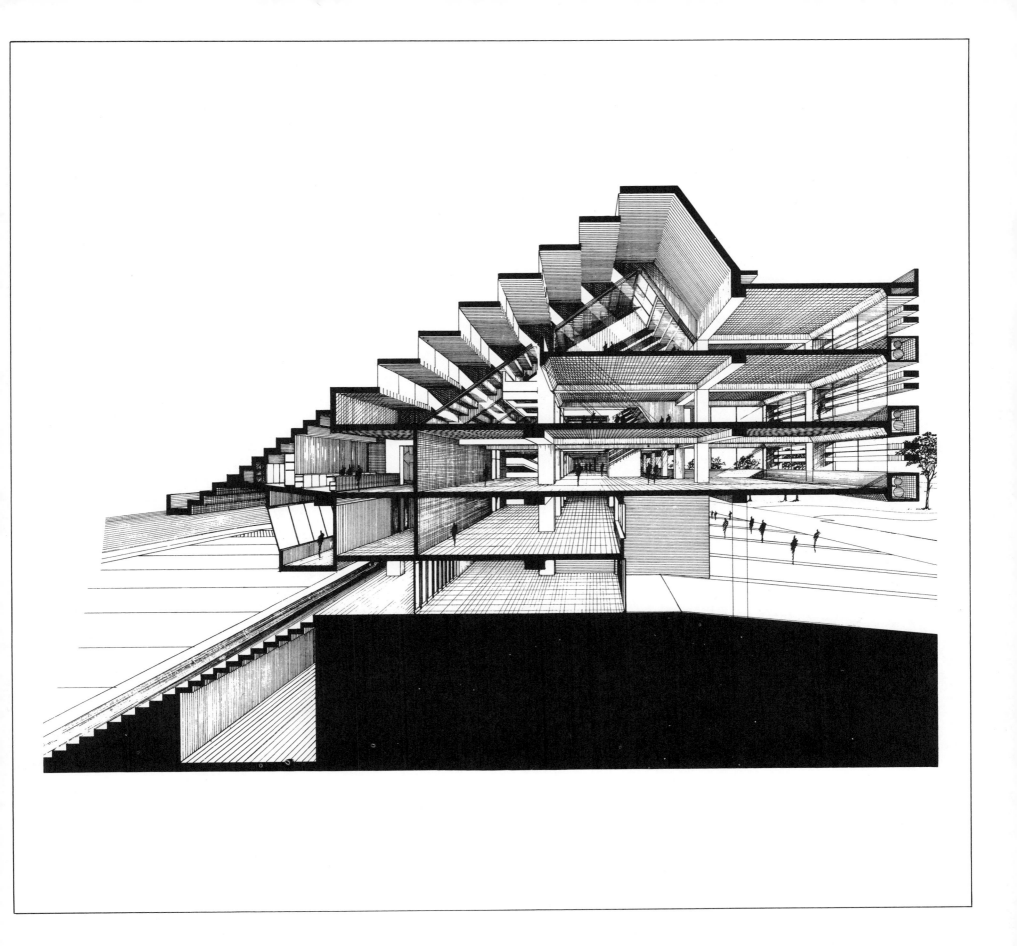

Bill Ross

Academic/Stadium Facility

Naramore, Bain, Brady & Johanson

Academy for Contemporary Problems

Naramore, Bain, Brady & Johanson

Carleton Kovell

Southwest Education Center

Naramore, Bain, Brady & Johanson

GIOVANNI
PASANELLA
ARCHITECT
A   I   A
154 WEST 57 STREET
NEW YORK CITY 10019
212   CIRCLE 7-7420

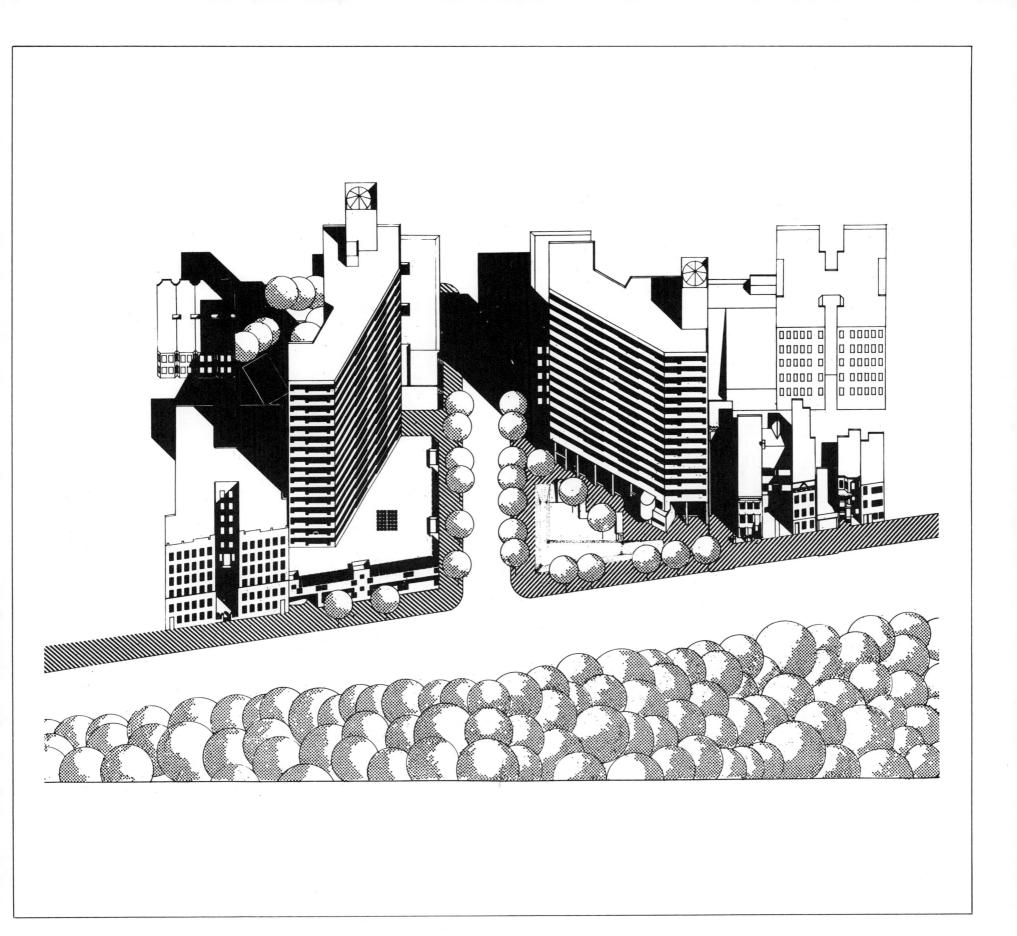

Thomas Stetz   Housing and School in Twin Parks   Giovanni Pasanella, Architect

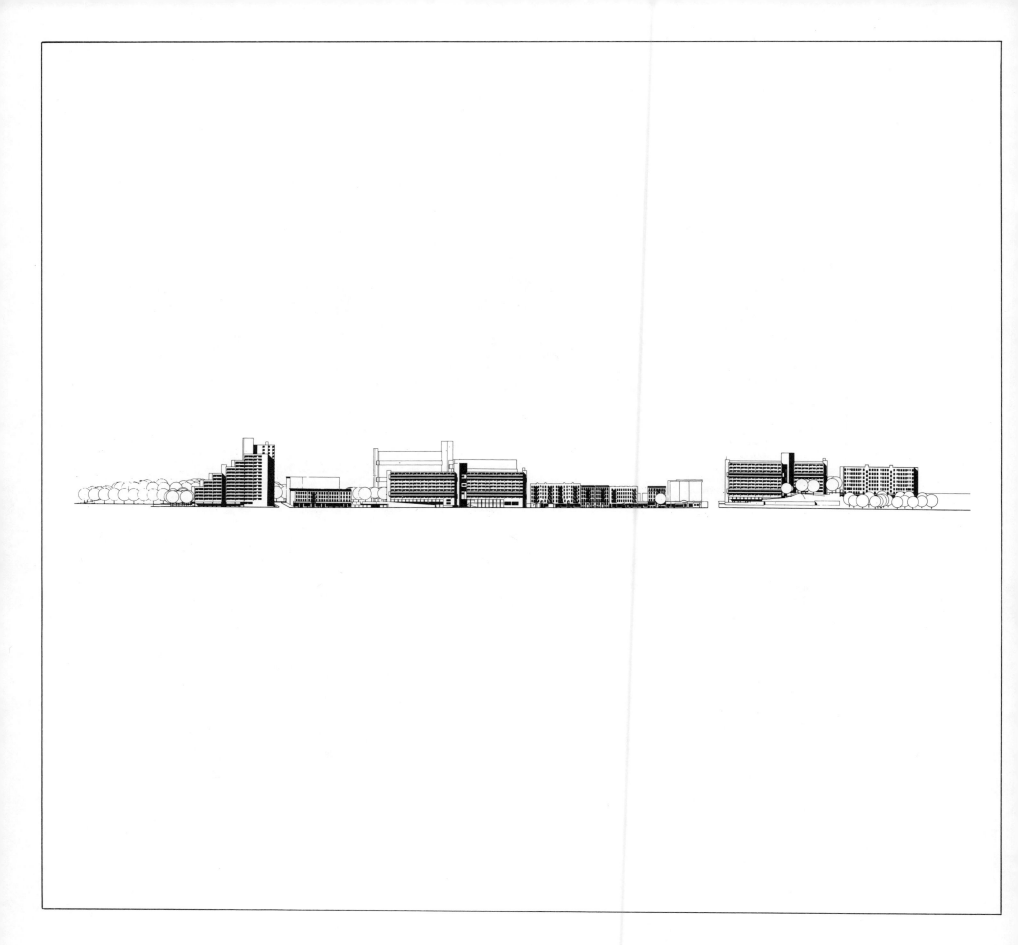

Housing for New York State

Giovanni Pasanella, Architect

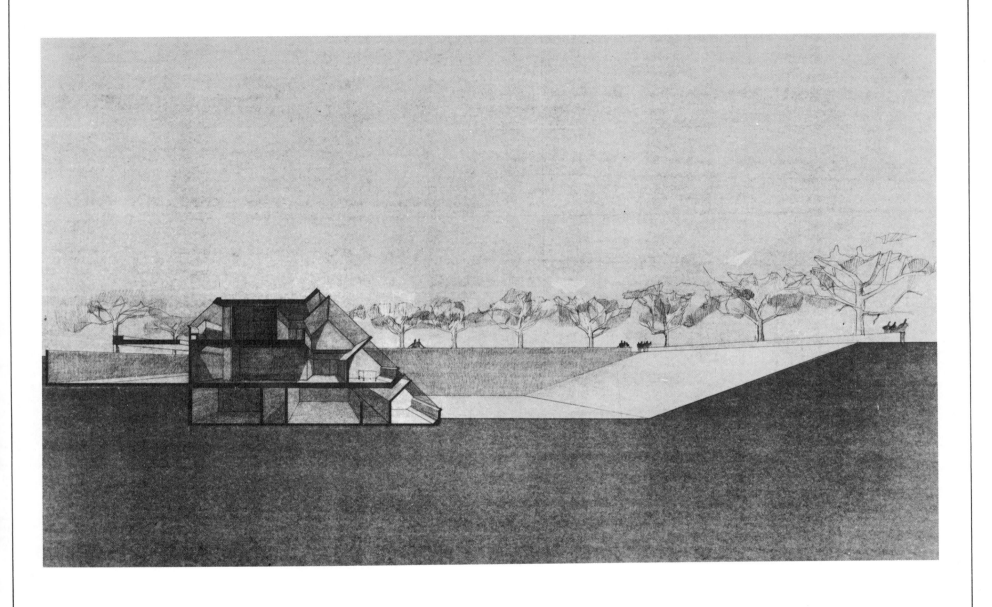

Giovanni Pasanella

Emergency Operations Center

Giovanni Pasanella, Architect

I. M. PEI & PARTNERS *Architects*

Steve Oles

National Gallery of Art

I. M. Pei & Partners

Mark deNalovy Rozvadovski

Bedford-Stuyvesant Superblock *(Detail)*

I. M. Pei & Partners

447

EVERSON MUSEUM

William Henderson

Everson Museum of Art, Syracuse, New York

I. M. Pei & Partners

448

Diedrich Praeckel   Washington Square East, Philadelphia, Pennsylvania   I. M. Pei & Partners

WILLIAM G. PERRY, F.A.I.A.
ROBERT C. DEAN, F.A.I.A.
CLIFFORD D. STEWART, A.I.A.
RICHARD G. SAWLER
CONOVER FITCH, JR., A.I.A.
RICHARD M. POTTER, A.I.A.
CHARLES F. ROGERS II

PERRY, DEAN AND STEWART, ARCHITECTS

955 PARK SQUARE BUILDING, BOSTON, MASSACHUSETTS 02116   617 482-9160

STANLEY S. SETCHELL, A.I.A.   JOHN F. CACHELIN   PETER A. RINGENBACH   DONALD B. ROBERTS   FRANK G. ST. PIERRE   HANS J. FINNE
JOSEPH TOMASELLO   PETER L. BUTLER   JAMES E. HEAVEY   ANDREW J. DEAN   BRUCE M. SCOTT   HEALTH FACILITIES
G. RICHARD DAVIS   GILBERT V. BORO   ROBERT MARKS   DONALD J. ROCHE   PAUL J. TRAPANI   PLANNER

Robert C. Dean

Andover Newton Theological School

Perry, Dean and Stewart, Architects

Zosar Fahmy

Newton High School

Perry, Dean and Stewart, Architects

Thomas Larson   Football Hall of Fame, Competition   Perry, Dean and Stewart, Architects

SUMMER CONCOURSE

WINTER ZOO

SERVICE AND PARKING

Steve Oles

454

Franklin Park Zoo

Perry, Dean and Stewart, Architects

CENTRAL AXIS

OTTER WALK

Steve Oles   Franklin Park Zoo   Perry, Dean and Stewart, Architects

455

TIMOTHY L. PFLUEGER 1892-1946

MILTON T. PFLUEGER   AIA ARCHITECT

580 MARKET STREET   SAN FRANCISCO, CALIFORNIA 94104   (415) 781-8872

MILTON T. PFLUEGER A.I.A.

LEFFLER B. MILLER A.I.A.
JOSEPH SCOMA A.I.A.
EDWARD M. HICKS A.I.A.
CARL H. RIESEN A.I.A.
WILLIAM A. HUTCHESON, JR. A.I.A.
LEE R. GREENFIELD R.A.
JOHN M. PFLUEGER A.I.A.
ROBERT COLBY A.I.A.
JAMES S. TULEY A.I.A.
RAPHAEL F. KEEGAN M.R.I.A.I.
DENIS BEATTY A.I.A.

Tim Casey

Lincoln University

Milton T. Pflueger

Leffler Miller

Office Building, Proposal

Milton T. Pflueger

458

Leffler Miller   Harbor Study   Milton T. Pflueger

WARREN PLATNER ASSOCIATES ARCHITECTS

18 MITCHELL DRIVE • NEW HAVEN, CONN. 06511 • 203/777-6471

J. Henderson Barr

Riverdale Country School

Warren Platner Associates, Architects

J. Henderson Barr

Harborside Pavillion

Warren Platner Associates, Architects

J. Henderson Barr   Harborside Pavillion   Warren Platner Associates, Architects

463

Riverdale Country School

Warren Platner Associates, Architects

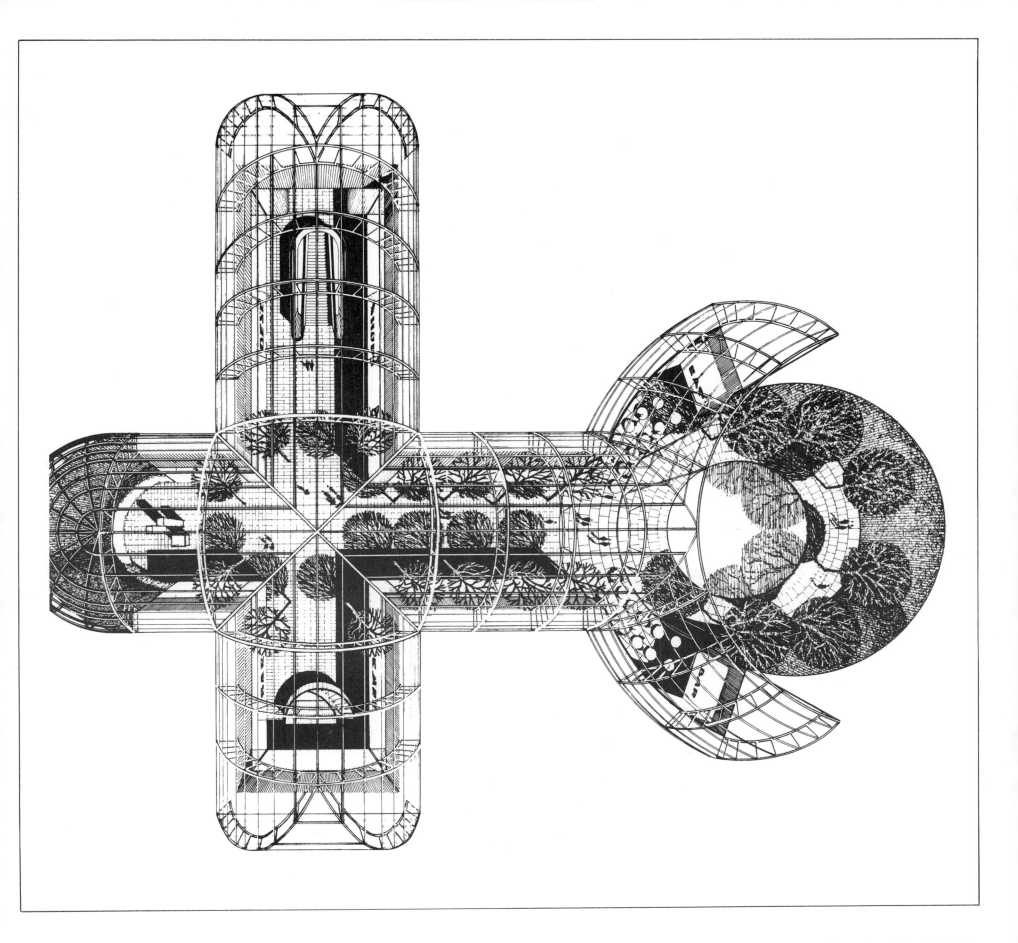

Richard Kaufman

Newark Airport Hotel

Warren Platner Associates, Architects

POMERANCE & BREINES

RALPH POMERANCE FAIA
SIMON BREINES FAIA
ARCHITECTS

MAX KANDEL AIA
MELVIN LESHOWITZ AIA
STEPHEN KAGEL AIA
ASSOCIATES

YUKON 6-5130   630 THIRD AVENUE, NEW YORK, N. Y. 10017

Ernest E. Burden

New York University College of Dentistry

Pomerance & Breines, Architects

467

Lee Harris Pomeroy   17th floor The Plaza
Architects-Planners   2 West 59th Street New York, N.Y. 10019 Telephone 212 838 6170

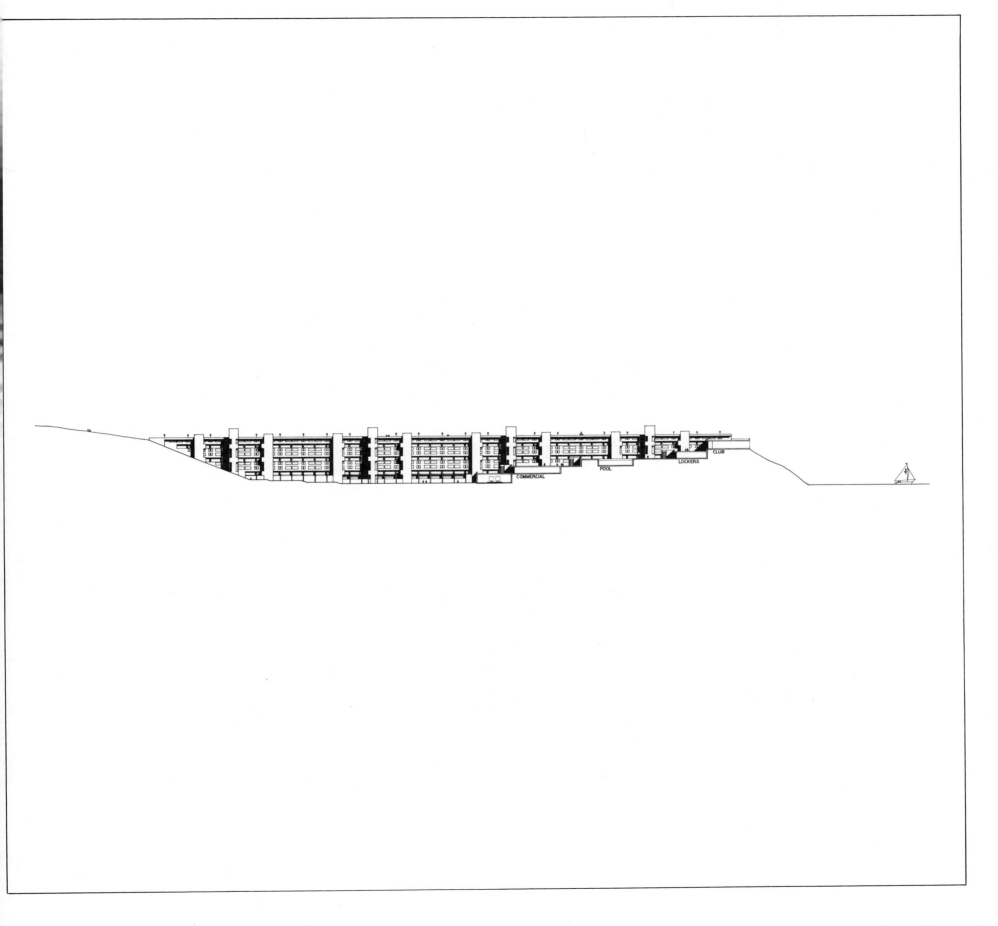

Robert Zimmerman

Manitou Station

Lee Harris Pomeroy, Architects—Planners

Bernard Stein

Pedestrian Mall in Trenton

Lee Harris Pomeroy, Architects—Planners

Bernard Stein

Pedestrian Mall in Trenton

Lee Harris Pomeroy, Architects—Planners

RALPH RAPSON AND ASSOCIATES, INC. ARCHITECTS AND PLANNERS 1503 WASHINGTON AVENUE S. MINNEAPOLIS, MINNESOTA 55404

RALPH RAPSON F.A.I.A.
KAY M. LOCKHART
RICHARD MORRILL
FRANK D. NEMETH
TIMOTHY L. STONE

Ralph Rapson

Hope Church

Ralph Rapson and Associates

Ralph Rapson

Proscenium Theatre

Ralph Rapson and Associates

474

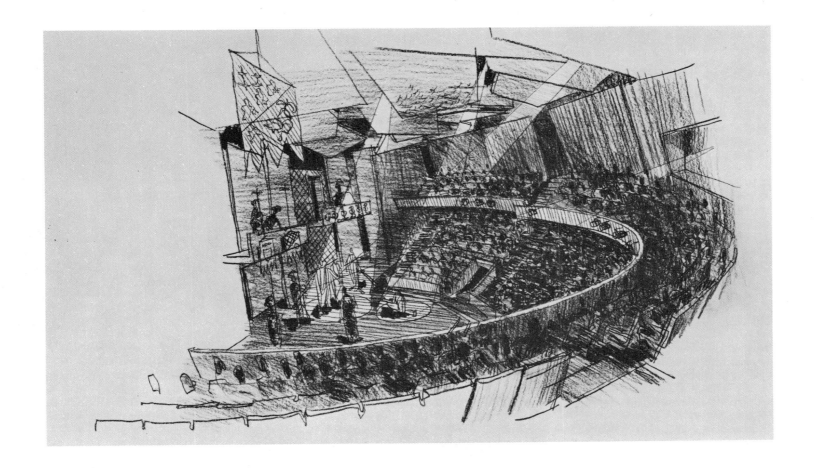

Ralph Rapson

Thrust Stage Theatre

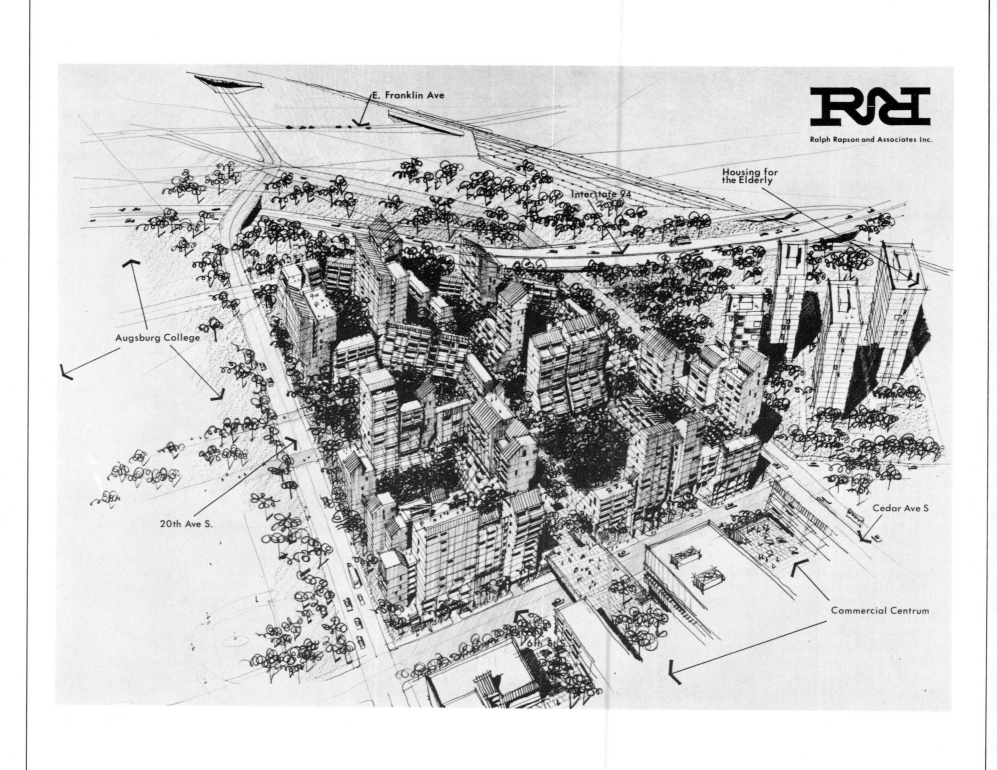

E. Franklin Ave

Interstate 94

Housing for
the Elderly

Augsburg College

20th Ave S.

Cedar Ave S

Commercial Centrum

6th St.

Ralph Rapson and Associates Inc.

Frank Nemeth

Cedar-Riverside Development

Ralph Rapson and Associates

Mike Gebhart

Teamsters Building

Ralph Rapson and Associates

477

ROCKRISE
ODERMATT
MOUNTJOY
AMIS

ARCHITECTURE   URBAN DESIGN   LAND PLANNING

GEORGE T. ROCKRISE, FAIA, AIP, ASLA   ROBERT A. ODERMATT, AIA   ROBERT C. MOUNTJOY, AIA   JAMES J. AMIS, AIA

ASSOCIATE: ALFRED A. STONE

405 SANSOME STREET, SAN FRANCISCO, CALIFORNIA 94111 · TELEPHONE (415) 392-3730

Colderon

Daly City, Master Plan

Rockrise, Odermatt, Mountjoy, Amis

PAUL RUDOLPH

A R C H I T E C T

54 West 57 Street
New York, New York   10019

Paul Rudolph

Interdenominational Chapel

Paul Rudolph, Architect

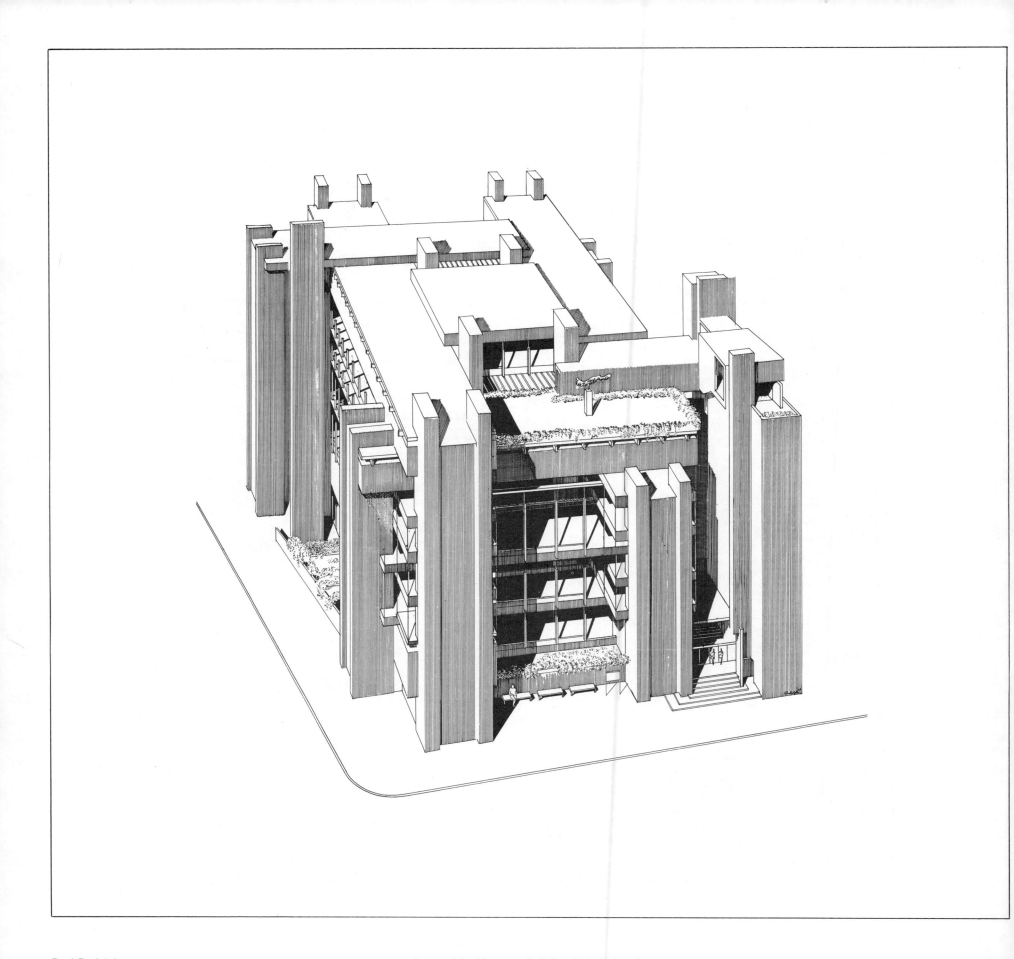

Paul Rudolph

Arts and Architecture Building, Yale University

Paul Rudolph, Architect

Paul Rudolph

Arts and Architecture Building, Yale University

Paul Rudolph, Architect

Paul Rudolph assisted by Makoto Miki

Town of Stafford Harbor, Virginia

Paul Rudolph, Architect

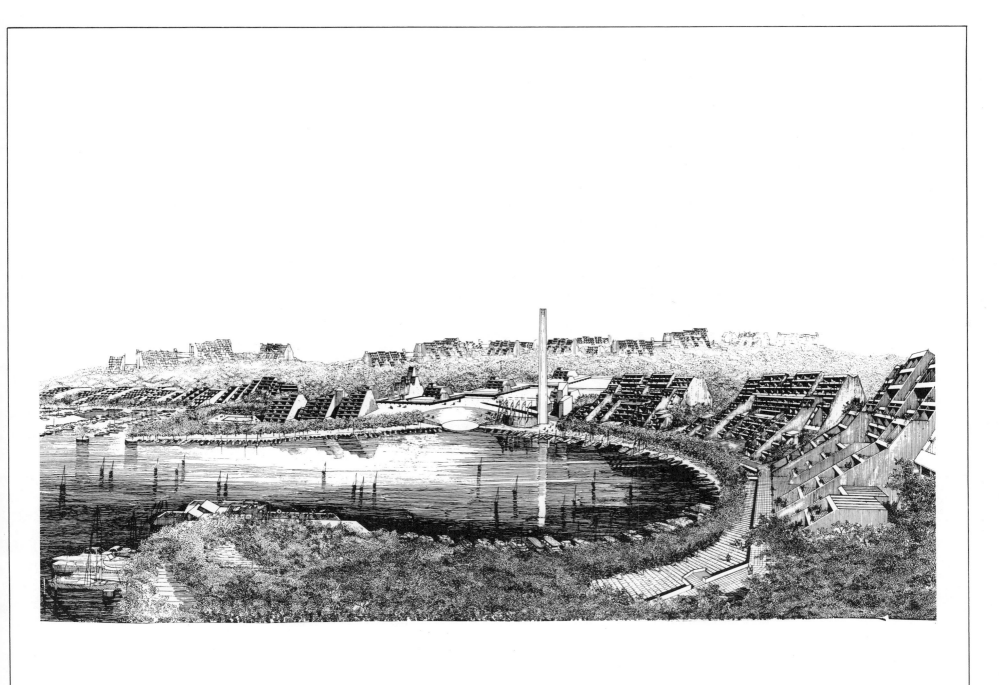

Paul Rudolph assisted by Makoto Miki

Town of Stafford Harbor, Virginia

Paul Rudolph, Architect

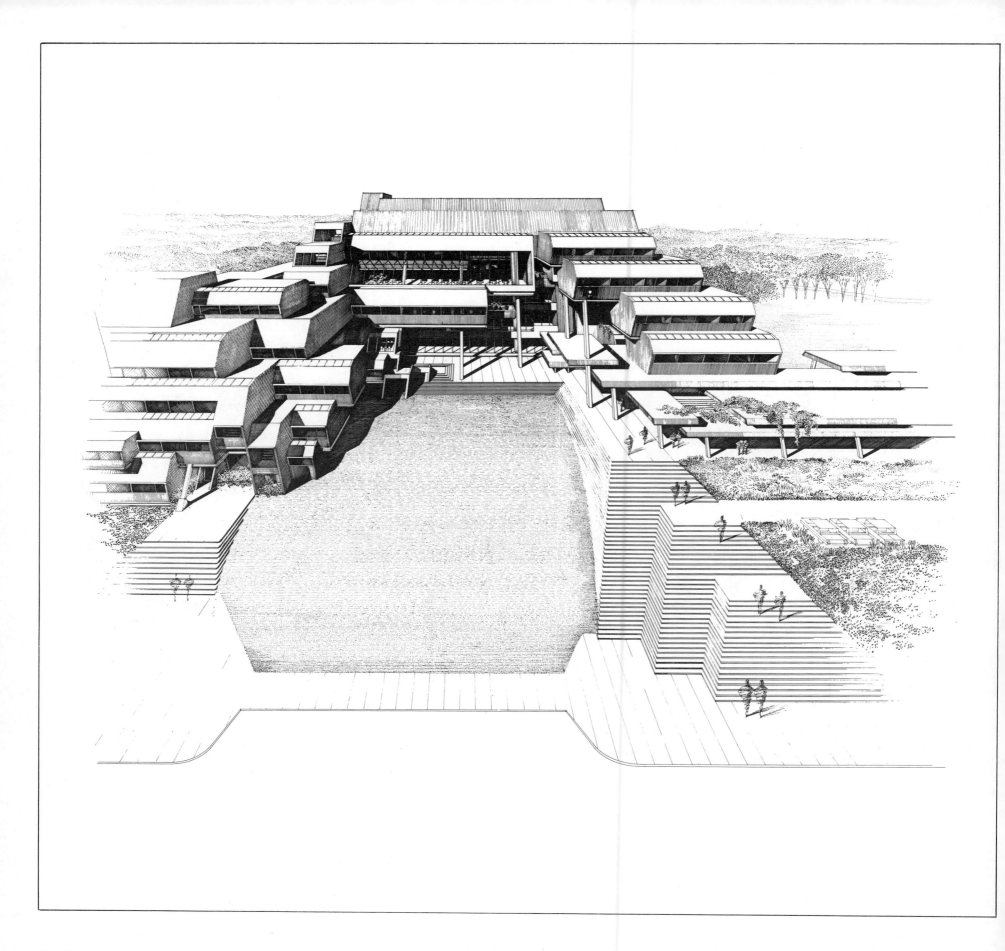

Paul Rudolph assisted by Robert Hill

Burroughs Wellcome Company, North Carolina

Paul Rudolph, Architect

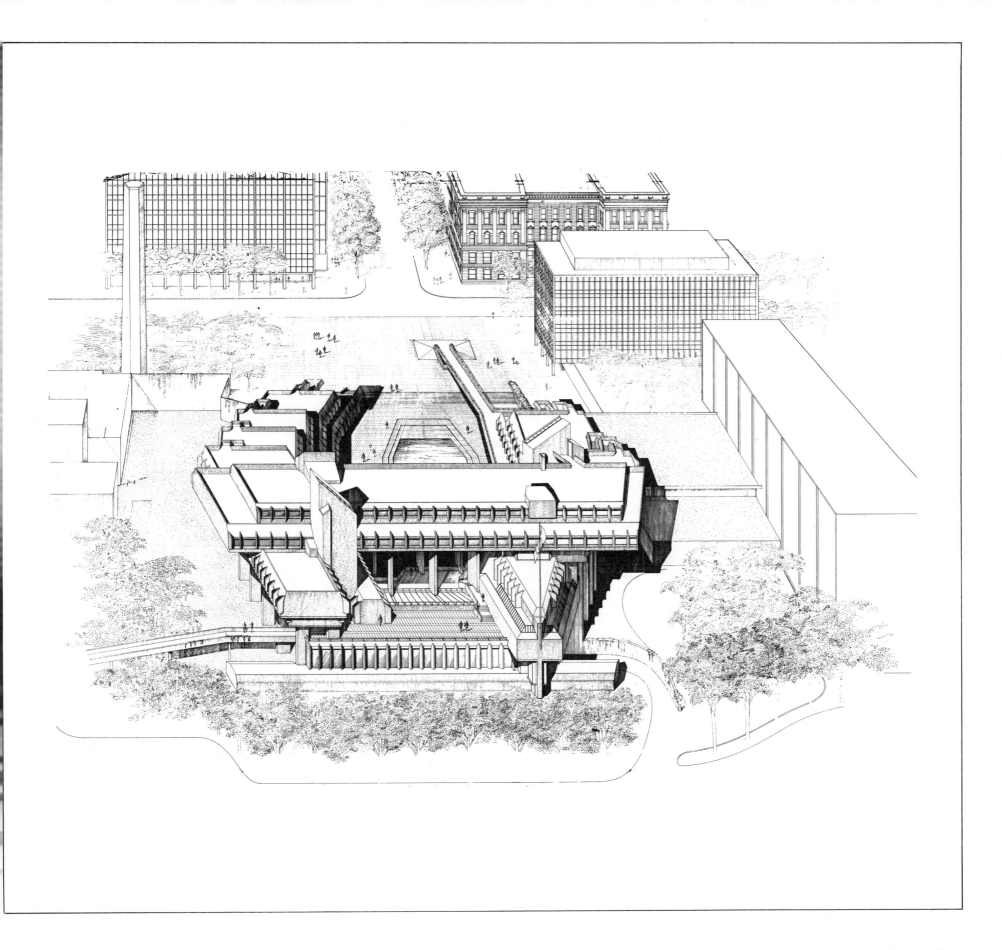

Paul Rudolph assisted by Joseph Huroitz

City Hall, Syracuse, New York

Paul Rudolph, Architect

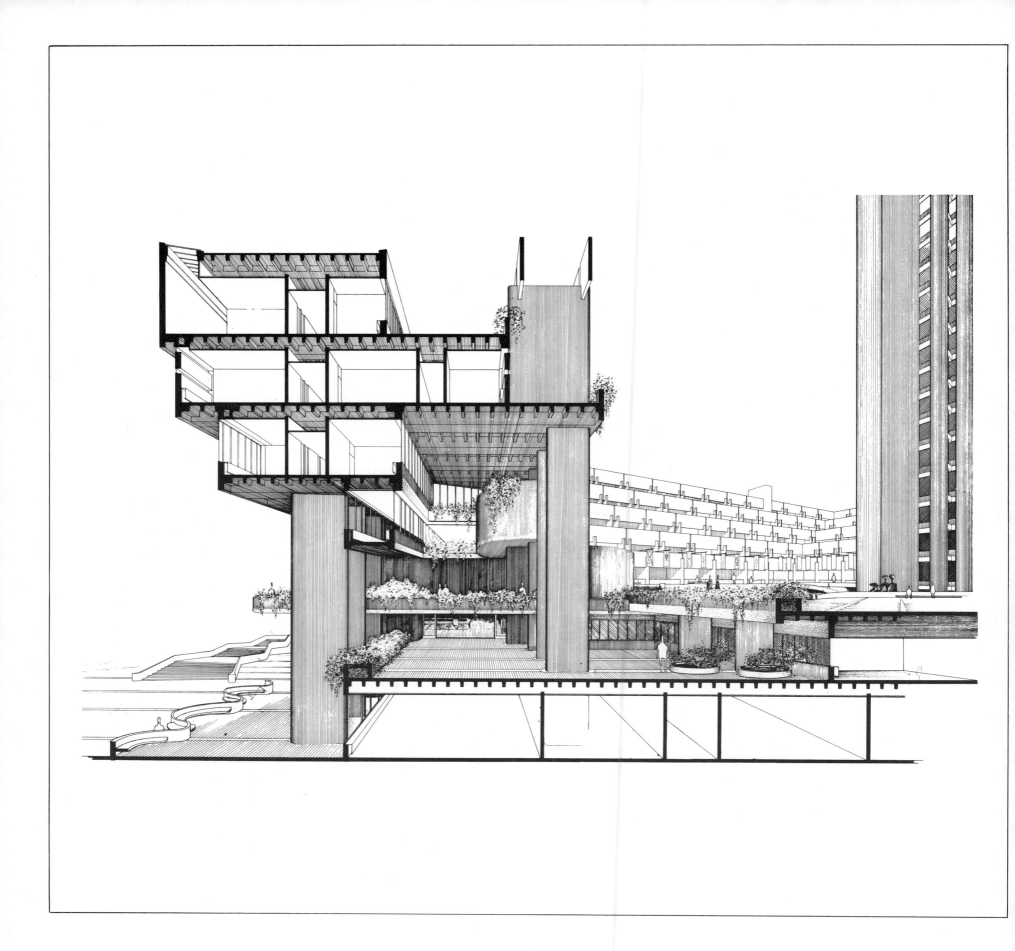

Paul Rudolph assisted by William Grindering

Boston Governmental Service Center

Paul Rudolph, Architect

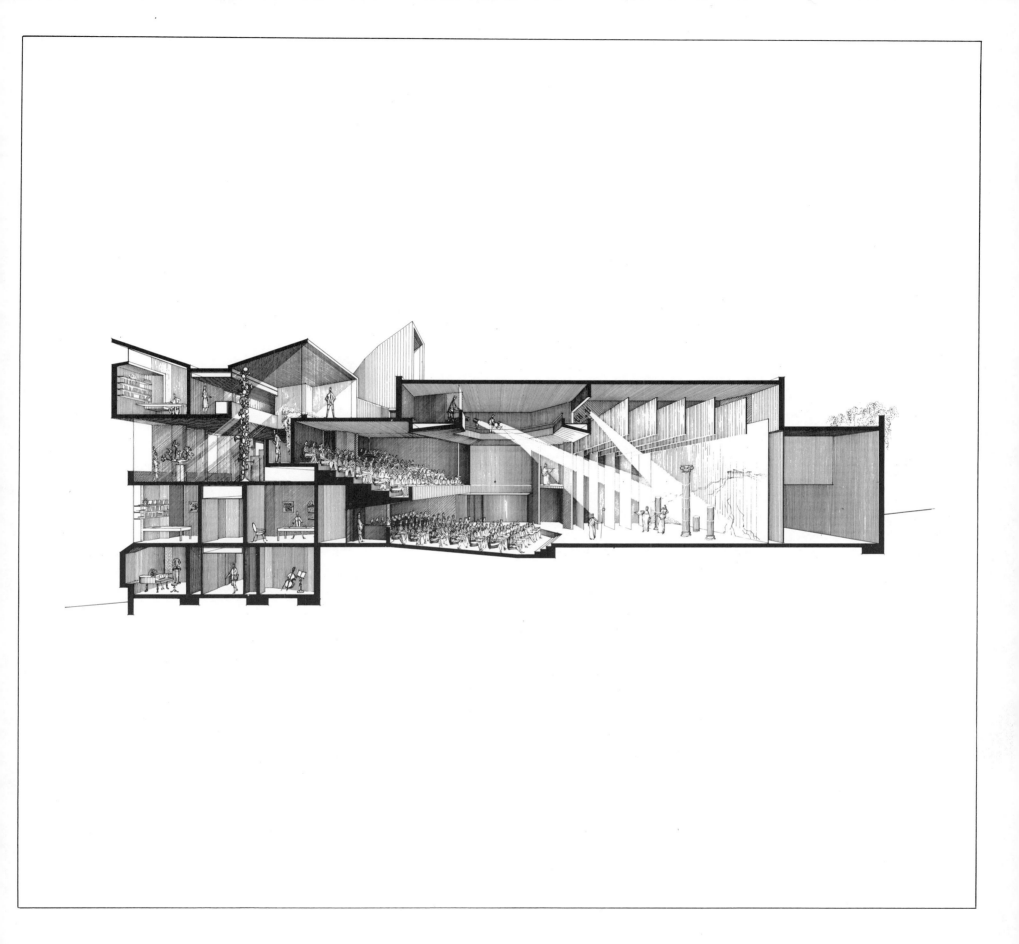

Paul Rudolph assisted by Davis Bite   Creative Arts Center, Colgate University   Paul Rudolph, Architect

RUMMELL
BOONE &
BROOKS
INC

ARCHITECTURE
ENGINEERING
&
PLANNING

320 WARD
HONOLULU
HAWAII 96814

TELEPHONE
537-2571

JOHN RUSSELL RUMMELL, AIA
WARNER G. BOONE, PRESIDENT
DESMOND K. BROOKS, VICE PRESIDENT

Warner G. Boone

Multi-Family Housing, Waikiki

Rummel, Boone & Brooks Inc.

Warner G. Boone

Kilauea Plantations

Rummel, Boone & Brooks Inc.

Warner G. Boone

Kilauea Plantations

Rummel, Boone & Brooks Inc.

GEORGE VERNON RUSSELL and associates

ARCHITECTS · ENGINEERS · PLANNERS

410 NORTH ROSENELL TERRACE / LOS ANGELES, CALIFORNIA 90026 / (213) 388-1281

GEORGE VERNON RUSSELL F. A. I. A. · BERNARD LEUIN A. I. A. · C. R. WOJCIECHOWSKI A. I. A.

E. D. DAVIES A. I. A. · JOHN H. HOOD M. E. · NIKOLAI KALIAKIN S. E.

George Vernon Russel

Office Building Study for Bunker Hill

George Vernon Russel & Associates

George Vernon Russel

Study for Geophysics and Planetary Sciences Laboratory
California Institute of Technology

George Vernon Russel & Associates

Tom Furishiro

Master Plan for Santa Cruz Island

George Vernon Russel & Associates

SARGENT
WEBSTER
CRENSHAW
& FOLLEY ARCHITECTS ENGINEERS PLANNERS

2112 ERIE BOULEVARD EAST
SYRACUSE, NEW YORK 13224

PARTNERS: D. KENNETH SARGENT FAIA   FREDERICK S. WEBSTER FAIA   THOMAS T. CRENSHAW AIA   MILO D. FOLLEY AIA   DARREL D. RIPPETEAU AIA   SARKIS M. ARKELL AIA
ROBERT W. MALMROS AIA   WM. STEVENSON YOUNG AIA   EDWIN B. BRUCE AIA   ARTHUR C. FRIEDEL JR. AIA   HERBERT BOERNER AIA   ARTHUR V. SERRANO PE
ASSOCIATES: DONALD P. BARNER AIA   JOHN H. DEIERLEIN AIA   ROBERT A. NEVIN PE   WILLIAM E. MARKLEY AIA   KENNETH R. BECKER LA   JOHN P. CHRISTEN PE
ARNOLD A. BITTERMAN PE   ROGER E. KAHN AIA   JOHN L. SALINSKY PE   ROBERT L. KELLY AIA   HARVEY H. KAISER AIA   CHARLES J. MACK AIA

SYRACUSE   WATERTOWN   SCHENECTADY   SAN JUAN, PUERTO RICO

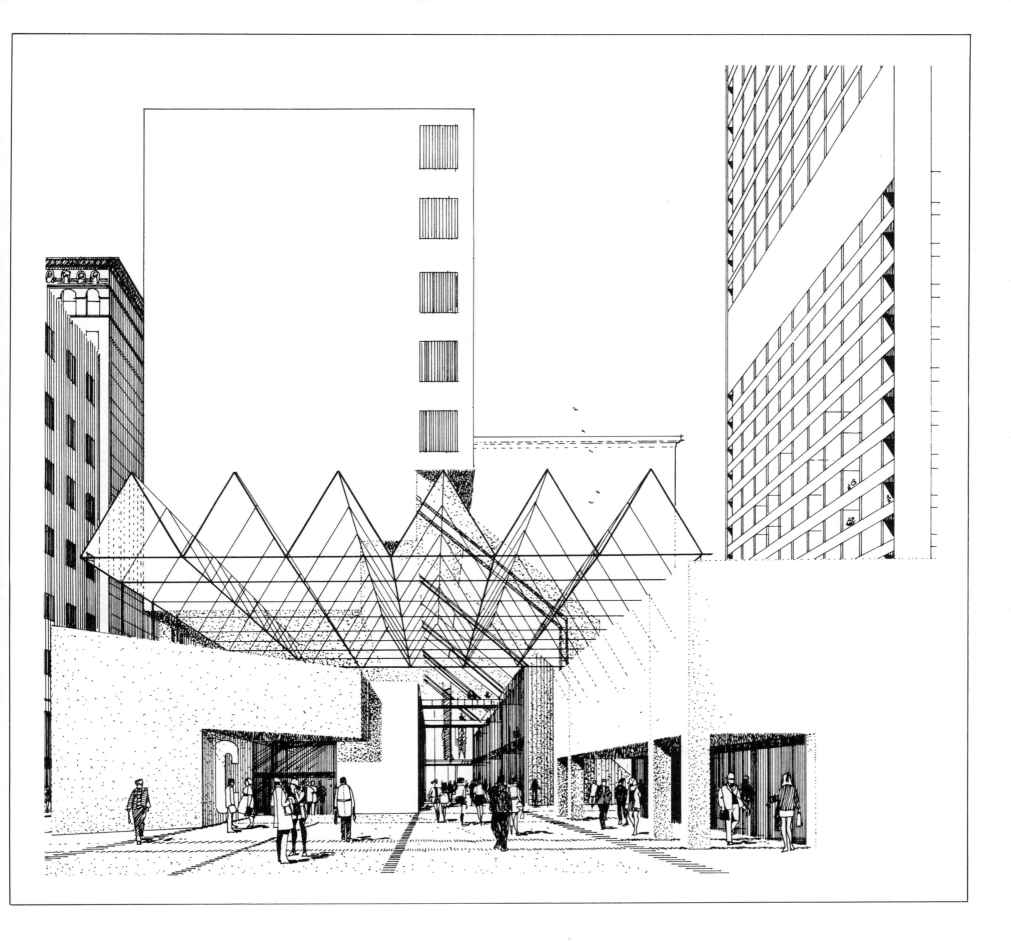

Ronald Love

First Trust Plaza, Syracuse

Sargent, Webster, Crenshaw & Folley

Ronald Love

Cayuga County Infirmary, Auburn

Sargent, Webster, Crenshaw & Folley

SHEPLEY BULFINCH RICHARDSON AND ABBOTT

ONE COURT STREET   BOSTON   MASSACHUSETTS 02108   RICHMOND 2-1400

JOSEPH P. RICHARDSON
JAMES FORD CLAPP, JR.
SHERMAN MORSS
JEAN PAUL CARLHIAN
HUGH SHEPLEY
OTIS B. ROBINSON

LLOYD PHELPS ACTON
RUSSELL G. BISHOP
DANIEL J. COOLIDGE
ROBERT T. HOLLORAN
W. S. MALLORY LASH
GEORGE R. MATHEY
ROBERT McINTOSH
ARVIDS A. SPIGULIS
WILLIAM R. SPILMAN
PAUL SUN
ROBERT A. TACCONI
RICHARD C. TOUSLEY
HERMAN J. VOSS

Paul Sun   Mass. Bay Community College   Shepley, Bullfinch, Richardson and Abbott

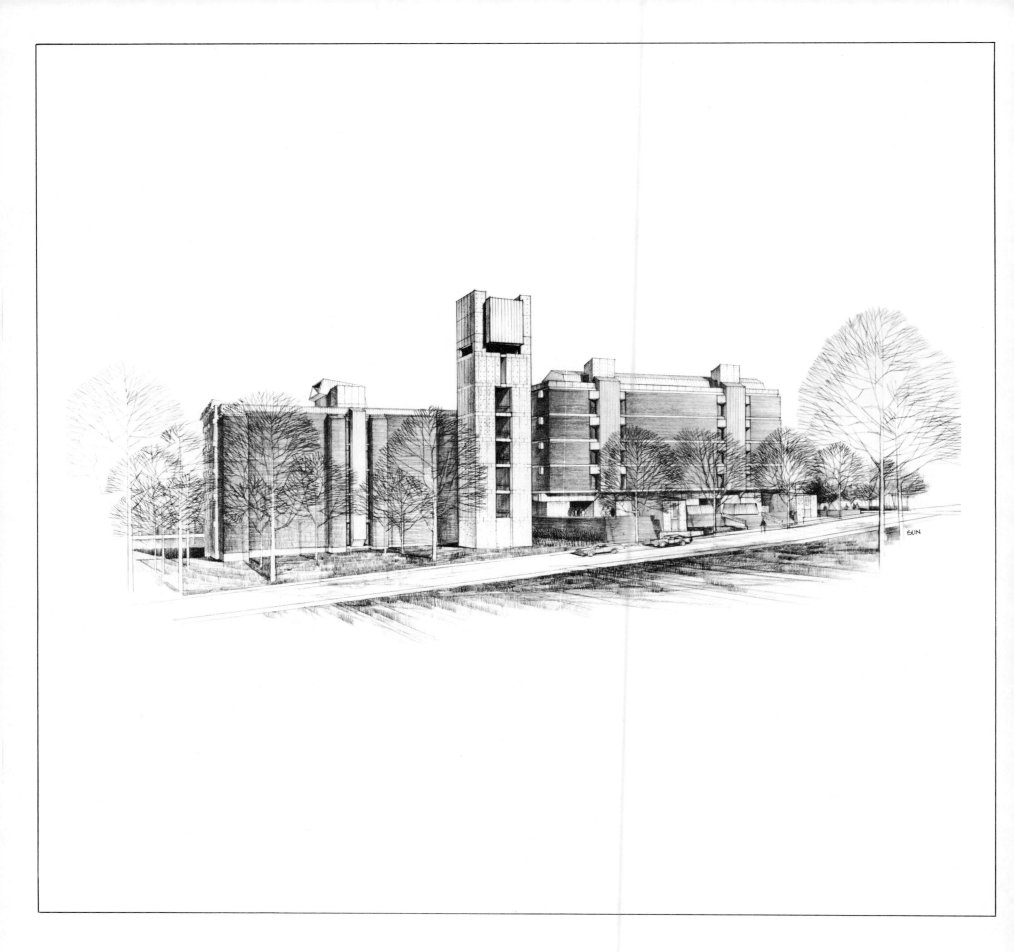

Paul Sun

Brown University, Bio-Medical Center

Shepley, Bullfinch, Richardson and Abbott

504

Paul Sun

Brown University, Graduate Center

Shepley, Bullfinch, Richardson and Abbott

Yale University, Math Building Competition

Shepley, Bullfinch, Richardson and Abbott

Paul Sun

Dartmouth Science Center, Hanover, New Hampshire

Shepley, Bullfinch, Richardson and Abbott

JACK SIDENER, architect / planner

lanai city, hawaii

John Torrey

Mililani Town

Jack Sidener, Architect

John Tatom

Oakland City Center Development

Jack Sidener, Architect

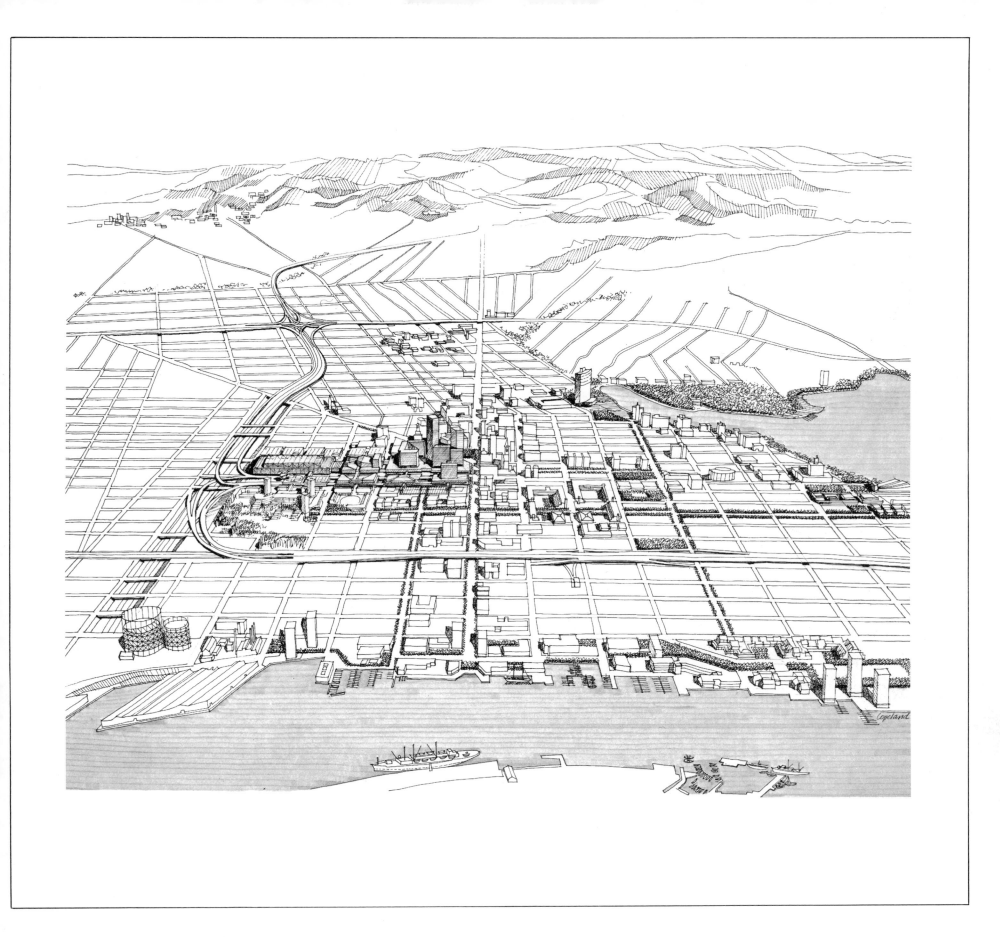

Lee Copeland

Oakland City Center Development

Jack Sidener, Architect

Skidmore, Owings & Merrill ARCHITECTS/ENGINEERS

ONE MARITIME PLAZA
SAN FRANCISCO, CALIFORNIA 94111

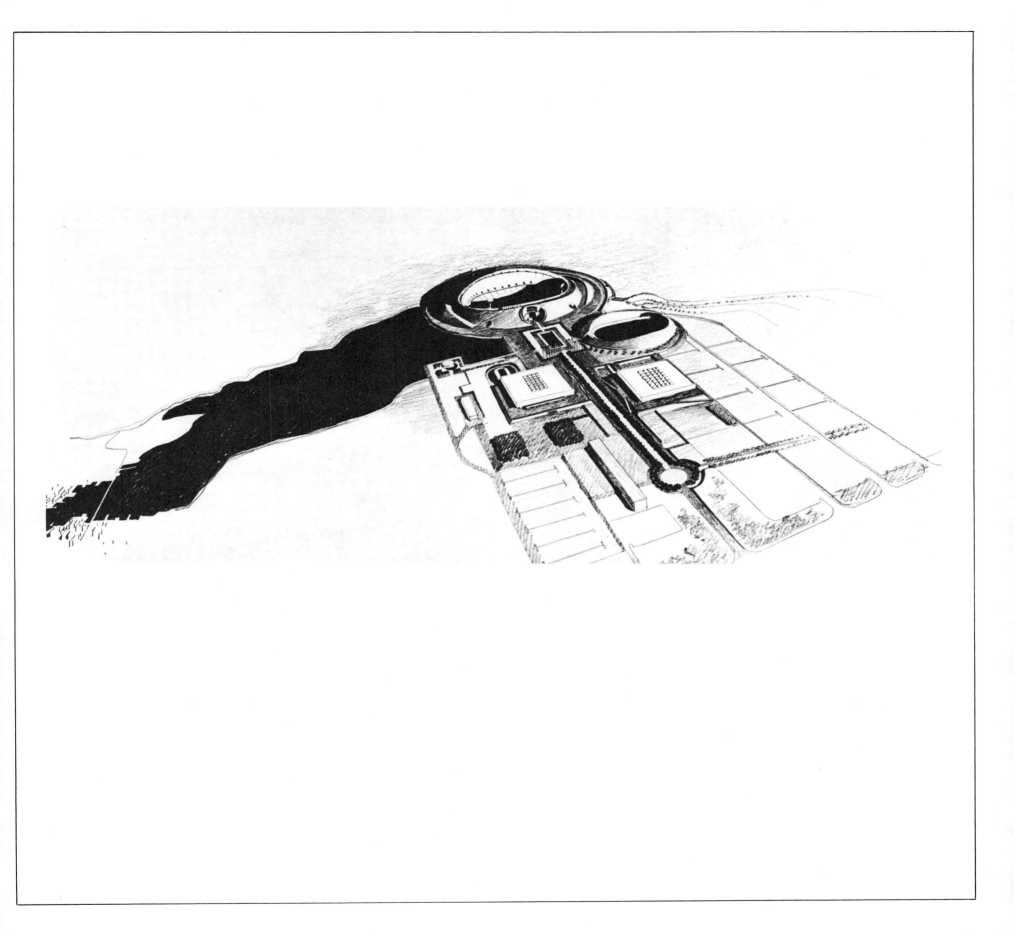

Roger Owen Boyer

Sports Center, Iran

Skidmore, Owings & Merril

Roger Owen Boyer

Sports Center, Iran

Skidmore, Owings & Merril

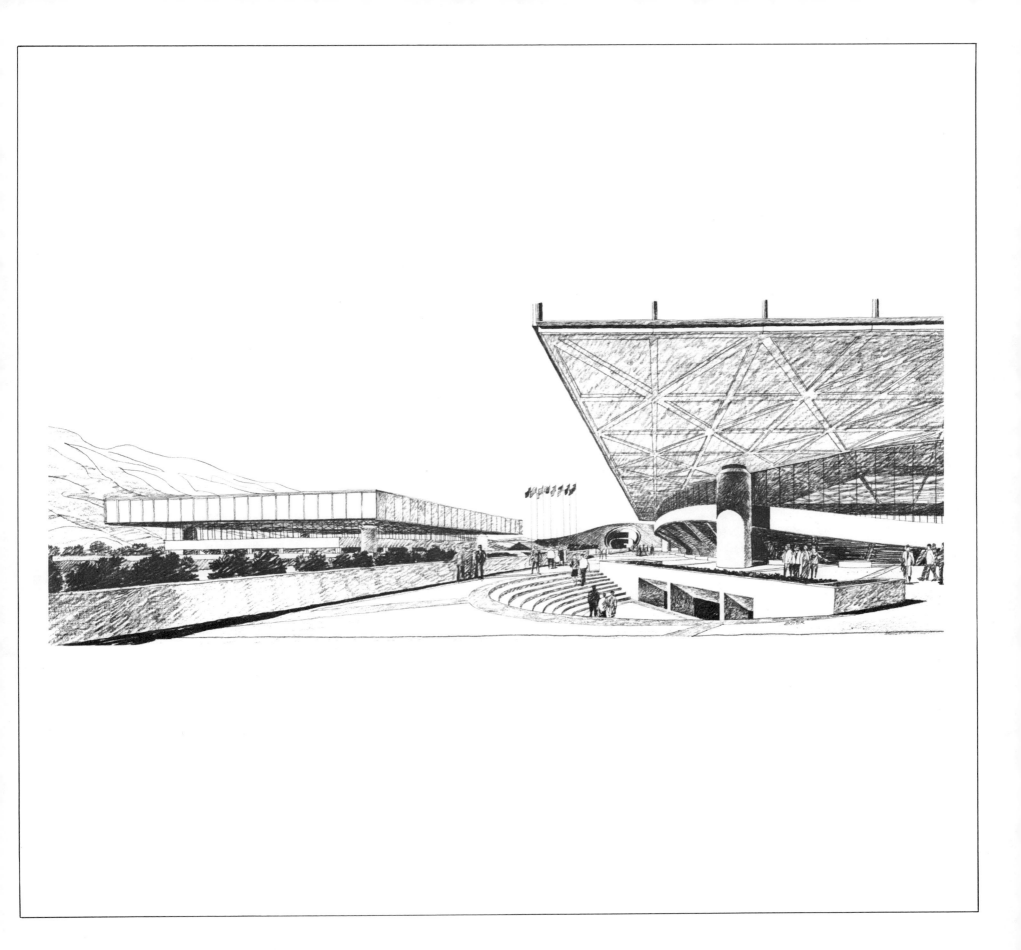

Roger Owen Boyer

Sports Center, Iran

Skidmore, Owings & Merril

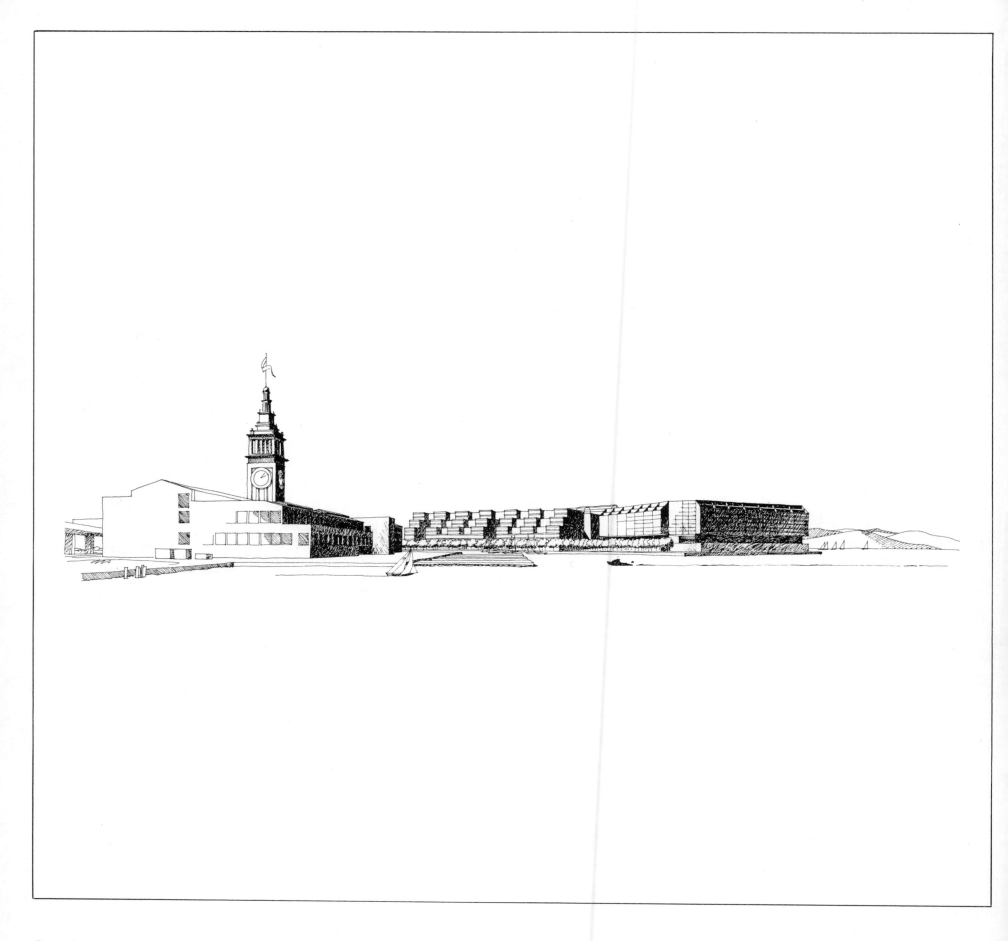

Roger Owen Boyer

Ferry Port Plaza

Skidmore, Owings & Merril

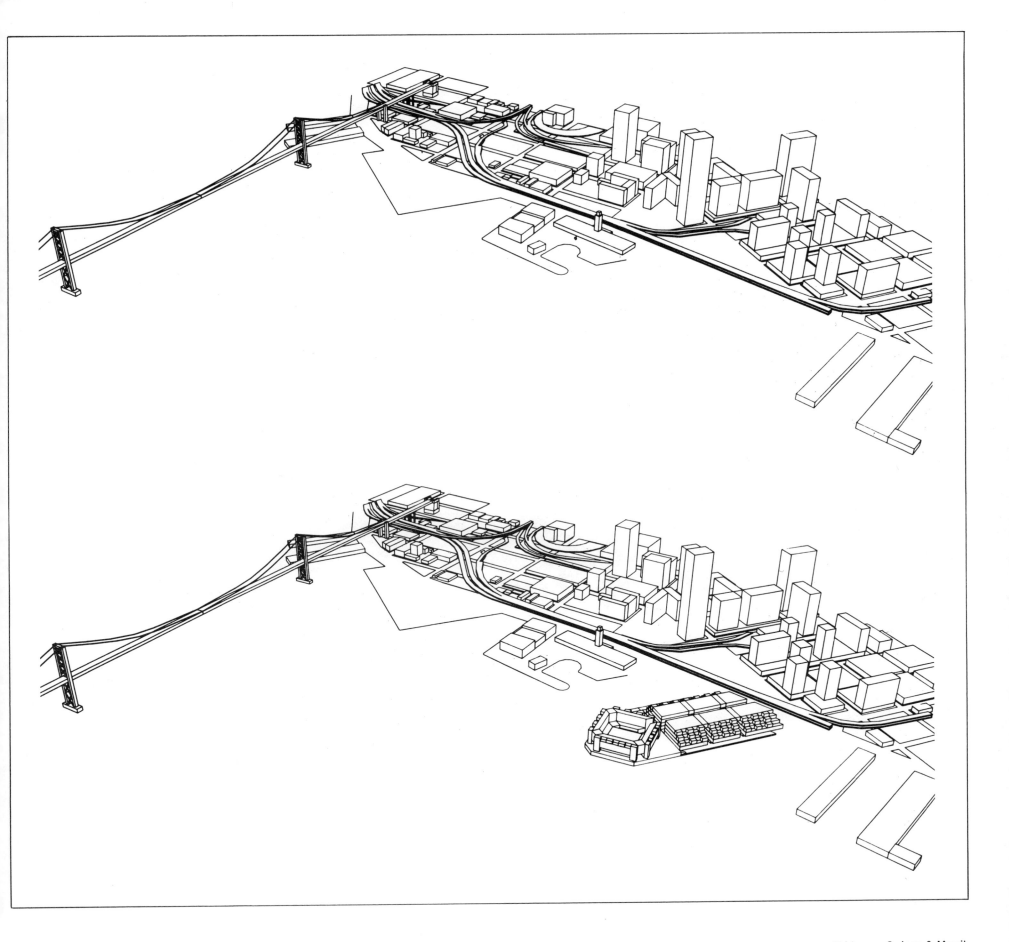

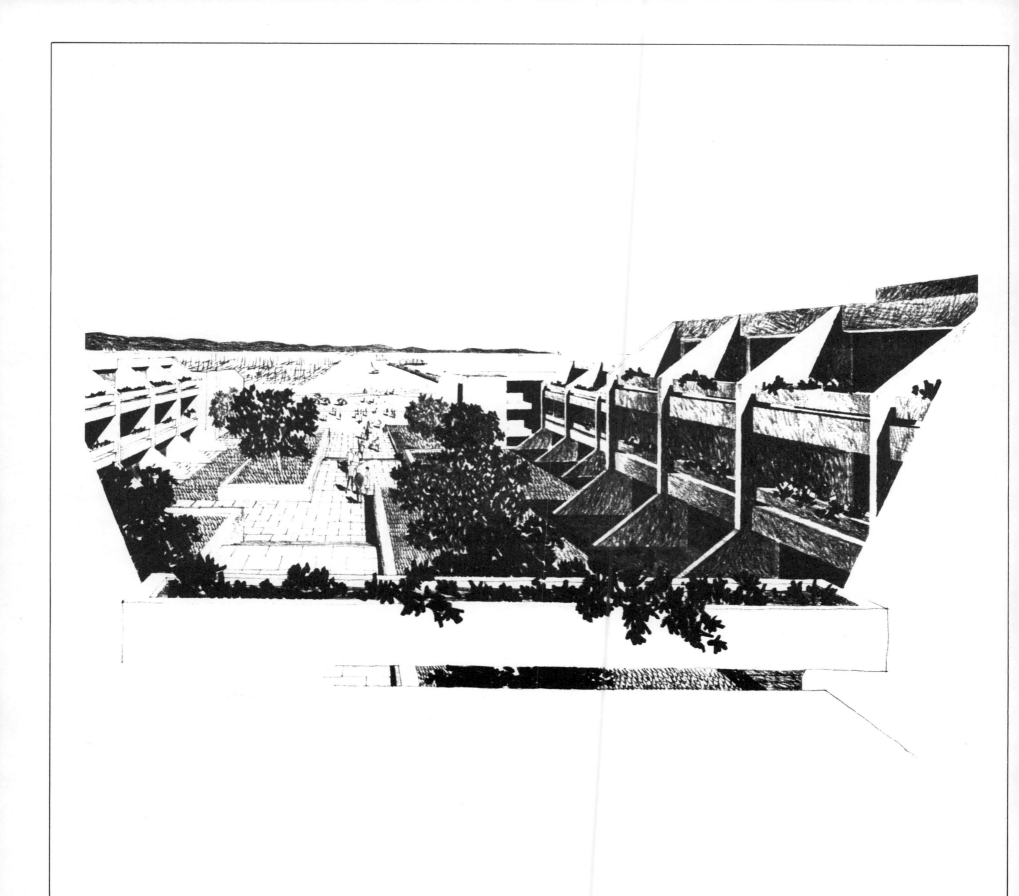

Roger Owen Boyer

Motel in Monterey

Skidmore, Owings & Merril

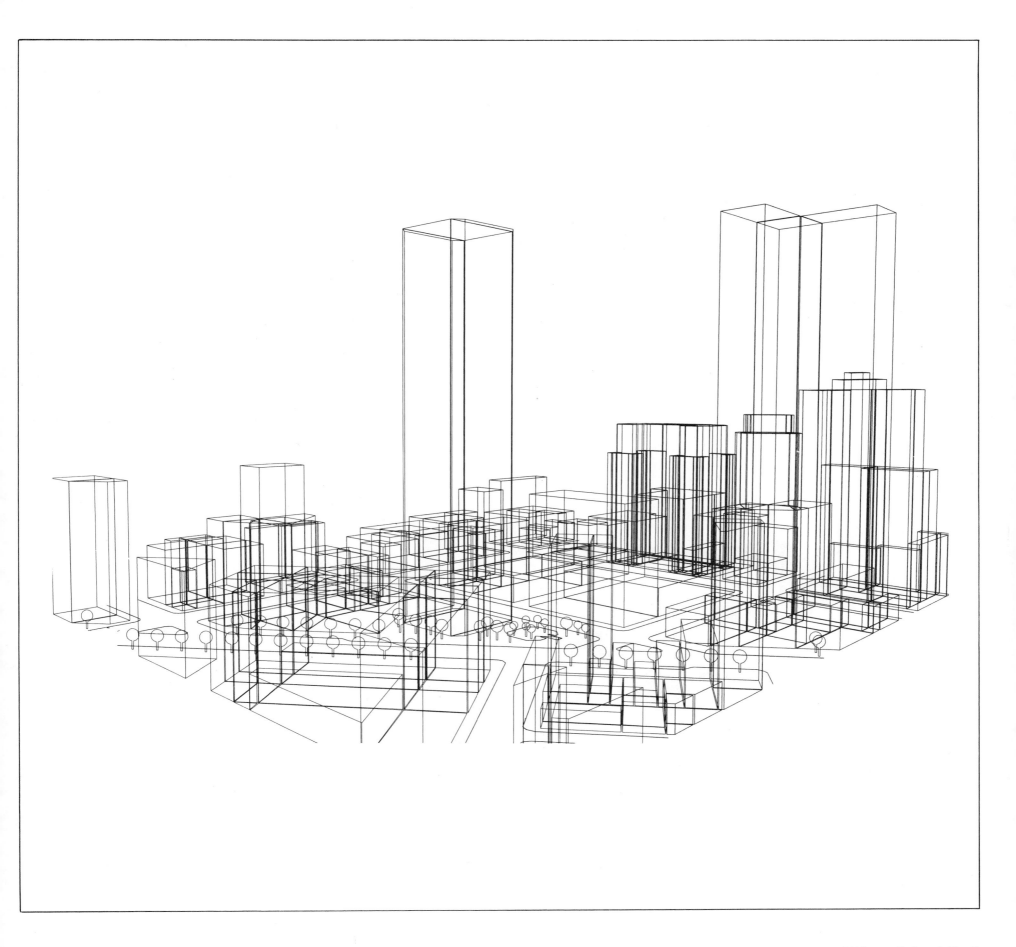

Transparent Aerial View, A Portion of Downtown San Francisco

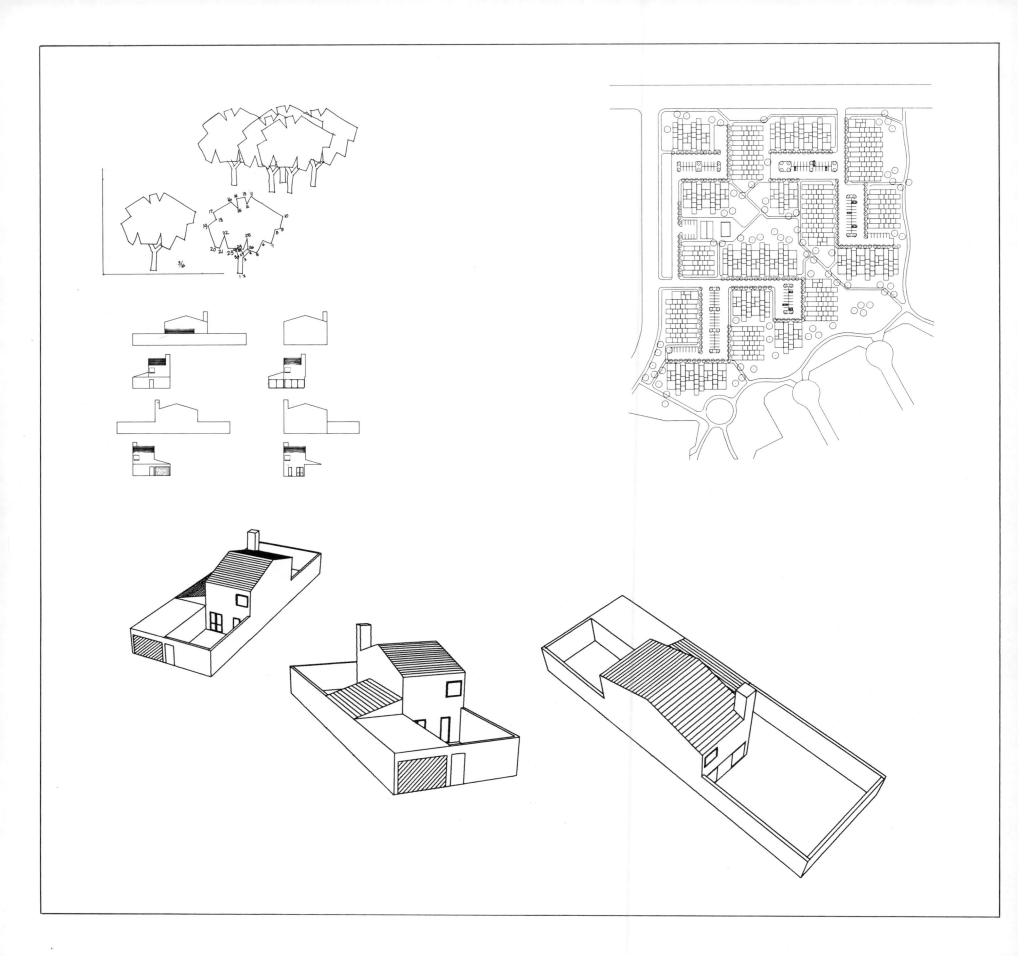

Housing Development, Pedestrian Views

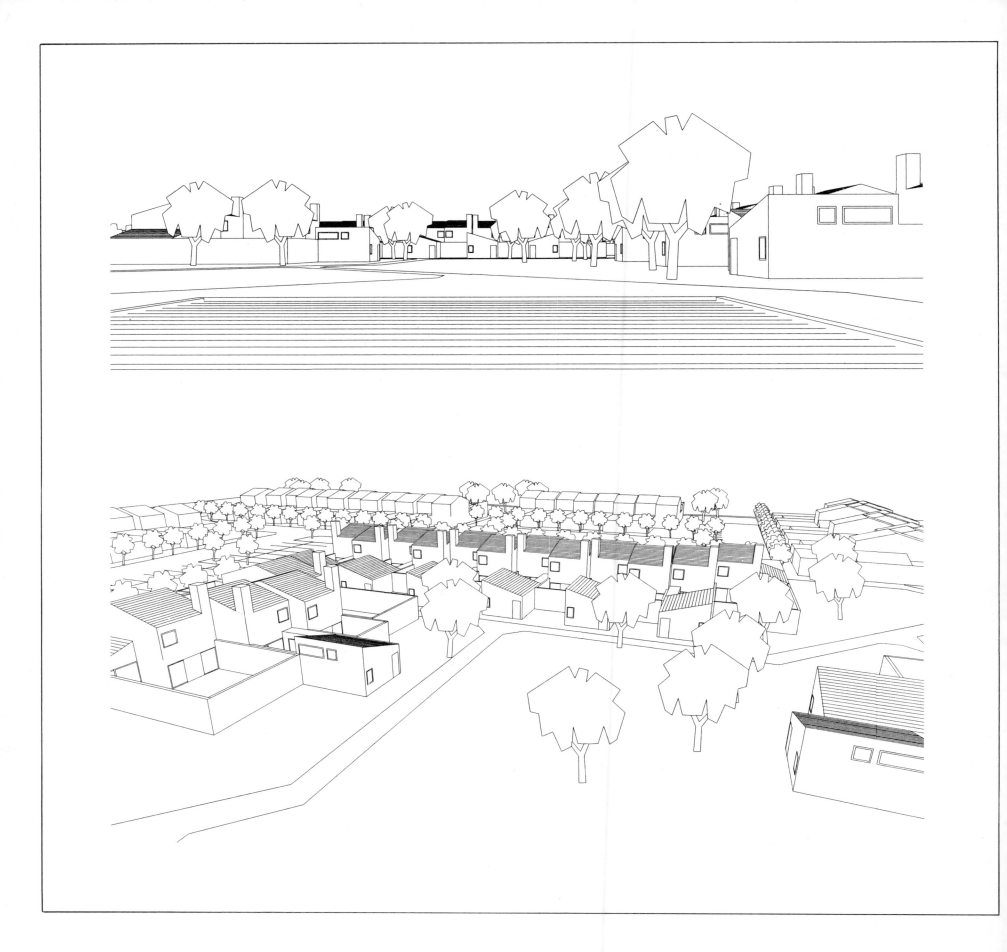

Housing Development, Pedestrian & Birdseye View

Skidmore, Owings & Merril

Dynamic Graphics

Housing Development, Aerial View

Skidmore, Owings & Merril

SMS Architects

Carrell S. McNulty, Jr. AIA
Willis N. Mills, Jr. AIA
Lester W. Smith FAIA
Gray Taylor AIA
A. Raymond von Brock AIA

William A. Briggs, Jr. AIA
Theodore E. Felker AIA
S. Timothy Martin AIA
Robert T. Packard AIA
Howard A. Patterson, Jr. AIA
Edward K. Scofield AIA
Robert C. Steinmetz AIA

777 Summer Street Stamford Connecticut 06901 Telephone 203 325-4141 New York Telephone 212 889-5383

Willis H. Mills, Jr.   Hudson River Museum   S.M.S. Architects

STEINMETZ

Robert C. Steinmetz

Dayton Avenue Medical Building

S.M.S. Architects

Willis H. Mills, Jr.

Pence Creek

S.M.A. Architects

Snibbe · Tafel · Lindholm

**Architects and
Planners Associates
74 Fifth Avenue
New York, N.Y. 10011
(212) 675-6991**
Richard W. Snibbe FAIA
Edgar Tafel AIA
Einar Lindholm AIA
Michael B. Gordon AIA
Associate

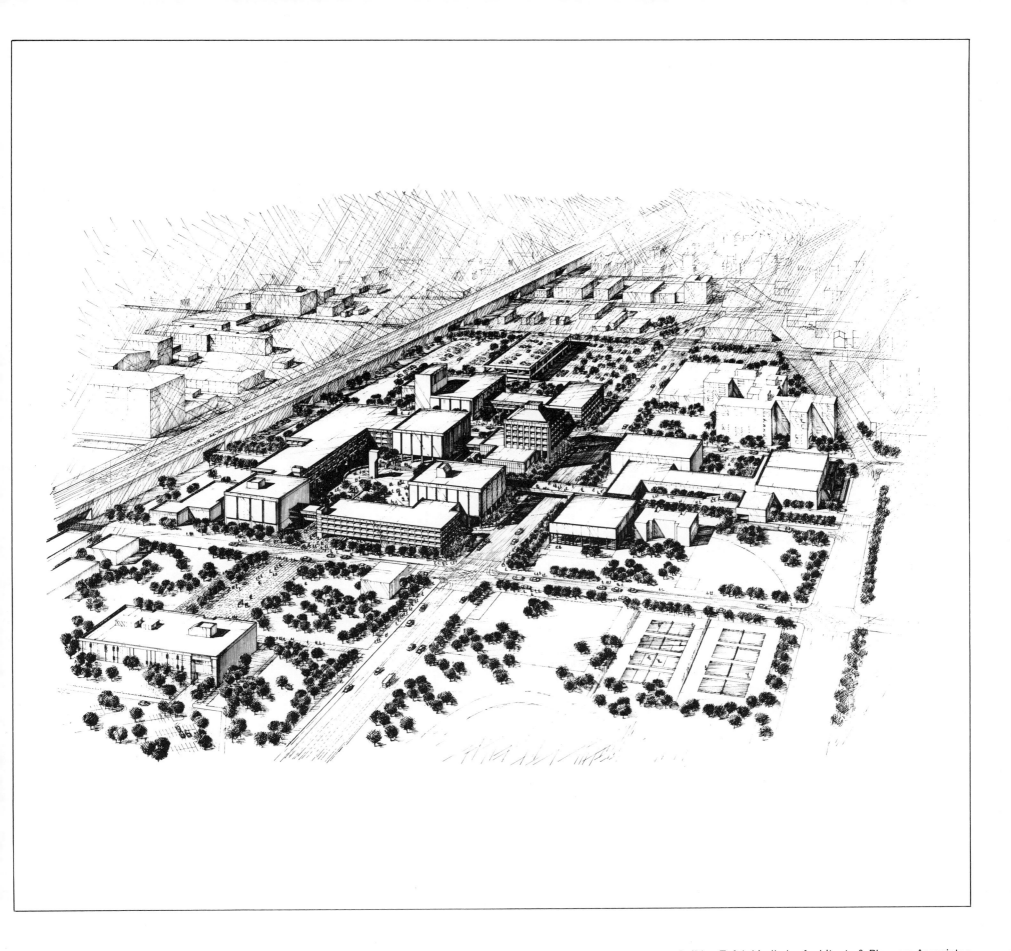

Mark deNalovy Rozvadovski

Aerial View of Campus

Snibbe, Tafel, Lindholm Architects & Planners Associates

Mark deNalovy Rozvadovski

Entrance at New York Boulevard

Snibbe, Tafel, Lindholm Architects & Planners Associates

530

Mark deNalovy Rozvadovski   New York Boulevard Looking South   Snibbe, Tafel, Lindholm Architects & Planners Associates

STAHL ASSOCIATES
A DIVISION OF STAHL/BENNETT, INC.
177 MILK STREET
BOSTON, MASS. 02109

Jack Hagan

Office Building, Boston

Stahl Associates

Jack Hagan

Ministerial Offices, Park Street Church

Stahl Associates

Helmut Jacoby

Central Services Building, Tufts University

Stahl Associates

535

Jack Hagan

Faneuil Hall, Markets Restoration

Stahl Associates

Jack Hagan

American Heritage Colony

Stahl Associates

537

STEVENS & WILKINSON / ARCHITECTS ENGINEERS PLANNERS INC. / 100 PEACHTREE ST. NW / ATLANTA, GA. 30303

Kehp Mooney   Birmingham-Jefferson Civic Center, Competition   Stevens & Wilkinson Architects, Engineers, Planners, Inc.

539

EDWARD DURELL STONE

745 FIFTH AVENUE   NEW YORK 10022

Vincent Furno and Henry Gazess

Standard Oil Building, Chicago

Edward Durell Stone

Ronald Love

Office Building, Canada

Edward Durell Stone

Vincent Furno and Henry Gazess

Standard Oil (Indiana) Building, Chicago

Edward Durell Stone

543

HUGH STUBBINS AND ASSOCIATES

ARCHITECTS, 1033 MASSACHUSETTS AVENUE, CAMBRIDGE, MASSACHUSETTS 02138   TELEPHONE (617) 491-6450

HUGH STUBBINS, FAIA

MERLE WESTLAKE, AIA
EDWIN F. JONES, AIA
PETER WOYTUK, AIA

NORMAN I. PATERSON, AIA
TETSUO TAKAYANAGI, AIA

STEVEN S. T. LO, AIA
PAUL JOHN GRAYSON, AIA
JOHN REUTLINGER, AIA
W. EASLEY HAMNER, AIA
MICHAEL J. KRAUS, AIA
AMIEL VASSILOVSKI, RA
JULIUS LOEWY, RA
ROBERT A. PALERMO, RA
EUGENE R. RACEK, RA
SEBASTIAN L. LaBELLA, AIA

EMMETT F. GLYNN, CSI

Jay Henderson Barr   Federal Reserve Bank of Boston   Hugh Stubbins and Associates

Michael F. Gebhart

Hampshire College

Hugh Stubbins and Associates

Michael F. Gebhart

Teacher's College, Columbia University

Hugh Stubbins and Associates

Michael F. Gebhart

Teacher's College, Columbia University

Hugh Stubbins and Associates

ALFRED SWENSON & PAO-CHI CHANG ARCHITECT/DESIGNER

5530 SOUTH SHORE DRIVE   CHICAGO, ILLINOIS 60637   (312) 288-6308

Alfred Swenson & Pao-Chi Change   Superframe Building, Chicago   Alfred Swenson and Pao-Chi Change, Architects

TIPPETTS - ABBETT - McCARTHY - STRATTON

ENGINEERS AND ARCHITECTS

345 PARK AVENUE, NEW YORK, N.Y. 10022

PARTNERS

ROBERT W. ABBETT, P. E.
GERALD T. McCARTHY, P. E.
EDWARD K. BRYANT, P. E.
FRANK LILIEN, P. E.
LEONARD A. LOVELL, P. E.
THOMAS J. FRATAR, P. E.
WALTHER PROKOSCH, R. A.
BARNETT SILVESTON, P. E.
JOHN LOWE, III, P. E.
WILSON V. BINGER, P. E.
ANDREW S. BALBIANI, P. E.
E. PER SORENSEN, P. E.
RAYMOND J. HODGE, P. E.
AUSTIN E. BRANT, JR., P. E.

PARTNERS (RETIRED)

ERNEST F. TIPPETTS, P. E.
JAMES H. STRATTON, P. E.

CONTROLLER

EDWARD T. SANDS, C. P. A.

TELEPHONE (212) 755-2000   CABLE: TAMSENG NEW YORK   TELEX: ITT 422188 / RCA 223055

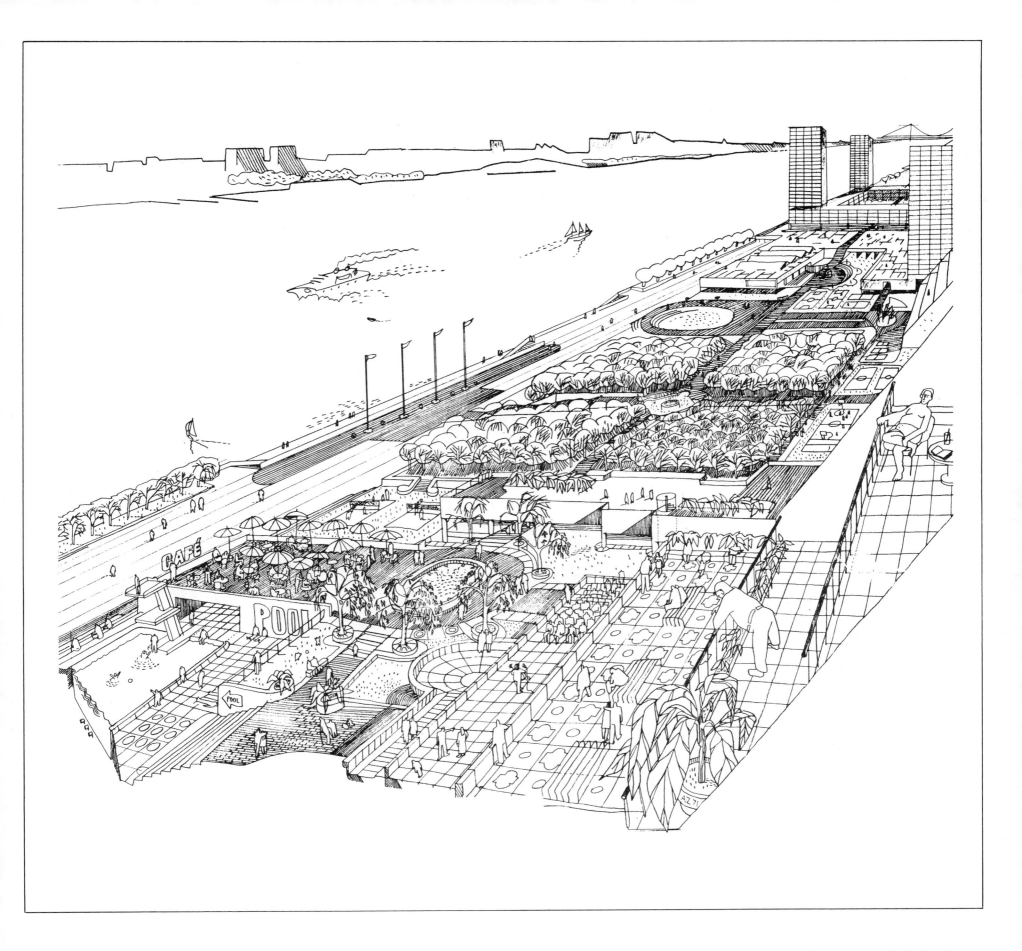

Andrew Zozienicki

Battery Park City, New York

Tippetts-Abbett-McCarthy-Stratton

553

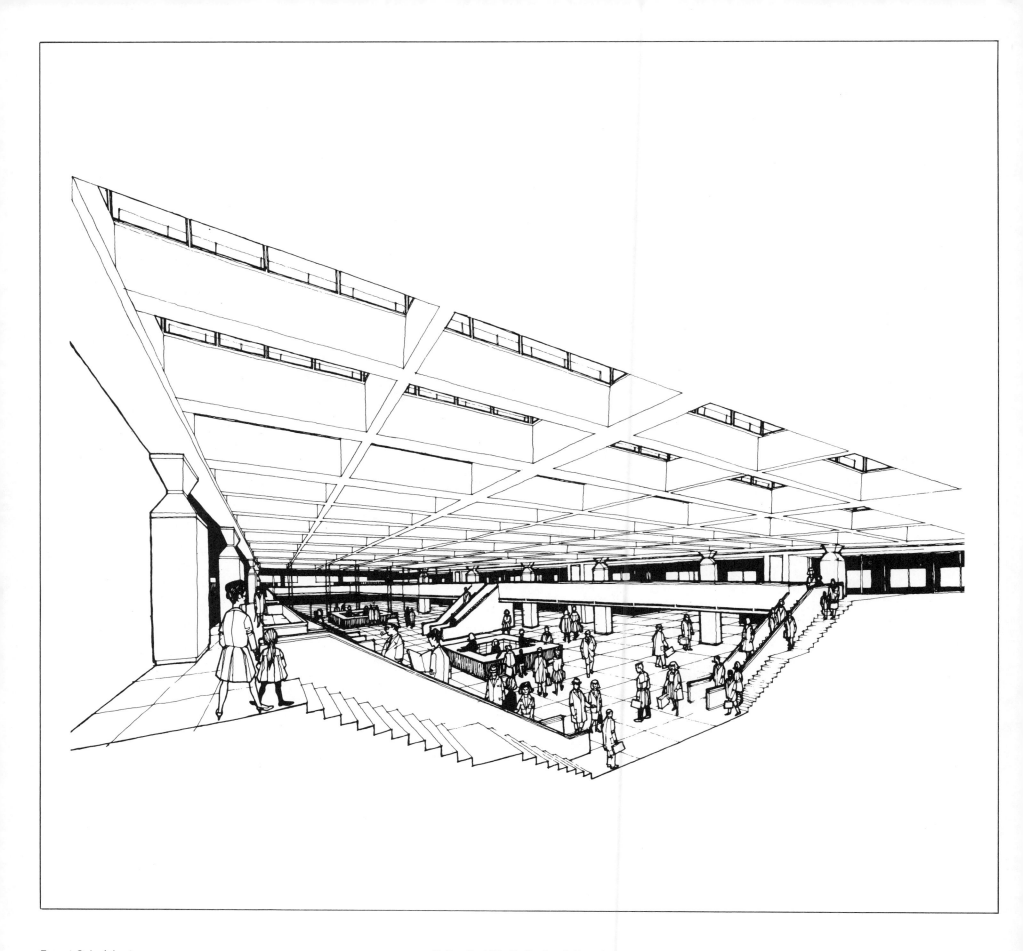

Zozislav Odesser

North River Pollution Control Plant

Tippetts-Abbett-McCarthy-Stratton

555

David Todd and Associates   Architects

David F. M. Todd, f.a.i.a., f.c.s.i.   Paul F. Basile, a.i.a.
Robert Cabrera, a.i.a.   F. Andrew Foord, a.i.a.
Eugene Jaffe, r.a., c.s.i.   Robin Wong, a.i.a.

303 East 65th Street, New York, New York 10021, 212 YUkon 8-8100

Kenneth Barricklo

Concourse Complex, State University at New Paltz, New York

David Todd and Associates, Architects

557

Kenneth Barricklo

Palmas Del Mar, Puerto Rico

David Todd and Associates, Architects

Kenneth Barricklo

Palmas Del Mar, Puerto Rico *(Detail)*

David Todd and Associates, Architects

JEFF J. VANDEBERG - ARCHITECT
240 EAST 15TH ST   NEW YORK, N Y 10003   (212) 673-5713

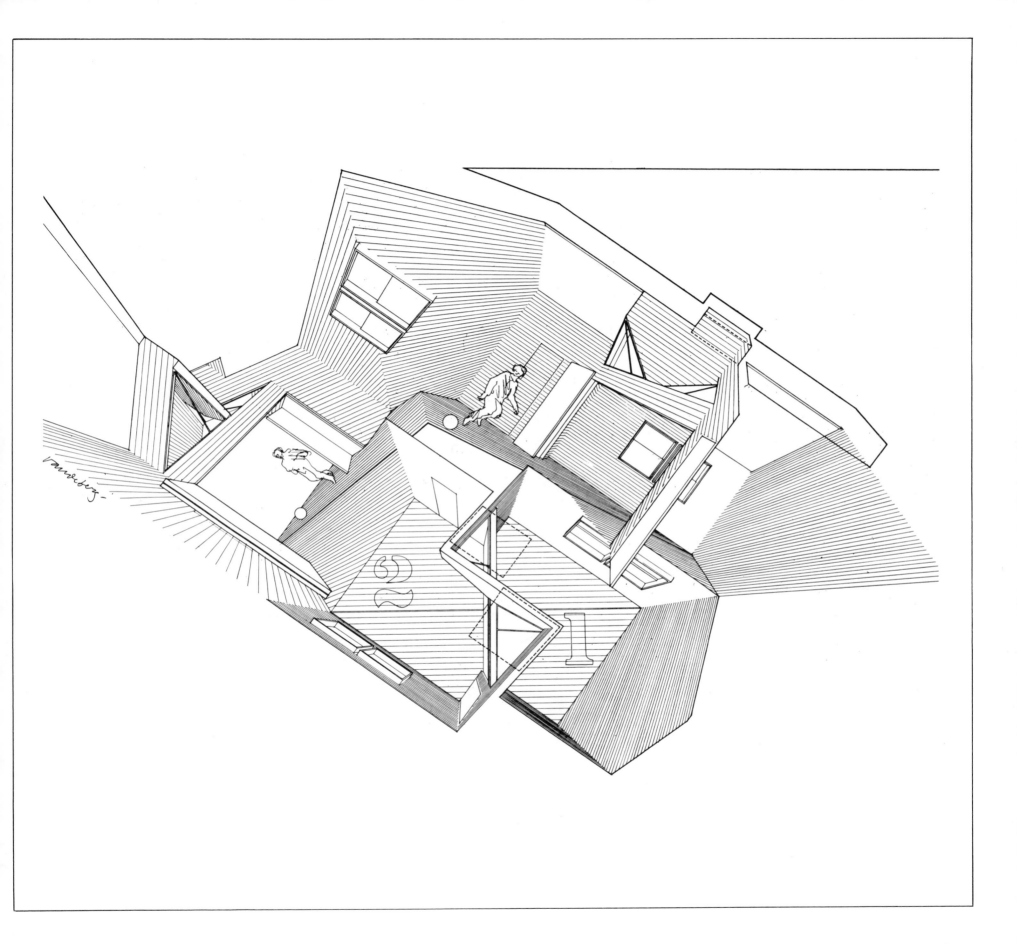

Jeff J. Vandeberg

Weis Residence

Jeff J. Vandeberg—Architect

Jeff J. Vandeberg

Uaxactun Acropolis, Reconstruction

Jeff J. Vandeberg—Architect (Blum & Amsden)

Jeff J. Vandeberg

Vienna U.N. *(Competition)*

Jeff J. Vandeberg—Architect (Stan Kan Dels)

Venturi and Rauch
Architects and Planners

Robert Venturi AIA
John Rauch AIA
Denise Scott Brown ARIBA
Gerod Clark

333 South 16th Street Philadelphia, Pa. 19102 Pe 5-5079

W. G. Clark

Yale Mathematics Building Competition

Venturi and Rauch, Architects

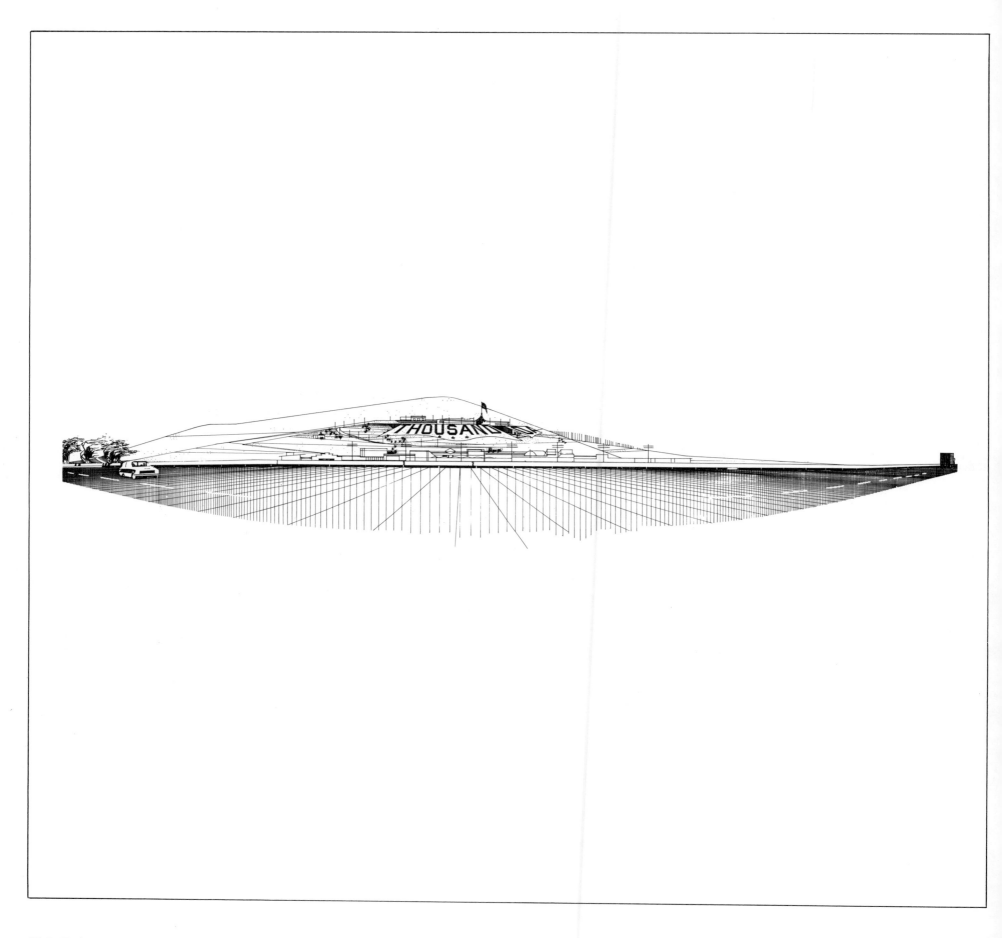

Civic Center Competition

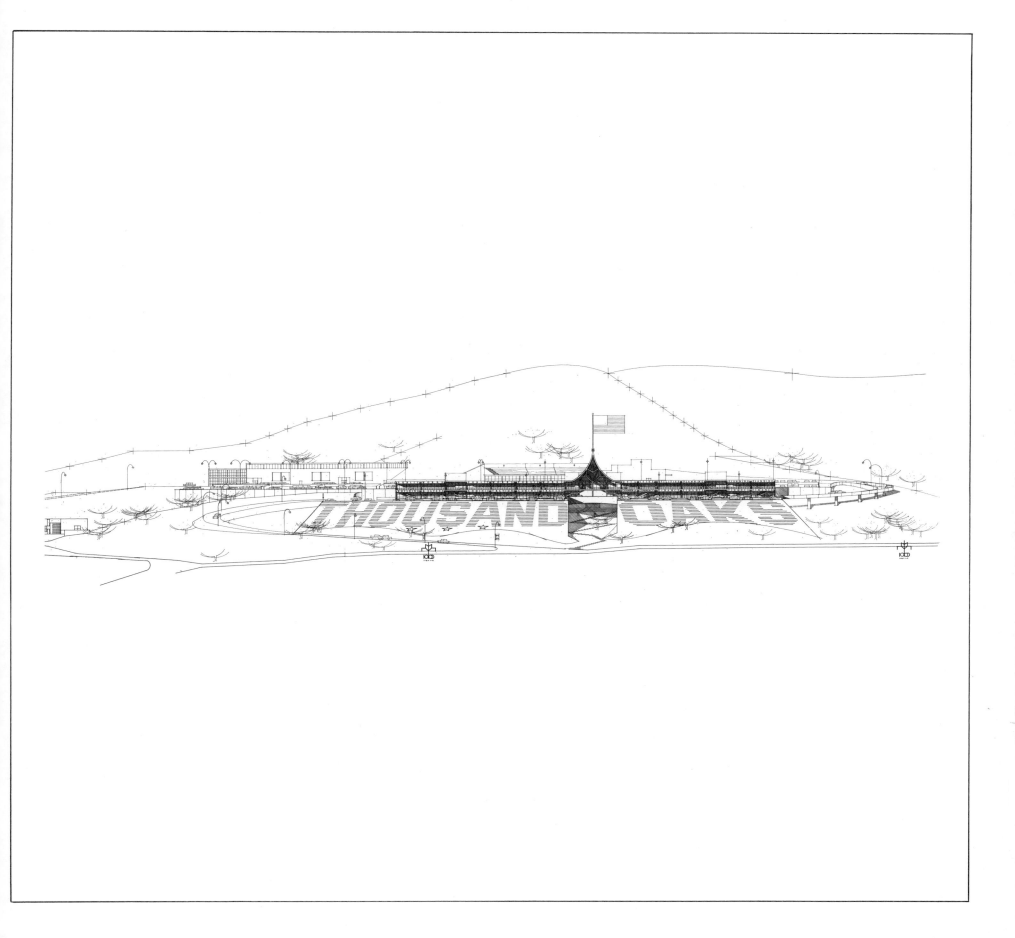

W. G. Clark

Venturi and Rauch, Architects

WALLACE, McHARG, ROBERTS AND TODD

ARCHITECTS / LANDSCAPE ARCHITECTS / URBAN AND ECOLOGICAL PLANNERS
1740 CHERRY STREET, PHILADELPHIA, PENNSYLVANIA 19103 / (215) 563-0890

David A. Wallace, FAIA, AIP/Ian L. McHarg, ASLA, AMTPI/William H. Roberts, RIBA, ASLA/Thomas A. Todd, AIA
Associates: David C. Hamme/Narendra Juneja, AIIA, ASLA/
Donald H. Brackenbush, AIA, /Michael G. Clarke/Charles B. Tomlinson, Jr./ Daniel Philip Busch

Thomas A. Todd

Bicentennial Proposal, Philadelphia

Wallace, McHarg, Roberts & Todd

Thomas A. Todd

Buffalo Downtown Plan, Main Street Mall

Wallace, McHarg, Roberts & Todd

Thomas A. Todd

Earl Estate Apartments

Wallace, McHarg, Roberts & Todd

Thomas A. Todd

New York Battery Park Proposal

Wallace, McHarg, Roberts & Todd

Thomas A. Todd   Inner Harbor Plan, Baltimore   Wallace, McHarg, Roberts & Todd

Thomas A. Todd   Views of "Constellation" (Frigate 1797)   Wallace, McHarg, Roberts & Todd

Thomas A. Todd

Inner Harbor Plan, Baltimore

Wallace, McHarg, Roberts & Todd

JOHN CARL WARNECKE AND ASSOCIATES

JOHN CARL WARNECKE, F.A.I.A.

CARL I. WARNECKE, A.I.A.

CARL RUSSELL, A.I.A.

A. EUGENE KOHN, A.I.A.

ARCHITECTS AND PLANNING CONSULTANTS, 61 NEW MONTGOMERY STREET, SAN FRANCISCO, CALIFORNIA 94105   (415) 397-4200

SAN FRANCISCO, CALIFORNIA   HONOLULU, HAWAII   NEW YORK, NEW YORK   WASHINGTON, D.C.

O. Dahlstrand
University of California, Santa Cruz Library
John Carl Warnecke and Associates

Hegenberger Overpass

John Carl Warnecke and Associates

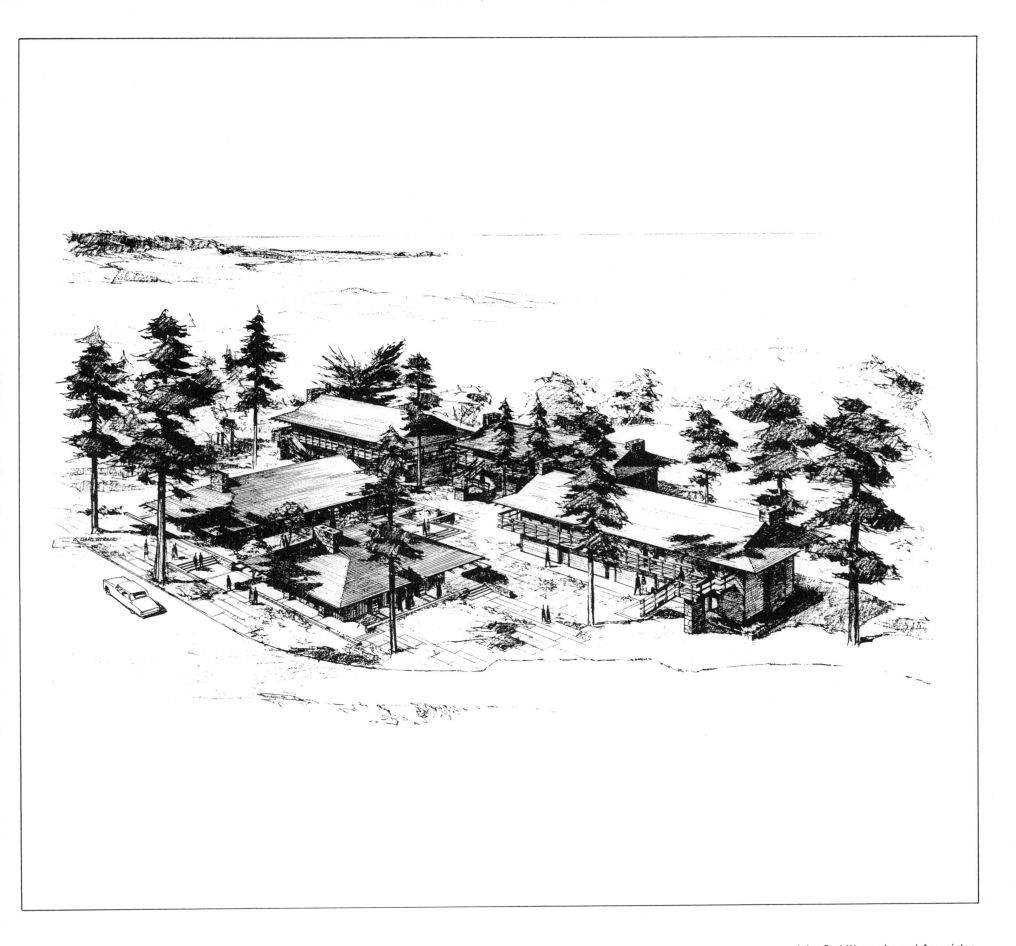

O. Dahlstrand

Hotel and Conference Grounds

John Carl Warnecke and Associates

WARNER
BURNS
TOAN
LUNDE

ARCHITECTS   724 FIFTH AVENUE, NEW YORK, N.Y. 10019   (212) 757-8900   CABLE: WARBURTOL   TELEX: 422512

Charles H. Warner, Jr.
Robert Burns
Danforth W. Toan
Frithjof M. Lunde

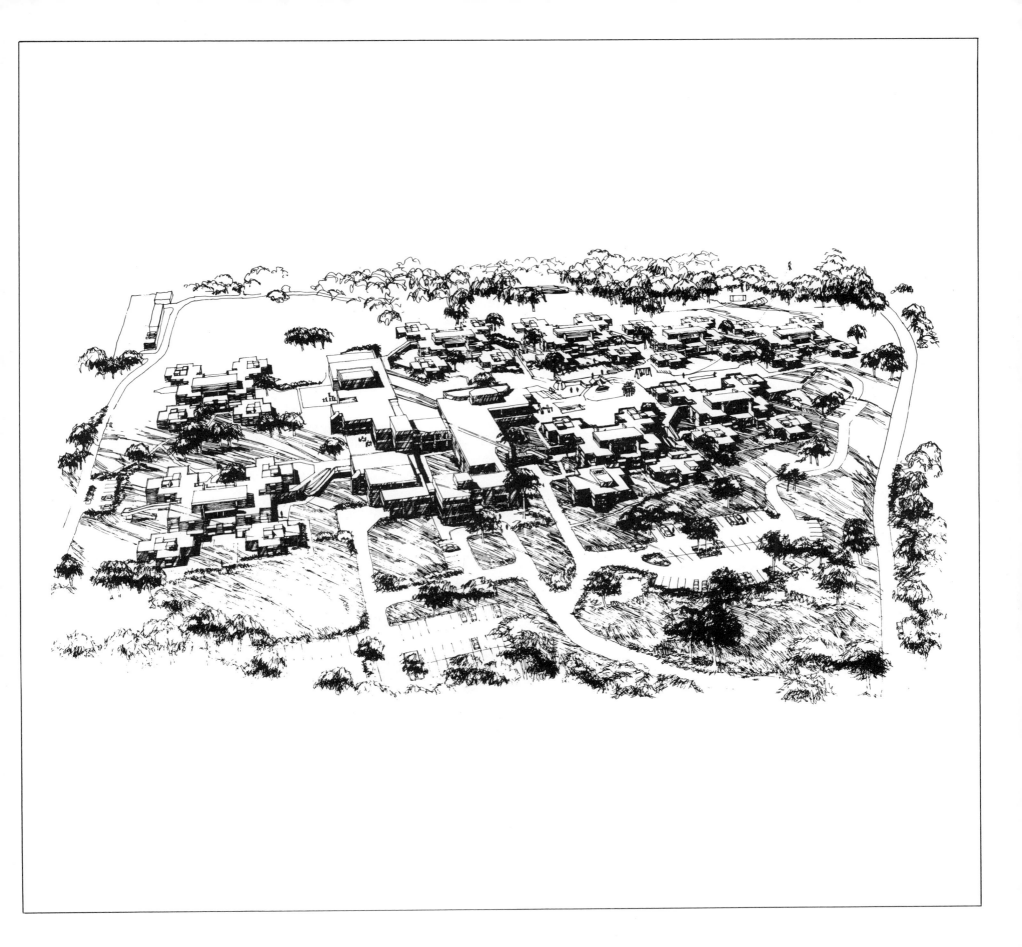

Jim Hadley

Tri-City State School

Warner, Burns, Toan, Lunde

581

Jim Hadley

Columbia University

Warner, Burns, Toan, Lunde

582

Jim Hadley

Genessee Hilton Hotel

Warner, Burns, Toan, Lunde

Alfred
Wastlhuber
Architect
AIA

2001 Grant Avenue · San Francisco · California · 94133 · Telephone 421-1698

Roger Owen Boyer

Santa Barbara Housing Development

Alfred Wastlhuber, Architect

Roger Owen Boyer

Santa Barbara Housing Development

Alfred Wastlhuber, Architect

Roger Owen Boyer   Santa Barbara Housing Development   Alfred Wastlhuber, Architect

**HARRY WEESE
& ASSOCIATES**

architects and engineers
10 west hubbard street
chicago   60610

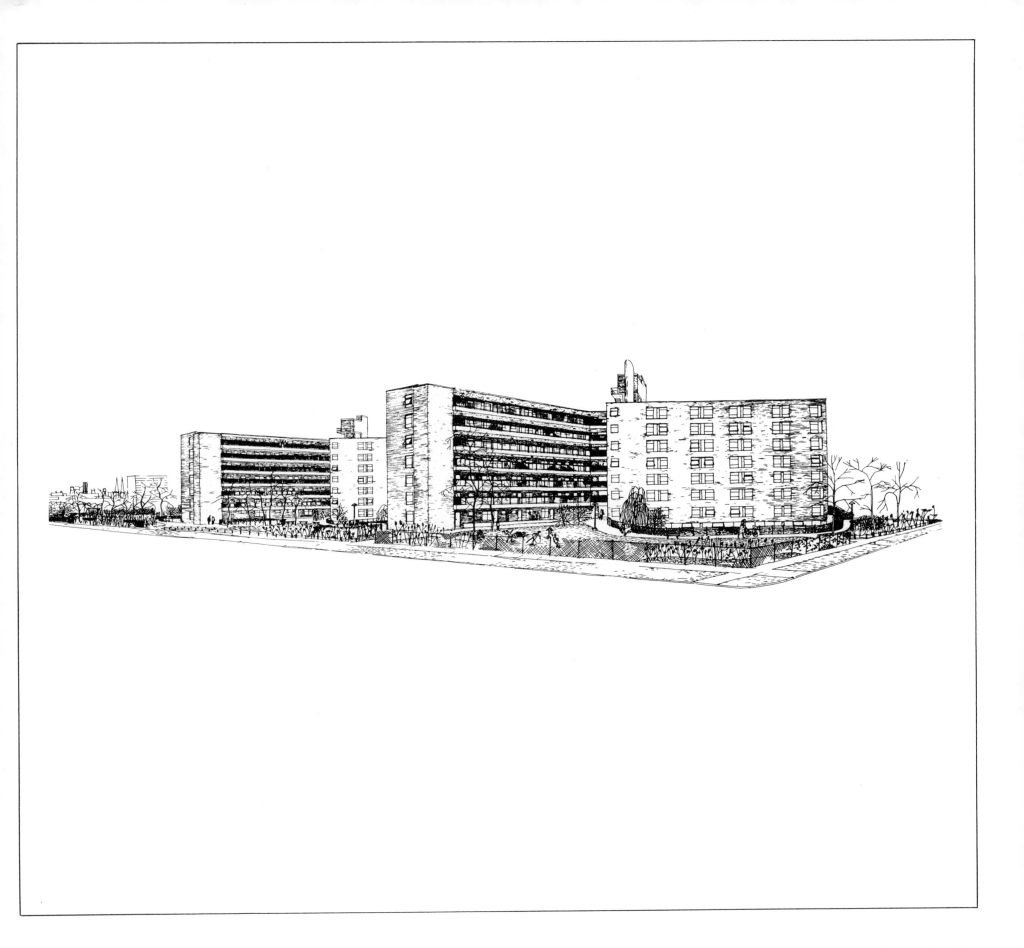

Harry Weese

Loomis Courts, Chicago

Harry Weese

Loomis Courts, Chicago

Harry Weese and Associates

ARCHITECTS
ENGINEERS
PLANNERS

ADRIAN WILSON ASSOCIATES

HOME OFFICE: 621 S. WESTMORELAND AVE. • LOS ANGELES, CALIFORNIA 90005
TELEPHONE: 386-7070 • AREA CODE 213 • CABLE: ADWIL

Shoji Shimizu

Seward's Success, Alaska

Adrian Wilson Associates

Escobar Valerio

Downey Theater

Adrian Wilson Associates

Shoji Shimizu

Los Angeles Civic Center Mall

Adrian Wilson Associates

595

WURSTER, BERNARDI AND EMMONS, INC., ARCHITECTS

1620 MONTGOMERY STREET SAN FRANCISCO CALIFORNIA 94111   (415) 397-6544

PRINCIPALS: WILLIAM WILSON WURSTER, F.A.I.A. THEODORE C. BERNARDI, F.A.I.A. DONN EMMONS, F.A.I.A.   ALLEN F. ROSENBERG, A.I.A.   RALPH O. BUTTERFIELD, A.I.A.

ASSOCIATES: ALBERT ARONSON, A.I.A.   DON E. STOVER, A.I.A.   ROBERT A. TOWLE, A.I.A.   PATRICK S. ZABALDO, A.I.A.   FREDERICK QUINTAL   ERIC R. BANCROFT, A.I.A.   LARRY L. CANNON, A.I.A.   GARTH COLLIER, A.I.A.

Carlos Diniz & Associates   Bank of America, World Headquarters   Wurster, Bernardi and Emmons, Inc. Architects

Carlos Diniz & Associates

San Francisco International Market Center

Wurster, Bernardi and Emmons, Inc. Architects

598

Gerald C. Taylor

Diablo Canyon PG&E Plant

Wurster, Bernardi and Emmons, Inc. Architects

George Taylor

Ghirardelli Square

Wurster, Bernardi and Emmons, Inc. Architects

George Albertus

Ghirardelli Square

Wurster, Bernardi and Emmons, Inc. Architects

Helmut Jacoby

Capital Towers

Wurster, Bernardi and Emmons, Inc. Architects

Helmut Jacoby

Capital Towers

Wurster, Bernardi and Emmons, Inc. Architects

**MINORU YAMASAKI
AND ASSOCIATES** ARCHITECTS
AND ENGINEERS
350 WEST BIG BEAVER ROAD
TROY, MICHIGAN 48084
313-689-3500

MINORU YAMASAKI HENRY J. GUTHARD AARON SCHREIER DANIEL L. TREACY ALVIN R. PREVOST WILLIAM KU HAROLD S. TSUCHIYA PETER TURNER MANUEL D. DUMLAO MODRIS PUDISTS
ROBERT L. MORRIS ROBERT A. PULLAR JOHN URBAN WALLACE K. KAGAWA ROBERT ORTEGA ROBERT H. DE VRIESE KIP W. SEROTA RAYMOND L. ANGERS GEORGE MOY DONALD LEE RALPH H. INSINGER

Carlos Diniz & Associates

World Trade Center

Minoru Yamasaki and Associates

Carlos Diniz & Associates

View from City Hall Park

Minoru Yamasaki and Associates

Carlos Diniz & Associates

World Trade Center, View from Governor's Island

Minoru Yamasaki and Associates

Carlos Diniz & Associates

Tower Lobby World Trade Center

Minoru Yamasaki and Associates

UNITED STATES CUSTOMS

Carlos Diniz & Associates

Plaza Entrance, World Trade Center

Minoru Yamasaki and Associates

Index of Renderers

Index of Architects